STATEGRAPHY

Studies in Social Analysis
General Editor: Martin Holbraad
University College London

Focusing on analysis as a meeting ground of the empirical and the conceptual, this series provides a platform for exploring anthropological approaches to social analysis while seeking to open new avenues of communication between anthropology and the humanities, as well as other social sciences.

Volume 1
Being Godless: Ethnographies of Atheism and Non-Religion
Edited by Ruy Llera Blanes and Galina Oustinova-Stjepanovic

Volume 2
Emptiness and Fullness: Ethnographies of Lack and Desire in Contemporary China
Edited by Susanne Bregnbæk and Mikkel Bunkenborg

Volume 3
Straying from the Straight Path: How Senses of Failure Invigorate Lived Religion
Edited by David Kloos and Daan Beekers

Volume 4
Stategraphy: Toward a Relational Anthropology of the State
Edited by Tatjana Thelen, Larissa Vetters, and Keebet von Benda-Beckmann

Volume 5
Affective States: Entanglements, Suspensions, Suspicions
Edited by Mateusz Laszczkowski and Madeleine Reeves

Volume 6
Animism beyond the Soul: Ontology, Reflexivity, and the Making of Anthropological Knowledge
Edited by Katherine Swancutt and Mireille Mazard

STATEGRAPHY
Toward a Relational Anthropology of the State

Edited by

Tatjana Thelen, Larissa Vetters,
and Keebet von Benda-Beckmann

berghahn
NEW YORK • OXFORD
www.berghahnbooks.com

First published in 2018 by

Berghahn Books

www.berghahnbooks.com

© 2018 Berghahn Books

Originally published as a special issue of *Social Analysis*, volume 58, issue 3.

All rights reserved.
Except for the quotation of short passages for the purposes of criticism and review, no part of this book may be reproduced in any form or by any means, electronic or mechanical, including photocopying, recording, or any information storage and retrieval system now known or to be invented, without written permission of the publisher.

Library of Congress Cataloging-in-Publication Data

Names: Thelen, Tatjana, editor. | Vetters, Larissa, editor. | Benda-Beckmann, Keebet von, editor.
Title: Stategraphy : toward a relational anthropology of the state / edited by Tatjana Thelen, Larissa Vetters, and Keebet von Benda-Beckmann.
Description: New York : Berghahn Books, 2017. | Series: Studies in social analysis | Includes bibliographical references and index.
Identifiers: LCCN 2017014899 (print) | LCCN 2017037523 (ebook) | ISBN 9781785337017 (ebook) | ISBN 9781785336997 (hardback : alk paper) | ISBN 9781785337000 (pbk. : alk. paper)
Subjects: LCSH: Political anthropology. | State, The.
Classification: LCC GN492 (ebook) | LCC GN492 .S74 2017 (print) | DDC 306.2–dc23
LC record available at https://lccn.loc.gov/2017014899

British Library Cataloguing in Publication Data

A catalogue record for this book is available from the British Library.

Contents

Introduction
Stategraphy: Relational Modes, Boundary Work, and Embeddedness   1
   Tatjana Thelen, Larissa Vetters, and Keebet von Benda-Beckmann

Chapter 1
Contingent Statehood: Clientelism and Civic Engagement as Relational
   Modalities in Contemporary Bosnia and Herzegovina   20
   Larissa Vetters

Chapter 2
The State, Legal Rigor, and the Poor: The Daily Practice of
   Welfare Control   38
   Vincent Dubois

Chapter 3
Relationships, Practices, and Images of the Local State in Rural Russia   56
   Rebecca Kay

Chapter 4
Acts of Assistance: Navigating the Interstices of the British State
   with the Help of Non-profit Legal Advisers   73
   Alice Forbess and Deborah James

Chapter 5
Images of Care, Boundaries of the State: Volunteering and Civil Society
   in Czech Health Care   90
   Rosie Read

Chapter 6
State Kinning and Kinning the State in Serbian Elder Care Programs   107
   Tatjana Thelen, Andre Thiemann, and Duška Roth

Chapter 7
Workings of the State: Administrative Lists, European Union Food Aid,
   and the Local Practices of Distribution in Rural Romania   124
   Ştefan Dorondel and Mihai Popa

Chapter 8
Creating the State Locally through Welfare Provision: Two Mayors,
   Two Welfare Regimes in Rural Hungary   141
   Gyöngyi Schwarcz and Alexandra Szőke

Index   159

INTRODUCTION
Stategraphy: Relational Modes, Boundary Work, and Embeddedness

Tatjana Thelen, Larissa Vetters, and Keebet von Benda-Beckmann

While the state had been a recurrent theme in anthropology (Bouchard 2011), the 1990s saw a new wave of interest in it. The efflorescence of the 'new' ethnography of the state has cast a spotlight on certain issues, while others have received less attention. Significantly, there has been a marked shift toward state images and representations in research and theorizing. In response, Anthony Marcus (2008) launched a fulminant critique against this development, which he described as the emergence of an 'orthodoxy' in (Anglophone) anthropological state theory. According to him, emphasizing the plurality of culturally constructed state representations without much reference to either power relations or larger social scientific discussions amounts to mere empiricism. We agree with Marcus that much of the recent anthropological literature has overemphasized cultural constructions, images, and discursive representations of the state, which, moreover, are often presented in a peculiarly monomorphic manner. The topic of state practices—perhaps more pronounced in European discussions—has not received appropriate attention in the strand of literature criticized by Marcus. More important, however, we believe that this development has resulted in a problematic theoretical void between state images and practices. The missing link makes it difficult to understand how specific state constellations and boundaries emerge and are reproduced or dissolved.

Notes for this section begin on page 16.

In this introduction, we propose a relational anthropology of the state as a way to bridge the gap between images and practices. While acknowledging that anthropologists have often stressed the embeddedness of the social phenomena they research, we argue that this has not yet been fully explored in the analysis of the state. Making relations the starting point of analysis can offer new insights into the workings of the state. We advance our argument in four interrelated sections.

First, we examine in greater detail the emergence of the analytical gap between state images and practices. This section does not intend to provide a comprehensive overview of the development of the anthropology of the state; instead, we focus on embedding the anthropological discussion within the wider domain of social scientific theorizing. Based on this analysis, we, secondly, outline the proposed relational approach, which we call 'stategraphy'. This section includes a working concept of the state and proposes three axes of analysis, namely, relational modalities, boundary work, and embeddedness of actors. Together they lay the foundation for the contributors' individual stategraphies, which we describe in the third section. All of the chapters in this book focus on social relations that simultaneously condition and emerge around one central field of state action, namely, welfare services. These redistributive relations constitute a crucial setting where state images and practices converge in the interactions of officials and other citizens. Although not the only possible entry point for a relational analysis, welfare services are especially suited to observe mechanisms of inclusion and identification, as claims and decisions are made about who belongs to a given community and who will have access to limited public resources.

The last part highlights how, read together, the collected chapters contribute not only to an understanding of the variety of constructions of the state but also to broader comparative topics. While many recent ethnographic studies of the state have concentrated on how the history of European state formation provided a powerful ideal for statehood in Africa, Asia, and elsewhere, the contributions in this volume concentrate on Eastern and Western Europe as well as Russia. The demise of socialism has called into question the former self-ascription of state functions and furthered the global hegemony of neo-liberal ideas that has also deeply affected Western European welfare practices. This development has included ideas about necessary state withdrawal from service provision and the introduction of new regulatory frameworks, turning the provision of welfare into important sites where the state redefines itself. Nevertheless, the Cold War dichotomy has not yet vanished (Chari and Verdery 2009), which leads to an often separated treatment of former socialist and capitalist states. Instead of taking the difference for granted, this book examines both post-socialist and post-welfare states as relational settings that demonstrate the fluidity and transformation of state structures, while simultaneously insisting on the particular historicity of each case. Thus, apart from the more general comparative conclusions that can be drawn from the relational approach, this volume seeks to contribute to a post–Cold War ethnography of the state.

The Emergence of a Dominant Dichotomy: State Images and Practices

The anthropological rediscovery of the state as a subject of research occurred at a time when other disciplines were already agonizing about the apparent withering away of the state. The following short overview of the broader interdisciplinary field shows that neither the timing nor the specific focus of this recent ethnography of the state was accidental.[1]

Up to the 1980s, political scientists and political sociologists engaged in intense debates about the nature of the state. In the 1960s and 1970s, the Marxist-oriented circles, especially those engaged in the 'Poulantzas-Miliband debate', discussed to what extent the state was exclusively an instrument of capitalist class interest (Miliband 1983; Poulantzas 1969, 1976).[2] In contrast, the largely American pluralist school of community studies of the time viewed the state as an extension of the power of either elitist or pluralist societal interest groups (Dahl 1961; Domhoff 1990). Finally, in the 1980s, neo-Weberian theorists sought to bring 'the state back in' (Evans et al. 1985) by treating it as an autonomous entity analytically separable from intra-societal power struggles. By the late 1980s, these approaches to the state had lost much of their appeal, and in the search for conceptual alternatives to overcome this theoretical stalemate, notions of ideology (Abrams 1988; Bourdieu 1994) and culture (Mitchell 1991, 1999; Steinmetz 1999a) took center stage.[3]

With the benefit of hindsight, one can now see how these developments provided an opening for the application of anthropological tools to the study of the state, while at the same time conditioning the form that this engagement would take. Looking back at Akhil Gupta's (1995) article "Blurred Boundaries," which is considered one of the founding texts of the new (Anglo-American) ethnography of the state, Gupta's insistence on the "analysis of the *everyday practices* of local bureaucracies and the *discursive construction* of the state in public culture" (ibid.: 375; emphasis in original) clearly fits into the broader cultural turn. More recently, two political scientists with an affinity for anthropological approaches, Migdal and Schlichte (2005: 15) proposed differentiating the idea of the state from state practices, thus drawing anthropology's contribution squarely into mainstream social science debates about the nature of the state. Even if the authors advocated investigating precisely the dynamics between state images and practices, they did not suggest a concrete way of how to proceed. In the end, it was rather the dichotomy between images and practices that became part and parcel of the 'new' anthropology of the state.

Prefigured by Gupta (1995), after the turn of the twenty-first century the new ethnographies of the state increasingly concentrated on the domain of representations.[4] In the introduction to their volume *States of Imagination*, Hansen and Stepputat (2001) opted for the formula 'languages of stateness' to capture both representations and practices of statehood. However, the volume's title and individual chapters document a tendency to emphasize cultural images and discourses of the state rather than concrete practices. Shortly afterward, Sharma and Gupta (2006) published a reader on the anthropology of the state, combining classic theoretical texts with recent ethnographic studies from diverse geographical settings. With older theoretical debates increasingly receding into the past and the question of when and by whom the state was really ever constructed as a coherent entity now often left unanswered, this volume quickly became the established canon. In yet another article, Gupta and Sharma (2006: 277) concluded that an "anthropological approach to the state differs from that of other disciplines by according centrality to the *meanings* of everyday practices of bureaucracies and their relation to *representations of the state*" (emphasis added). Seemingly unwittingly, proponents of the new anthropology of the state have fulfilled the expectations of other disciplines in that they have contributed to the established schools of thought—Marxist, (neo-)Weberian, pluralist—by emphasizing the culturally constructed images of the state.

A distinct line of inquiry still consistent with the emphasis on images of the state was taken by scholars who focused on the idea of the nation-state in building communities and, ultimately, national identities. For instance, Herzfeld (1992) demonstrated that both nation-state bureaucracies and local-level societies put the symbolism of family and the language of blood and race in the service of building, maintaining, and manipulating classificatory systems of inclusion and exclusion. Similarly, Borneman (1992) shows how ideas of kin, state, and nation were mutually constructed in former East and West Germany, which constantly mirrored each other in their efforts to create specific self-understandings by regulating the life courses of their respective citizens. Although these insights clearly speak to the imaginative side of state formation, they have not—apart from a few passing references—been fully incorporated into contemporary mainstream ethnography of the state.

One reason for this omission may have to do with the fact that much of the new anthropology of the state focuses explicitly on non-European marginal sites. Das and Poole (2004b: 6) describe the task of the anthropologist as first having to detect the state in "parochial sightings." A similar move away from centers of state power can be observed in discussions of globalization. Trouillot (2001: 132) observes that "state power is being redeployed, state effects are appearing in new sites, and, in almost all cases, this move is one away from national sites to infra-, supra-, or transnational ones." Large parts of the literature on sovereignty have also stressed new forms of sovereignty outside or below the confines of the national state.[5] In addition, many of the studies on specific state activities have focused on coercive sides of the state, such as war, counterinsurgency, and surveillance measures (Aretxaga 2003; Das and Poole 2004a), thereby neglecting the more benevolent side of the state. The stress on often excluded minorities and antagonistic state representations might be due to a certain tradition in peasant studies (Scott 1998). A second influence can be found in Foucauldian thinking, which emphasizes the omnipresence of governmental technologies and techniques in managing (deviant) populations (e.g., Gupta 2012).

Although subscribing to studying the state from its margins, the recent collection of ethnographies of French state institutions by Didier Fassin et al. (2015) is insofar an exception, as it attempts to grasp moral economies and moral subjectivities "at the heart of the state" by studying interactions between state actors and marginalized populations (Fassin 2015: 3). As such, it comes much closer to the relational approach we advocate below.

So far, two lines of criticism have been advanced to counter the emphasis on the fragmentation of state power and the linked methodological recommendations for approaching the state from its margins. Bierschenk (2010: 4) calls the latter a "classical anthropological reflex" that "leads to a tendency to re-invent the wheel and to exoticise states of the South" (ibid.: 3; see also Bierschenk and Olivier de Sardan 2014a: 52–54). Kapferer (2005) and Marcus (2008) contend that this approach takes a pluralist understanding of the state for granted, which in and of itself is an ideology that must be questioned. While non-state actors have undeniably taken over former state responsibilities in many places around the globe, this approach might underestimate the degree to which these processes not only weaken or even deconstruct the state but also contribute to its continuity and strength as both a representation and a political formation (Kapferer 2005: 286–287). In addition, talking about state effects and new sites of sovereignty runs the risk of juxtaposing globalization with an ideal of the sovereign nation-state in much the same way that non-European states were measured against the template of the Weberian ideal type modern state (Migdal and Schlichte 2005: 3; Steinmetz 1999a: 22). To these criticisms we add a third point: the anthropological stress on cultural representation has shifted the weight from state practices toward state images. And despite the stress on the diversity of cultural representations and the co-production of state images by state subjects, the state images described often appear to be rather monolithic, coherent, and unified across the respective society under study. Furthermore, the emphasis on images—first attributed to anthropology by other disciplines in their attempt to overcome the theoretical stalemate in the late 1980s, and then actively appropriated within the new studies of the state in the 1990s—not only rendered state practices the junior partner but also left the void between state images and practices unexplored.

The smaller strand of literature that explicitly focuses on state practices often follows a Weberian tradition with its emphasis on mechanisms of state power. Casting the state largely as a stable political formation, James Scott (1998), for example, took this perspective to the forefront in exploring state practices of making populations and territory legible. In the field of peasant studies, Norman Long's (1989) concept of an 'interface' between the life-worlds of peasants, bureaucrats, and experts also contributed to the study of state practices. Finally, several authors researching particular bureaucratic institutions or sets of actors were inspired by Michael Lipsky (1980), who emphasized the role played by street-level bureaucrats in giving concrete shape to abstract state policies in their encounters with clients. Stressing the structural embedding of state actors, Dubois (2010) studied encounters in French welfare offices, while Bierschenk and Olivier de Sardan (2014b) with their collaborators examined practices of judges and teachers in West Africa. Heyman (1995) explored interactions at the US Immigration and Naturalization Service, and Eckert (2009) analyzed interactions between police officers and poor citizens in Mumbai. Frykman et al. (2009), Larsen (2011), and Olwig (2011) described forms of integration into local communities through welfare provision in Scandinavia. In all of these studies, local state actors play a pivotal role in determining state practices, which contributes significantly to our understanding of the working of the state. Nevertheless, these findings are discussed only sporadically under the heading 'anthropology of the state', and some remain largely confined to the realm of applied anthropology (e.g., Heyman 2004).[6] More importantly, what is often missing here as well is the explicit link to how state actors' practices are shaped by the relational setting.

To conclude, recent ethnographic approaches have greatly advanced our understanding of state formations. However, the methodological stress on marginal sites and state images, combined with the theoretical emphasis on diversity, fragmentation, and disaggregation, leaves some questions unanswered with regard to the stability and the apparent coherence of images and the solidity of the organizational entity called 'state'. In addition, the core distinction between state images and state practices brushes over an analytical void by not clearly demonstrating how they are linked. With this book, we propose to return to the crucial aim identified by Migdal and Schlichte (2005) by exploring these linkages through a relational approach. We thereby combine the emphasis of the practice-oriented studies on bureaucracies as emergent organizational forms with scholarly insights into state images. In the following section, we outline the contours of this relational anthropology of the state, suggesting that it can bridge the gap without abandoning ethnography based on micro-level perspectives.

Stategraphy: Toward a Relational Anthropology of the State

With Max Weber, Georg Simmel, and Norbert Elias usually listed as its forefathers, relational theorizing can hardly be thought of as 'new' in the social sciences (Häußling 2010; see also Emirbayer 1997). However, its potential has not yet been rendered fully prolific for the anthropology of the state. In the following, we seek to outline the main trajectories and specific insights to be gained from such an approach. Investigations into the potency of images and the inherently processual nature of ever-changing forms has made the endeavor to define this shifting and polymorphous entity called 'state' inherently difficult and perhaps ultimately doomed to fail (Jessop 2008: 1). With this in mind, we nevertheless put forward a working concept of the state for the purpose of comparing relational settings. We distinguish three analytical axes that support the indispensable effort to 'relationalize' data gathering and analytical proceedings.

The earliest relational approaches in political anthropology were introduced by the Manchester School. Especially in the African Copperbelt, seemingly fixed categories of religious, ethnic, or clan membership no longer were thought to provide a satisfactory explanation for social phenomena. Researchers turned from actors' individual attributes, such as gender or age, to their personal embeddedness as the focal point of analysis (e.g., Bott 1957; Kapferer 1972). Furthermore, Gluckman (1963) argued that political systems gain their stability through the establishment and re-establishment of cross-cutting ties among social actors.[7] However, shortly after its inception, social network analysis turned to quantification and ventured into structural determinism, while explicit relational theory remained marginal within anthropology.[8] With our approach, we wish to keep the focus on what happens between actors and thereby view such relations as decisive in shaping state formations, images, and practices.

We seek to retain the earlier insights into the importance of embeddedness and complement it with the above-mentioned emphasis on state representations. As Hansen and Stepputat (2001: 6) have argued, the idealized Weberian image of the state as a sovereign entity that reigns over a specific territory by means of a monopoly of violence and rational bureaucracy has influenced state images worldwide.[9] Such expectations of what the state is or what functions it should fulfill feed into the relations between governments and populations as described by Chatterjee (2004). The relational approach adds to these insights by turning the gaze toward the question of how the images themselves are shaped in a concrete web of relations.

In political science, the first explicit articulation of a relational approach to the state was made by Poulantzas (1969), who advanced the idea that the state is a 'social relation'.[10] Although he was less interested in the analysis of the state as such (Hansen and Stepputat 2001: 3), his proposition was taken up by Bob Jessop (2008), who developed it into a 'strategic-relational approach'. This and other relational approaches in sociology and political science usually analyze aggregated levels of nation-states and international relations. Taking a more transactional perspective, Frödin (2012: 271) claims that the state can be "best understood in terms of aggregated patterns of interaction among individuals with different rights and obligations, defined by an immense set of constitutive and regulative rules." This view of the state as 'aggregated structures of interaction' is comparable to the structures of networks found by early network theorists. We complement this perspective by maintaining a processual focus in which relational modalities and the influence of embeddedness become palpable in the multitude of recurrent face-to-face encounters.

Accordingly, we can describe the state as a relational setting that cannot be categorized according to simple hierarchies or a governing center,[11] but that exists within the relations between actors who have unequal access to material, social, regulatory, and symbolic resources and who negotiate over ideas of legitimate power by drawing on existing state images—at once reaffirming and transforming these representations within concrete practices. Such a conceptualization does not attach any regulative functions or source of authority per se to the state. States are viewed not as being characterized by static ties but as being processual in nature. From that perspective, states can be understood as ever-changing political formations with institutional settings that are structured by social relations in interactions characterized by different state images.

A first avenue of analysis is thus a focus on different relational modalities. Such modalities draw on differing normative concepts of what a state should be and how it should act and embody past experiences in structural environments that translate into contingent expectations for the future. Consequently, we do not take the attribute 'relational' to designate a specific monomorphic concept of the state, as Levi-Faur (2013) critically remarks for the concept of a regulatory state. Instead, we understand the state generally as polymorphic and as being created by, and experienced through, different relational modalities. To be sure, actual state practices most often do not conform to images, hopes, or wishes for a coherent state. Relations mediate the apparent mismatch between practices and images and, as such, constitute the interceding link. State formations can be seen as emerging through these relational modalities.

A second avenue of analysis focuses on boundary work, which, heeding Mitchell's (1991) call, we consider central to any state theory. As part of a relational analysis, this boundary work is implicated in the constant negotiation of state images in and through social relations that bring states into being. Two fields of boundary work stand out: that between family/kinship and the state and that between civil society and the state. Both are predicated on the dominant Western interpretation of states. Accordingly, earlier anthropological understandings of states were influenced by the powerful dichotomy between state-based and kin-based societies (e.g., Fortes and Evans-Pritchard 1940), which has been heavily criticized in more recent studies (Thelen and Alber 2017). Nonetheless, both this dichotomy and the concept of civil society as comprising forms of social organization other than the state (Hann 1996) have continued to influence self-understandings of Western societies. Such conceptualizations not only obscure particular social relations as constitutive of the workings of the state, but are in themselves a part of the negotiations and struggles over the power to define how the (legitimate) state should be seen and work.

Besides relational modalities and boundary work, we thirdly emphasize the need to observe different sets of actors and their personal embedding within state hierarchies as well as within other networks. 'Embeddedness' here not only describes the norms and interests of different actors; 'relational embeddedness' is also seen as decisive for practices and decisions (Granovetter 1985). A classic article by Gluckman et al. (1949: 93) describes the irreconcilable demands arising from this double embeddedness in different relational logics as the 'dilemma of the village headman'. Being locally entangled in kinship relations, and being a political representative of this same group of people vis-à-vis the colonial state, made the headman's position difficult, but it also left room for maneuver (Kuper 1970). This by now classical topic, foreshadowed in Weber's notion of pre-modern notables, has lost none of its urgency. Local state actors struggle with structural constraints and their discretionary powers while being embedded in many other relations within the local community that involve different sets of norms. In this regard, Franz and Keebet von Benda-Beckmann's (1998) description of 'state' and 'off-state' activities of state actors in rural Indonesia prefigures the transition from the above-mentioned ethnographic studies of bureaucracies to a relational perspective.

The relations between differentially embedded actors link individuals as well as groups of actors in webs characterized by differences in power and access to diverse resources. Interactions within these webs (re)create boundaries of inclusion and exclusion as expressions of power differentials. By foregrounding concrete social relations and how they adhere in recurring interactions over the life of the individual, we can begin to understand how such situational power differentials might sediment into larger political formations and lend the state as a political formation an appearance of coherence through time.

The relational approach is not intended to gloss over the existing differentiated concepts of statehood, such as the distinction between legislative, executive, and judicial power; between central government and local authorities; between service provision and coercive intervention; and between the regulation, financing, and implementation of specific state tasks by different actors. But it accentuates how this variety feeds into the empirically traceable notions of statehood that emerge in interactions between state and non-state actors. Using a relational perspective, we come to understand that who is locally seen to be a representative of state power can vary and is contingent on particular configurations of state functions, institutional arrangements, and the social relations within which these are embedded. It should therefore be clear that when using the term 'local state' or 'local state actors', our analytical interest lies not with bounded local communities but with grounded social interactions and relations.

By focusing on concrete social relations, it becomes possible to see both the processual nature of state formation and how images become generalized and concretized. Moreover, stategraphy as a relational approach encourages inquiry into the negotiation of the tension between what actors see state agents do and what they think those actors ideally should be doing. By focusing on contradictory moments and conflicting images as they become apparent in interactions, we can move away from seemingly straightforward, unified cultural representations in order to appreciate fully the diversity and contradictory nature of existing state images as well as the role of long-term historical and global processes in bringing about such images (Krohn-Hansen and Nustad 2005: 7).

Stategraphy: The Relational Approach Applied

The relational approach that we have thus far outlined has governed the analysis in the chapters in this volume. Rather than anchoring this book in one area-based interpretative framework, we start from the common ground of what we have called 'stategraphy'. Each individual case study is characterized by a core commitment to a view of the state as a relational setting, ethnographically analyzing how the state is understood, experienced, and reproduced in everyday encounters. These findings are grouped around the three interrelated areas of analysis outlined above—relational modalities, boundary work, and embeddedness—each of which is foregrounded to varying degrees in the contributions to this volume.

In contrast to the aforementioned focus on the coercive sides of the state in many ethnographic studies, the main thematic focus here is on relations within the field of welfare—what could be viewed as a benevolent side of the state, although it clearly has its own coercive dimension. Welfare is a core field of analysis since different state images and state practices come together in negotiations of citizens and local state actors. On the one hand, welfare "managers and protagonists generally undertake action in order to shape their recipients in the light of their own moral motivations" as Kalb (1997: 205) has argued. On the other hand, citizens also actively engage in the field of welfare, making claims for inclusion. Referring to examples from South Africa, James Ferguson (2013: 259) has insisted on the growing importance of social service provision as a site of politics. It is a field in which citizens are not only disciplined or subordinated to state measures, but can use bureaucratic technologies to make the state 'see them' and act as desired (Jansen 2014; Street 2012).

Relational Modalities

In most of the chapters, specific state images embedded in historical trajectories play an important role in citizens' and state actors' use of particular relational modalities. They figure most prominently in Vetters's case study on housing assistance in post-war Mostar (Bosnia and Herzegovina), which documents two ends of a relational continuum. On one end, the state is envisaged as a paternalistic figure that cares for deserving citizens and brings state officials and citizens into personal relationships. In public discourse, this modality is known as clientelism. The opposite end offers a set of practices and images that are associated with civil society. This is represented as relying on the opposing logic, that is, on a clear separation of local government and citizens. Premised on citizens' desire to relate to state authorities, both modalities facilitate communication and interaction between citizens and authorities despite their apparent opposition. Socio-political transformation along this relational continuum occurs contingently, leading to a temporary stabilization of an otherwise fragmented and increasingly dysfunctional post-war Bosnian statehood.

While also stressing recent historical developments, Dubois's chapter has the relational modality of French welfare controllers as the starting point of analysis. The modalities employed by the controllers in their interactions with clients depend on their embeddedness within their respective institutions as a result of differential career perspectives. This resembles the distinct relational modalities employed by the Hungarian mayors described by Schwarcz and Szőke in this book's last chapter. One mayor enacts a paternalistic and hail-fellow-well-met modality in relating to the local public workers, while the other adopts a more distanced educative modality in interacting with his co-villagers. Like the case of the French welfare controllers, the variation of local modalities in Hungary does not contradict central policy aims or contribute inevitably to state fragmentation.

Contrary to the emphasis on discrete modalities employed by specific actors in these ethnographic accounts, Kay's stategraphy concentrates on how a variety of modalities are employed between local state actors and other villagers, between local state actors and officials *within* the social sector, and between local state actors and higher-level authorities in rural western Siberia. These modalities depend on different—at times contradictory—state images, but they are not discrete. Instead, they are combined into hybrid modalities or used consecutively, thereby reinforcing one another. Similar to both Vetters and Dubois, Kay argues that rather than being imperfections or anomalies, such combined relational modalities bridge the gap between images and practices of the state.

The legal advisers of the two London non-profit legal service providers described by Forbess and James in their contribution also employ different relational modalities that range from adversarial to cooperative. They put citizens into contact with various state actors and enable different state actors to communicate among themselves. In this way, the case resembles the accounts of Kay and Vetters, who describe how 'getting things done' through personalized relations makes the state tangible in practice. However, these processes also increasingly blur the boundaries between state and civil society. Ultimately, this might weaken the position of legal advisers, whose power is based on the construction of a separate sphere of civil society. This chapter directs us to the question of how these boundaries are recreated in specific interactions.

Boundary Work

Boundary work is a central topic in Read's relational analysis of volunteering in three Czech hospitals. The chapter demonstrates how volunteering as an instantiation of civil society is distinguished from the state. The volunteer coordinators forge relationships with a variety of state actors, including hospital managers and officials in local and central government. Although the volunteers' success depends heavily on material resources and moral backing from the state, Read emphasizes the ongoing reproduction of the ideological boundary between state and civil society. She shows how this apparent contradiction is mediated and resolved within the relationships between volunteer coordinators and state actors.

Using the example of two elder care projects in Serbia, Thelen, Thiemann, and Roth explore yet another prominent field of boundary work—that between state and family. In one project, state-paid carers come to be included as members of the kinship networks of the recipients. In another project, foster families for the elderly are organized and financed through a state program. These practices stand in stark contrast to the prevailing image of an unresponsive and distant Serbian state. By reframing state support in terms of kinship, state care becomes acceptable while simultaneously sustaining an ideological separation of the realms of state and family.

All of these contributions hint at the crucial importance of actors' embeddedness in a wide range of relations. This determines not only the implementation and outcome of central state policy, but also how state images and practices are either reconciled or challenged in concrete social relations.

Embeddedness

In Vetters's case study of housing in Mostar, citizens' employment of different relational modalities depends on which social relations they are able to mobilize based on their embeddedness in particular socially and politically structured webs of relations in a divided city. Read's contribution reveals how the differentiated embedding of volunteer coordinators leads to more or less successful programs. Similarly, Dubois's chapter on controllers and Forbess and James's chapter on legal advisers show how state actors' specific positions enable them to make the state 'work'. In both cases, these actors' practices make complex circumstances decipherable for higher state officials. Through their practices of putting their clients into contact with different state agencies, the legal advisers, in fact, create new webs of relations for them.

Further exploring aspects of embeddedness, Dorondel and Popa focus on how local state actors translate a central policy by relying on local notions of deservingness. Their relational analysis examines the discretionary practices of local bureaucrats in implementing an EU food aid program in two different sites in Romania. The double embeddedness of local state actors poses a dilemma (as described by Gluckman et al. 1949), but it also enhances those actors' power and discretion. Thus, similar to Dubois, the authors argue that individual discretion in combination with a transnational policy does not necessarily undermine state power.

In the final chapter in this book, Schwarcz and Szőke compare how the embeddedness of two Hungarian village mayors relates to their distributive practices. At one site, the mayor, in line with national trends, favors individual lower-middle-class local citizens, whom he considers to be 'self-advancing' (as opposed to the poor villagers). By contrast, the mayor of the second village organizes state programs in a more expansive manner, ensuring that the members of the marginalized Roma minority in the village have access to the benefits as well. This mayor adheres to a vision of the state as the guarantor of social peace and advocates a sense of community that includes the Roma.

Many of these individual contributions focus on inner-country comparisons, mainly pointing to dissimilarities within a supposedly similar national setting on the basis of different relational patterns. An understanding of statography as a grounded analysis of particular relational settings defines these localities as sites for the manifestation of states, but this owes less to their bounded, small-scale nature or their legally defined degrees of local autonomy. Rather, these sites derive their significance through the convergence of ever-changing regulatory frameworks, actors, resources, and interpretations, actualized in webs of social relations at particular conjunctions of time and space. Thus, our contributors find plural manifestations of the state in one locality (Vetters) and within one state territory (Schwarcz and Szőke). Likewise, actors switch between and combine different images of the state (Kay) and exploit supra-national programs to enhance their role as state actors in the local context (Dorondel and Popa). Such insights gained from an analysis of relational modes, boundary work, and actors' embeddedness can contribute to broader discussions about the workings of the state. In our concluding section, we therefore seek to open up this perspective by pointing to larger patterns and global historical contexts.

Comparative Outlook and Concluding Remarks

Based on a comparative reading of the individual contributions, we outline some possible, but by no means exhaustive, insights about the issues of local state manifestations and welfare transformation, as well as an analysis of power and patterns of inclusion and exclusion, as an invitation for further comparative work that reaches beyond the confines of country or regional area studies.

Throughout this collection of relational analyses, boundary work leading to local manifestations of the state permeates not just interactions between elected or appointed state agents and welfare recipients in which it is clear who represents the state. As demonstrated in the chapters by Forbess and James, by Read, and by Thelen, Thiemann, and Roth, boundary work also pervades interactions involving a broad array of intermediaries receiving varying degrees of state funding. Such intermediaries often emerge to facilitate connections between citizens and various state agencies, sometimes allowing for personalized relationships that would be impossible in direct interactions between state agents and citizens. The resulting complex webs of state and state-like agencies that are together responsible for the provision of welfare have a counter-intuitive implication. As it is often difficult to determine unambiguously whether or not an actor is part of the state, these relations contribute to the blurring of the state's boundaries. Yet as these contributions also demonstrate, intermediaries are often most effective when they discursively distance themselves from the state, thereby recreating the image of a coherent state entity.

The selection of case studies from diverse settings (Russia, Eastern Europe, the western Balkans, Western Europe) shows how the relationships between state institutions at various levels and the constraints posed by welfare restructuring condition how state officials interact with welfare recipients. As a whole, the chapters allow for a more nuanced understanding of change and continuity that challenges the all-too-familiar grand narratives of East-West difference. As demonstrated in some of the ethnographies, the restructuring of the Western European welfare state undermines old certainties and forces the painful negotiation of new, frequently improvised scripts (Dubois, chap. 2; Forbess and James, chap. 4). Along the same lines, the contributions dealing with post-socialist countries—in two cases they are also post-war societies—provide an avenue for studying the state as a process, itself subject to deep historical transformations (Thelen et al., chap. 6; Vetters, chap. 1).

The chapters furthermore illustrate how state agents who attempt to shape the behaviors of welfare recipients with respect to moral notions implied in welfare programs sometimes assume a coercive capacity, patrolling the borders of belonging and making decisions about a given community's inclusion or exclusion by granting or withholding benefits. But the authors also point out the diversity that arises when welfare policies are concretely implemented, which in turn affects images of the state and notions of deservingness. Thus, Thelen, Thiemann, and Roth portray a process characterized less by coercion and more by a mutual co-optation of values in which care recipients reframe state-funded support in terms that are acceptable to them. The British legal advisers studied by Forbess and James challenge what they perceive as unfair decisions made by state officials on behalf of their clients. Domination and resistance as analytical categories in these instances cannot be easily attributed to clear-cut sides but emerge as properties of social relations.

Through their shared commitment to relating micro-level social relations to macro-level configurations of state, welfare, and political systems, the authors contribute to the larger analysis of power. The chapters by Dorondel and Popa and by Schwarcz and Szőke analyze how, in post-socialist contexts, changes in welfare systems (through the EU as a transnational welfare provider in one case and the decentralization of welfare provision in the other) are utilized by elected state actors to reproduce local communities and their hierarchies. These hierarchies are tied in complex ways to the reproduction of power relations at the national level. In the cases described by Dorondel and Popa, the local practice of symbolic acts of 'gifting' to specific individuals and groups—instead of 'granting' rights to legally eligible recipients—not only enhances state actors' personal standing in their respective communities, but also serves to garner political support for ruling national parties in the upcoming presidential elections. Thus, these acts at the same time strengthen the embeddedness of state actors within local and supra-local networks of power, thereby contributing to the consolidation of central authority. In one of Schwarcz and Szőke's cases, we see a similar yet different effect. The devolution of central regulative power to municipalities allows for some degree of deflection from nationally dominant discourses of deservingness in so-called disadvantaged areas with a Roma majority: the mayor of one such village has established a paternalistic, inclusive practice of granting benefits. However, admitting such local variances also absolves the central government from the responsibility of preventing widespread poverty and demonstrates its compliance with neo-liberal notions of workfare and reduced public spending.

It is instructive to compare this last case with Dubois's case study of the role of control as an instrument of social policy that has become central to the remodeling of the French welfare system. In an urban setting at the heart of a capitalist Western state and in a context structured by new public management reforms of the welfare sector, we find that paternalistic practices are reintroduced and institutionalized within the boundary zones of the state apparatus in interactions between controllers and benefit recipients. Rather than being inclusive, these practices and the relations on which they are predicated serve the structural rationale of the post-welfare era. As "a consistent mode of governance in which discretion and leeway accorded to street-level bureaucrats are necessary for the state to exert power over citizens' behaviors" (Dubois, chap. 2), they reveal the coercive side of welfare provision.

In conclusion, we have argued that the historical positioning of the new anthropology of the state within the wider social sciences and within specific anthropological traditions has produced a one-sided emphasis on the state as cultural representation, contributing to the emergence of an analytical gap between state images and state practices. We have furthermore proposed that a relational approach can tie these strands together, thereby bridging the established divide between state images and practices and showing how both are negotiated, approved, and transformed in everyday interactions within webs of relations. Together, the chapters in this book make a strong case for comparative ethnographic research that investigates different relational modalities, the (re)production of state boundaries, and forms of embeddedness. The relational perspective highlights similarities in such processes without neglecting structural as well as historical particularities. We believe that, applied in a variety of settings, stategraphy as a relational anthropology of the state can yield a number of comparative insights that can enrich current debates about the nature of the state.

Acknowledgments

This book is based in part on papers presented at the conference "Local State and Social Security: Negotiating Deservingness and Avenues to Resources in Rural Areas," which took place in Halle from 30 June to 2 July 2011. We would like to thank the Max Planck Institute for Social Anthropology and the Volkswagen Foundation for the intellectual and financial support that enabled this workshop to take place. We also thank Ștefan Dorondel, Julia Eckert, Mihai Popa, and Andre Thiemann for comments on earlier drafts of the introduction; Benjamin White and Gita Rajan for careful language editing; and Christof Lammer and Patrick Muigg for support with formatting and preparing the bibliography.

Tatjana Thelen is a Full Professor in the Department of Social and Cultural Anthropology, University of Vienna. In 2016–2017, she was a Fellow at the Center for Interdisciplinary Research, Bielefeld University, leading the research group on "Kinship and Politics." Her areas of interest include the state, property, welfare and care, and kinship and family. She is the co-editor of a special section of *Focaal* entitled "Social Security and Care after Socialism" (2007) and of *Reconnecting State and Kinship* (2017).

Larissa Vetters currently acts as a Research Coordinator of the Law and Society Institute at the Humboldt University of Berlin. She previously worked as a Coordinator of the project "Local State and Social Security in Rural Hungary, Romania and Serbia" carried out at the Max Planck Institute for Social Anthropology (2009–2011) and as a Lecturer at the Institute of Social and Cultural Anthropology of the Martin Luther University of Halle-Wittenberg (2011–2013). Her research focuses on processes of (external) state building in Bosnia and Herzegovina and, more recently, on migrants' encounters with the German state in the frame of administrative court cases.

Keebet von Benda-Beckmann is a Professor Emeritus, the former Head of the Project Group Legal Pluralism, and currently an Associate in the Department of Law and Anthropology at the Max Planck Institute for Social Anthropology. Recent publications include the co-edited *Rules of Law and Laws of Ruling: On the Governance of Law* (2009) and the co-authored *Political and Legal Transformations of an Indonesian Polity* (2013).

Notes

1. One might argue that this 'new' anthropology of the state took after its 'elder brother', political anthropology, by exhibiting an ignorance of the original anthropology of the state, which was mainly concerned with the origins of the state, and ignoring debates about the colonial state as discussed in the works of the early Manchester School (Gluckman 1963; Gluckman et al. 1949). On the relation between political anthropology and the ethnography of the state, see also Thomassen (2008).
2. Strikingly, Marcus's (2008) critique of the new anthropology of the state resembles Poulantzas's criticism of Miliband. For a review on the debate, see also Laclau (1975).
3. This turn had some antecedents in both Marxist (Althusser 1971; Gramsci 1992) and neo-Weberian or neo-institutionalist (Nettl 1968) paradigms, but also took up Foucault-inspired post-structuralist approaches.
4. See Thomassen (2008) for more a more detailed analysis of the new dominance of representational approaches.
5. On Africa, see Mbembe (2005). On graduated sovereignty in Southeast Asia, see Ong (2000). On transnational sovereignty, see Sassen (2004), and on fractured sovereignty in India, see Randeria (2007).
6. Similarly, the predominant focus of the growing sub-field of the anthropology of policy in 'advanced' Western societies (Shore et al. 2011) seems to have hindered the full incorporation of this body of literature into the new anthropology of the state.
7. On the insights of the Manchester School, see also Thomassen (2008: 266).
8. On the development of network analysis in anthropology, see Schweizer (1996).
9. Despite Weber's interpretative approach, his ideal type state took on a life of its own, leading to a largely objectivist understanding of the Weberian state.
10. Although Weber (1978: 14) had already paid a good deal of attention to the problem of how agency and authority are attributed to collective entities such as nation-states, which, empirically speaking, are constituted by individual interactions, he did not develop an explicitly relational perspective on the state.
11. For a similar description of society as a relational setting, see Somers (1994: 70–72). For a relational view on the state from an actor-network theory (ANT) perspective, see Passoth and Rowland (2010). Although we acknowledge the importance of the specific materiality of state bureaucracies, we concentrate on interpersonal relations in our approach.

References

Abrams, Philip. 1988. "Notes on the Difficulty of Studying the State." *Journal of Historical Sociology* 1 (1): 58–89.

Althusser, Louis. 1971. *Ideology and the Ideological State Apparatuses: Lenin and Philosophy and Other Essays*. Trans. Ben Brewster. New York: Monthly Review Press.

Aretxaga, Begoña. 2003. "Maddening States." *Annual Review of Anthropology* 32: 393–410.

Benda-Beckmann, Franz von, and Keebet von Benda-Beckmann. 1998. "Where Structures Merge: State and Off-State Involvement in Rural Social Security on Ambon, Indonesia." In *Old World Places, New World Problems*, ed. Sandra N. Pannell and Franz von Benda-Beckmann, 143–180. Canberra: Australian National University, Centre for Resource and Environmental Studies.

Bierschenk, Thomas. 2010. "States at Work in West Africa: Sedimentation, Fragmentation and Normative Double-Binds." Department of Anthropology and African

Studies, Johannes Gutenberg University, Working Paper No. 113. http://www.ifeas.uni-mainz.de/Dateien/AP113.pdf (accessed 27 March 2012).

Bierschenk, Thomas, and Jean-Pierre Olivier de Sardan. 2014a. "Ethnographies of Public Services in Africa: An Emerging Research Paradigm." In Bierschenk and Sardan 2014b, 35–65.

Bierschenk, Thomas, and Jean-Pierre Olivier de Sardan, eds. 2014b. *States at Work: Dynamics of African Bureaucracies*. Leiden: Brill.

Borneman, John. 1992. *Belonging in the Two Berlins: Kin, State, Nation*. Cambridge: Cambridge University Press.

Bott, Elizabeth. 1957. *Family and Network: Roles, Norms, and External Relationships in Ordinary Urban Families*. London: Tavistock.

Bouchard, Michel. 2011. "The State of the Study of the State in Anthropology." *Reviews in Anthropology* 40 (3): 183–209.

Bourdieu, Pierre. 1994. "Rethinking the State: Genesis and Structure of the Bureaucratic Field." *Sociological Theory* 12 (1): 1–18.

Chari, Sharad, and Katherine Verdery. 2009. "Thinking between the Posts: Postcolonialism, Postsocialism, and Ethnography after the Cold War." *Comparative Studies in Society and History* 51 (1): 6–34.

Chatterjee, Partha. 2004. *The Politics of the Governed: Reflections on Popular Politics in Most of the World*. New York: Columbia University Press.

Dahl, Robert A. 1961. *Who Governs? Democracy and Power in an American City*. New Haven, CT: Yale University Press.

Das, Veena, and Deborah Poole, eds. 2004a. *Anthropology in the Margins of the State*. Santa Fe, NM: School of American Research Press.

Das, Veena, and Deborah Poole. 2004b. "State and Its Margins: Comparative Ethnographies." In Das and Poole 2004a, 3–34.

Domhoff, G. William. 1990. *The Power Elite and the State: How Policy Is Made in America*. New York: Aldine de Gruyter.

Dubois, Vincent. 2010. *The Bureaucrat and the Poor: Encounters in French Welfare Offices*. Farnham: Ashgate.

Eckert, Julia. 2009. "The Virtuous and the Wicked: Anthropological Perspectives on the Police in Mumbai." Habilitation, Martin Luther University of Halle-Wittenberg.

Emirbayer, Mustafa. 1997. "Manifesto for a Relational Sociology." *American Journal of Sociology* 103 (2): 281–317.

Evans, Peter B., Dietrich Rueschemeyer, and Theda Skocpol, eds. 1985. *Bringing the State Back In*. Cambridge: Cambridge University Press.

Fassin, Didier. 2015. "Introduction: Governing Precarity." In Fassin et al. 2015, 1–11.

Fassin, Didier, Yasmine Bouagga, Jean-Sébastian Eideliman, et al. 2015. *At the Heart of the State*. Trans. Patrick Brown and Didier Fassin. London: Pluto Press.

Ferguson, James. 2013. "Reply to Comments on 'Declarations of Dependence.'" *Journal of the Royal Anthropological Institute* 19 (2): 258–260.

Fortes, Meyer, and E. E. Evans-Pritchard, eds. 1940. *African Political Systems*. London: Oxford University Press.

Frödin, Olle J. 2012. "Dissecting the State: Towards a Relational Conceptualization of States and State Failure." *Journal of International Development* 24 (3): 271–286.

Frykman, Jonas, Mia-Marie Hammarlin, Kjell Hansen, et al. 2009. "Sense of Community: Trust, Hope and Worries in the Welfare State." *Etnologia Europaea* 39 (1): 7–46.

Gluckman, Max. 1963. *Order and Rebellion in Tribal Africa*. London: Cohen & West.

Gluckman, Max, James C. Mitchell, and John A. Barnes. 1949. "The Village Headman in British Central Africa." *Africa: Journal of the International African Institute* 19 (2): 89–106.

Gramsci, Antonio. 1992. *The Prison Notebooks*. New York: Columbia University Press.
Granovetter, Mark. 1985. "Economic Action and Social Structure: The Problem of Embeddedness." *American Journal of Sociology* 91 (3): 481–510.
Gupta, Akhil. 1995. "Blurred Boundaries: The Discourse of Corruption, the Culture of Politics, and the Imagined State." *American Ethnologist* 22 (2): 375–402.
Gupta, Akhil. 2012. *Red Tape: Bureaucracy, Structural Violence, and Poverty in India*. Durham, NC: Duke University Press.
Gupta, Akhil, and Aradhana Sharma. 2006. "Globalization and Postcolonial States." *Current Anthropology* 47 (2): 277–293.
Hann, Chris. 1996. "Introduction." In *Civil Society: Challenging Western Models*, ed. Chris Hann and Elizabeth Dunn, 1–26. London: Routledge.
Hansen, Thomas B., and Finn Stepputat, eds. 2001. *States of Imagination: Ethnographic Explorations of the Postcolonial State*. Durham, NC: Duke University Press.
Häußling, Roger. 2010. "Relationale Soziologie." In *Handbuch Netzwerkforschung*, ed. Christian Stegbauer and Roger Häußling, 63–87. Wiesbaden: VS Verlag.
Herzfeld, Michael. 1992. *The Social Production of Indifference: Exploring the Symbolic Roots of Western Bureaucracy*. Chicago: University of Chicago Press.
Heyman, Josiah McC. 1995. "Putting Power in the Anthropology of Bureaucracy." *Current Anthropology* 36 (2): 261–287.
Heyman, Josiah McC. 2004. "The Anthropology of Power-Wielding Bureaucracies." *Human Organization* 63 (4): 487–500.
Jansen, Stef. 2014. "Hope For/Against the State: Gridding in a Besieged Sarajevo Suburb." *Ethnos* 79 (2): 238–260.
Jessop, Bob. 2008. *State Power: A Strategic-Relational Approach*. Cambridge: Polity Press.
Kalb, Don. 1997. *Expanding Class: Power and Everyday Politics in Industrial Communities in the Netherlands, 1850–1950*. Durham, NC: Duke University Press.
Kapferer, Bruce. 1972. *Strategy and Transaction in an African Factory: African Workers and Indian Management in a Zambian Town*. Manchester: Manchester University Press.
Kapferer, Bruce. 2005. "New Formations of Power, the Oligarchic-Corporate State, and Anthropological Ideological Discourse." *Anthropological Theory* 5 (3): 285–299.
Krohn-Hansen, Christian, and Knut G. Nustad. 2005. "Introduction." In *State Formation: Anthropological Perspectives*, ed. Christian Krohn-Hansen and Knut G. Nustad, 3–26. London: Pluto Press.
Kuper, Adam. 1970. "Gluckman's Village Headman." *American Anthropologist* 72 (2): 355–358.
Laclau, Ernesto. 1975. "The Specificity of the Political: The Poulantzas-Miliband Debate." *Economy and Society* 4 (1): 87–110.
Larsen, Birgitte R. 2011. "Drawing Back the Curtains: The Role of Domestic Space in the Social Inclusion and Exclusion of Refugees in Rural Denmark." *Social Analysis* 55 (2): 142–158.
Levi-Faur, David. 2013. "The Odyssey of the Regulatory State: From a 'Thin' Monomorphic Concept to a 'Thick' and Polymorphic Concept." *Law & Policy* 35 (1–2): 29–50.
Lipsky, Michael. 1980. *Street-Level Bureaucracy: Dilemmas of the Individual in Public Services*. New York: Russell Sage Foundation.
Long, Norman, ed. 1989. *Encounters at the Interface: A Perspective on Social Discontinuities in Rural Development*. Wageningen: Wageningen Agricultural University.
Marcus, Anthony. 2008. "Interrogating the Neo-pluralist Orthodoxy in American Anthropology." *Dialectical Anthropology* 32 (1–2): 59–86.
Mbembe, Achille. 2005. "Sovereignty as a Form of Expenditure." In *Sovereign Bodies: Citizens, Migrants, and States in the Postcolonial World*, ed. Thomas B. Hansen and Finn Stepputat, 148–166. Princeton, NJ: Princeton University Press.

Migdal, Joel S., and Klaus Schlichte. 2005. "Rethinking the State." In *The Dynamics of States: The Formation and Crises of State Domination*, ed. Klaus Schlichte, 1–40. Aldershot: Ashgate.

Miliband, Ralph. 1983. *Class Power and State Power*. London: Verso.

Mitchell, Timothy. 1991. "The Limits of the State: Beyond Statist Approaches and Their Critics." *American Political Science Review* 85 (1): 77–96.

Mitchell, Timothy. 1999. "Society, Economy, and the State Effect." In Steinmetz 1999b, 76–97.

Nettl, John P. 1968. "The State as a Conceptual Variable." *World Politics* 20 (4): 559–592.

Olwig, Karen F. 2011. "'Integration': Migrants and Refugees between Scandinavian Welfare Societies and Family Relations." *Journal of Ethnic and Migration Studies* 37 (2): 179–196.

Ong, Aihwa. 2000. "Graduated Sovereignty in South-East Asia." *Theory, Culture & Society* 17 (4): 55–75.

Passoth, Jan-Hendrik, and Nicholas J. Rowland. 2010. "Actor-Network State: Integrating Actor-Network Theory and State Theory." *International Sociology* 25 (6): 818–841.

Poulantzas, Nicos. 1969. "The Problem of the Capitalist State." *New Left Review* 58: 7–78.

Poulantzas, Nicos. 1976. "The Capitalist State: A Reply to Miliband and Laclau." *New Left Review* 95: 63–83.

Randeria, Shalini. 2007. "Legal Pluralism, Social Movements and the Post-Colonial State in India: Fractured Sovereignty and Differential Citizenship Rights." In *Another Knowledge Is Possible: Beyond Northern Epistemologies*, ed. Boaventura de Sousa Santos, 41–74. London: Verso.

Sassen, Saskia. 2004. "Beyond Sovereignty: De-Facto Transnationalism in Immigration Policy." In *Worlds on the Move: Globalization, Migration, and Cultural Security*, ed. Jonathan Friedman and Shalini Randeria, 229–249. London: Tauris.

Schweizer, Thomas. 1996. *Muster sozialer Ordnung: Netzwerkanalyse als Fundament der Sozialethnologie*. Berlin: Reimer.

Scott, James C. 1998. *Seeing Like a State: How Certain Schemes to Improve the Human Condition Have Failed*. New Haven, CT: Yale University Press.

Sharma, Aradhana, and Akhil Gupta, eds. 2006. *The Anthropology of the State: A Reader*. Malden, MA: Blackwell Publisher.

Shore, Cris, Susan Wright, and Davide Però, eds. 2011. *Policy Worlds: Anthropology and the Analysis of Contemporary Power*. New York: Berghahn Books.

Somers, Margaret R. 1994. "Rights, Relationality, and Membership: Rethinking the Making and Meaning of Citizenship." *Law & Social Inquiry* 19 (1): 63–112.

Steinmetz, George. 1999a. "Introduction: Culture and the State." In Steinmetz 1999b, 1–49.

Steinmetz, George, ed. 1999b. *State/Culture: State-Formation after the Cultural Turn*. Ithaca, NY: Cornell University Press.

Thelen, Tatjana, and Erdmute Alber. 2017. "Reconnecting State and Kinship: Temporalities, Scales, Classifications." In *Reconnecting State and Kinship*, ed. Tatjana Thelen and Erdmute Alber, 1–35. Philadelphia: University of Pennsylvania Press.

Street, Alice. 2012. "Seen by the State: Bureaucracy, Visibility and Governmentality in a Papua New Guinean Hospital." *Australian Journal of Anthropology* 23 (1): 1–21.

Thomassen, Bjorn. 2008. "What Kind of Political Anthropology?" *International Political Anthropology* 1 (2): 263–274.

Trouillot, Michel-Rolph. 2001. "Anthropology of the State in the Age of Globalization." *Current Anthropology* 42 (1): 125–138.

Weber, Max. 1978. *Economy and Society: An Outline of Interpretive Sociology*. Ed. Guenther Roth and Claus Wittich. Berkeley: University of California Press.

Chapter 1

CONTINGENT STATEHOOD
Clientelism and Civic Engagement as Relational Modalities in Contemporary Bosnia and Herzegovina

Larissa Vetters

On a winter day in January 2006, 12 years after the Bosnian War had ended, a protest meeting took place in Mostar's inner city on Šantićeva Street. This street runs parallel to the former military front line, which separates the Croat side to the west of the city from the predominantly Bosniak side to the east. Signs of the war were visible here, and many apartment blocks remained in ruins. On that day, former residents rallied for reconstruction of the buildings and publicly decried the passivity of the local authorities. Approximately 40 people had assembled in front of the ruins of their apartments, holding up signs with the slogan "Raseljeni u svom gradu" (Displaced in our own town), when the mayor of Mostar arrived and issued a statement. He reiterated the local

Notes for this chapter begin on page 35.

government's support for the reconstruction of war-damaged housing despite municipal budget restrictions and waning support from international donors. After a brief question-and-answer session with protestors and journalists, he quickly departed. Thereupon, the protest organizers announced that the residents of Šantićeva would henceforth gather publicly every two weeks to draw attention to their cause.

The problem of housing was at the core of another meeting with state officials, which 60-year-old Alma Dedič[1] described to me in the summer of 2006. She had heard about a state-run reconstruction and return program in the neighboring, predominantly rural municipality. Under this program, beneficiaries who qualified as displaced persons (*raseljeni*) were able to secure grants to rebuild and return to their original homes, as long as they fell into the category of 'minority returnees'. Brokered by Nezad, the leader of the neighborhood cell of the locally dominant political party and a good friend, the Dedič family applied for the program and claimed reconstruction aid for their weekend home (*vikendica*) in this municipality, now largely populated by Croats. To this end, they declared the *vikendica* to have been their regular pre-war residence. Again, with the help of friends in the administration of the neighboring municipality, they managed to obtain proof of pre-war residence, which then allowed them to register as potential returnees eligible for reconstruction aid. To further advance Alma's chance of success, Nezad arranged for her to meet with the federal minister for human rights and refugee affairs, whose ministry was responsible for selecting beneficiaries. Alma had clearly been impressed with the minister. He had actively sought information from her about the situation of each family member—employment, education, wartime experiences—and had promised help. This meeting had restored Alma's trust in at least some politicians and her hope that finally some sort of help would come through. In her eyes, such support would acknowledge her service as a volunteer toward the preservation of a Bosnian state during the war.

• • •

This chapter examines how the contemporary state of Bosnia and Herzegovina (BiH) is coming into being as an idea, a political formation, and an institutional framework. As an ethnography of the aggregate effects of interactions between state agents and ordinary citizens over time, it explores the interplay between actually existing politico-administrative structures, state practices, and state representations of bureaucrats, politicians, and other citizens.

In what follows, I start with a brief introduction to the post-war governance structure in Mostar and then present detailed case studies involving the Dedič family and the residents of Šantićeva. Based on ethnographic fieldwork[2] and secondary sources, I demonstrate that residents of Mostar are affected by two important spatial configurations. Housing policies during the socialist era affirmed spatially structured state imaginaries of redistribution[3] that engendered distinct notions of rural and urban, whereas violent ethno-nationalist policies that came into force during the war created a socio-politically divided post-war city space. Distinctive relational modalities evolve as citizens inhabiting particular positions within the divided space of the city resort to the rural-urban imaginary of state redistribution in their interactions with state representatives. Supplicants such as the Dedič family go about it individually, using personalized relations and hoping for assistance from what is imagined to be a caring and paternalistic state represented by powerful patrons. The residents of Šantićeva organize a public protest and cast themselves as representatives of civil society in order to stake a collective claim to an initially unresponsive state. In juxtaposing these two cases, I aim to unsettle scholarly and popular depictions of clientelism and civil society as diametrically opposed social forms of state-society relations (see also Kay, chap. 3; Read, chap. 5). I argue that a relational 'stategraphy' offers deeper insights into the modalities that are available to citizens, or sought out by them, for interacting with state officials along a relational continuum (see also the introduction to this volume). Placing citizens' relational modes in the wider historical context of post-socialist and post-war transformation reveals that they are differentially embedded in the socio-political city space and affected by current and past legal concepts and regulations. These embedded positionalities enable and constrain citizens in different ways. Such a diachronic and processual approach centered on citizens' relational work ultimately sheds light on the dynamics of state transformation[4] and leads to a more nuanced assessment of the contemporary Bosnian state.

Housing Insecurities in Post-war Bosnia and Herzegovina

The war in Bosnia wrought massive destruction on both urban and rural housing stock between 1992 and 1995. The violent consolidation of ethno-national territories forced large segments of the population to relocate. As a result, the occupation and ownership structures of individual family houses and collective apartment buildings changed radically. International donors stepped in after the war, offering assistance for reconstruction and the return of former residents, while socially owned[5] housing came to be privatized. Nevertheless, for many families the housing situation remained unclear and unresolved. In an era of socio-economic insecurity, residential property became a much-valued and sought-after asset.

Bosnia is now also grappling with a highly complex governance structure[6] and the ambiguities of externally dictated state-building processes. A special international authority, the Office of the High Representative (OHR), holds far-reaching powers to intervene in all matters pertaining to the implementation of the civilian aspects of the Dayton Peace Agreement, which ended the war in 1995. Contemporary Bosnian politics is driven by identity politics, with prominent leaders representing each of Bosnia's three constituent peoples (Bosnian Serbs, Bosnian Croats, Bosniaks)[7] in the framework of a consociational political system that many observers describe as dysfunctional. Ethno-national political tensions, international interventions, and the paralysis of the formal political decision-making process are all particularly evident in the city of Mostar.

Spanning both sides of the Neretva River, Mostar is the urban industrial center of the Herzegovina region and had long been regarded as one of the most multi-ethnic cities in former Yugoslavia (Bose 2002: 99). During the violent dissolution of the Socialist Federal Republic of Yugoslavia, Mostar witnessed some of the region's most intense hostilities and destruction, consequently dividing the city into a Croat-dominated West and a Bosniak-dominated East. Separate wartime administrations were established for each territory, and members of ethno-national groups opposed by the dominant ethno-national military organizations within the respective territories left, either voluntarily or through forced expulsion. The conflict drastically altered the composition of Mostar's population.[8] Most Serbs had left Mostar, people relocated from one side of the city to the other, many Mostarians took refuge in foreign countries, and there was a massive influx of displaced persons from surrounding areas into both sides of the city.

Despite extensive physical reconstruction carried out between 1994 and 1996 under the mandate of the European Union Administration of Mostar, numerous private houses and collective housing blocks remained in ruins, and persistent ethno-political divisions forestalled attempts to formulate an integrated housing reconstruction policy for the entire city. Instead, Croat authorities on the western bank and Bosniak authorities on the eastern bank pursued ethno-nationally motivated policies of return and settlement for internally displaced persons (IDPs) within the framework of housing reconstruction. A small central zone, which both parties had agreed to administer jointly, became a highly contested space and an administrative no-man's-land (Yarwood 1999).

The *Vikendica* as a Second Home: Tapping into Reconstruction Funds for Rural Returnees

Constraints and Opportunities for Obtaining Housing Assistance in a Divided City

The iconic inner-city neighborhood on Mostar's eastern bank where the Dedič family resides represents the heartland of the Bosniak territory. This neighborhood is dominated by the major ethno-nationalist-oriented Bosniak Party, which draws its legitimacy from having played a leading role in mobilizing and organizing the defense of this part of town against the Serb and Croat attacks between 1992 and 1994. As we saw in the opening vignette, Alma Dedič referred to her participation in these efforts to demonstrate her family's deservingness to receive state assistance to the federal minister for human rights and refugee affairs, who belongs to the same party.

Alma began to seek funding to rebuild the family's *vikendica* at a time when her eldest son planned to marry and establish his own household. Both he and his fiancée lived with their respective parents. The Dedič household spanned three generations, all living together in crowded conditions. Alma was the only household member holding a salaried job: her husband and his parents received minimal pensions, and her son worked informal jobs whenever the opportunity arose. Although their house had been heavily damaged during the war, the Dedič family claimed never to have received reconstruction aid. According to Alma, reconstruction programs prioritized IDPs from rural areas, and because Alma's family had remained in Mostar throughout the war, they did not count as *raseljeni*. By claiming the *vikendica* as their regular pre-war residence and the house in Mostar as their post-war residence, they finally found a way to access reconstruction aid targeted for rural areas. Once it was rebuilt, Alma and her husband planned to relocate to the *vikendica* after retirement, thereby making room for the young couple to live in the city house.

Raseljeni *as a Recent Category of Entitlement for Post-war Housing Assistance*

The categories of 'refugee' (*izbeglice*) and 'internally displaced persons' (transliterated as *raseljeni*) were first introduced in Annex 7 of the Dayton Peace Agreement. These categories were meant to address and reverse large-scale internal displacements within BiH as well as settlement abroad. These two categories and the related legal category of 'returnee' (*povratnik*) implied entitlement to property restoration or compensation, as well as allied benefits in the form of temporary housing, reconstruction aid, and in-kind assistance. In the immediate post-war environment, international organizations took the lead in defining and implementing these categories. Later on, local authorities were charged with implementing Annex 7, and the measure was integrated into local legal frameworks and administrative procedures. A statewide Refugee Return Fund that pooled international donor contributions and local funds was formed as a financing and coordinating instrument for various return programs (cf. Vetters 2007: 192–195). Support for refugees and returnees thus became a domain of state activity and, together with other war-related state provisions (such as veterans' care), blended into the overall welfare system. With the widespread administrative use of *raseljeni* as a category of entitlement, people began to pay attention to and embody these categories. All three categories—refugee, IDP, returnee—were incorporated into folk discourses about deservingness to receive state assistance. As the following examples demonstrate, Alma was not alone in feeling that rural refugees and IDPs were unfairly prioritized in the distribution of housing assistance.

In particular, IDPs from surrounding villages who have remained in Mostar since the war are perceived as not belonging to the community of true Mostarians. Senad, a Bosniak man in his fifties and a self-declared "true Mostarian," told me: "They have taken over the town. They have all built their nice houses here with donation money, and now they run the town. They don't know how to behave in a city. They built their houses illegally, and you see what the results are." Here, Senad was referring to displaced Bosnian Muslims from the rural neighboring municipalities that are now controlled by Bosnian Serbs. Instead of returning home, they had diverted reconstruction funds meant to rebuild their pre-war rural houses into new home constructions in Mostar. As we walked through the neighborhood, Senad explained how the new houses constructed without permits on the hillside had caused mudslides during heavy storms. He pointed to the lack of sewage infrastructure as yet another sign of unvarnished peasant sensibilities. The newcomers had built their houses "just like in the village," demonstrating no concern for urban planning and infrastructure.

Croat Bosnians showed a similar disdain for new settlements in the south of Mostar that had been built by the wartime Herceg-Bosnia leadership for Croat IDPs from Central Bosnia with the intent of consolidating Croatian dominance in the area. Passing by such a settlement, a middle-aged Croat woman explained to me: "The Croat government built these settlements and resettled displaced persons here during the war. You see how big the houses are? Who owns a house with two floors nowadays? But it is good that they have been settled outside of the city. They are people from the country, and it will take them a generation or so to get used to the city." Moreover, particular mentalities and forms of political behavior are attributed to the newly settled IDPs. Contemporary Mostarian folk discourse faults displaced persons from rural areas with having taken over and corrupted local politics and bureaucracy, resulting in the continued dominance of ethno-nationalist wartime political parties. In Mostar, the toponym Podvelež (a dispersed rural settlement in the mountains above Mostar) has become synonymous with such conceptual associations. When employees of the city administration criticize colleagues or clients who do not conform to official procedures, they might say, "She acts like a Podveležian" or "What can you do? He's from Podvelež!"

As we can see from these quotations, the figure of the refugee or the displaced person is fundamental to public discourses about belonging, deservingness, and state assistance that center on a morally charged distinction between rural and urban.[9] In an interview with the regional office of the United Nations High Commissioner for Refugees (UNHCR) in Mostar, both the international head of office and his local co-worker confirmed that the criteria for reconstruction aid, developed by the UNHCR and its donor partners, privileged the reconstruction of private houses in remote and agricultural areas. The latter explained that this mostly had been a function of chronology. IDPs who had fled to the cities during the war first had to be transferred to their pre-war homes. Only then could the apartments and houses that they had occupied in cities be returned to their pre-war inhabitants, who themselves were either internally displaced or living abroad and awaiting return to Bosnia.

The tendency to target rural displaced persons for support was coupled with another policy priority, namely, minority return. This refers to the right of displaced persons to return to pre-war municipalities that are now dominated by other ethno-national groups. It is meant to reverse the effects of wartime ethnic cleansing and to recreate pre-war mixed residential patterns. Many donors made minority return a precondition to receive their support for financing reconstruction and return programs. The program that the Dedič family applied for—financed by the statewide Refugee Return Fund and administered by the Federal Ministry for Displaced Persons and Refugees—also prioritized minority return.

In prioritizing the return of rural refugees/IDPs and making minority status a criterion for selection, post-war reconstruction was spatially structured and became integrated into a popular spatial imaginary built around the rural-urban dichotomy. The Dedič family developed its strategy for obtaining housing in this particular context, while also drawing on earlier experiences with socialist housing policies and practices. As I will show in the next section, the rural-urban dichotomy had its roots in pre-war socialist housing policies.

Socialist-Era Housing in the City and Countryside

Socialist Housing Policy and the Rural-Urban Dichotomy

Socialist state intervention in the field of housing stands in stark contrast to post-war assistance for reconstruction and return. As in other socialist states, socialism in Yugoslavia was based on an ideology of modernization and progress. From the 1950s onward, economic and social policies aimed for (and achieved) rapid industrialization accompanied by a rapid growth of cities. For planners and policy makers all over Eastern Europe, the city was the primary site in which the new 'socialist man' (Fisher 1962) would be formed. Yugoslavia shared this focus on the city as a site of massive social transformation with extensive urban housing provision directed toward this end. Although the degree to which the state services extended to the countryside had been impressive (especially in the educational and health sectors) and rural towns had been modernized, housing in the villages predominantly remained a private and individual concern resolved through inheritance or self-financed construction with the help of relatives, neighbors, and friends (Gantar and Mandič 1991).

Although regulated differently, socialist rural and urban spaces had been linked by the widespread migration from rural to urban areas and by the movement of urban dwellers to rural weekend homes beginning in the late-socialist era. Rural to urban migration reached its heights between the late 1950s and early 1980s (Spangler 1983: 83). This trend drew extensive scholarly and public interest, much of which focused on peasant migrants' adaptation to modern socialist city life (Simić 1973, 1983; Spangler 1983). Initially, rural migrants were lauded for maintaining kinship ties, as it was believed that these relations facilitated settlement, employment, and integration in the city (Simić 1983: 203). Beginning in the 1970s, public wisdom on this matter began to change, and rural migrants were increasingly assailed for clinging on to the negative aspects of peasant behavior in the urban context. In the early 1980s, Andrei Simić emphasized what he perceived as the maladaptive aspects of traditional (peasant) social structures and associated values, contrasting them with the values of rationality, progress, and modernity. In particular, Simić (1983: 215–221) contended that 'traditional' kinship ties and personalized relationships facilitated corruption and hindered modern institutions from taking form. The city, in this view, was falling prey to kinship solidarity and to clientelism, which had originated in the village and was being brought to the city by rural migrants.

A different discourse about rurality and urbanity evolved around the weekend homes maintained by city dwellers. Beginning with party leaders and functionaries who built or acquired holiday cottages in the late 1950s, the *vikendica* soon became an object of desire for white-collar workers and intellectuals as well. In the 1970s, *vikendicas* boomed in all strata of society, largely through self-construction or the renovation of abandoned village homes, sometimes with generous support received from friends, colleagues, and neighbors (cf. Taylor 2010).

The *vikendica* phenomenon ran counter to the core tenets of socialist planning and ideology. As a form of private property that displayed personal enrichment and conspicuous consumption, it made social inequalities manifest and led to spatial segregation. Nevertheless, it was (uneasily) accommodated by party ideologists and policy makers, who presented the proliferation of *vikendicas* as evidence of a successful Yugoslav socialist economy that allowed for satisfactory consumption levels, creative self-initiative, and free choice in the sphere of leisure. Popular discourse also emphasized the benefits of spending leisure time at the *vikendica*. Depictions of gardening and subsistence activities as positive and of the countryside as healthy and wholesome further contributed to the legitimacy of the *vikendica*, even as its legal and administrative status remained fuzzy (Taylor 2010: 173–174).

Socialist-Era Housing Practices between City and Countryside

Vikendicas, however, provided more than just leisure opportunities outside of the city. They also served socio-economic purposes, ranging from homegrown produce exchange networks to household living arrangements and investments in property. In the face of urban housing shortages, *vikendicas* played a critical role in intergenerational housing arrangements. Legally, ownership of housing property was allowed for personal and family use, but was restricted to one housing unit in addition to a socially owned apartment (cf. Mandič 1990; Taylor 2010: 180, 195). *Vikendicas* were left unregulated. As part of housing reforms introduced in the 1970s, credit was made available for the self-construction of family houses and commissioned apartments in order to alleviate housing shortages in urban centers. However, these resources were often informally invested in building rural *vikendicas* rather than in housing solutions for the city, as envisioned by policy makers. Another common strategy used by residents was to declare a (former) family house in the vicinity of one's place of residence as a *vikendica* and not a family home, allowing residents to obtain socially owned apartments (Taylor 2010: 197–198). In the 1980s, when housing shortages and housing inequality in urban centers had become more apparent, a statewide campaign was started under the slogan "Imaš kuču, vrati stan!" (You have a house, return your [socially owned] flat!).

As a result of the campaign, more people declared their homes a *vikendica* and altered their official household registration (ibid.: 198n69). Owing to long waiting periods for state-provisioned housing, families combined the *vikendica* and socially owned apartments (and, in some cases, family homes) to address housing problems when younger family members matured and sought to live on their own. Families creatively moved between places of residence and reassigned household membership in order to provide housing for all members and procure space for married children, all the while circumventing property laws.

Continuity and Transformation, Representation, and Practice in the Housing Strategy of the Dedič Family

We can now situate the Dedič family's housing strategy in a broader historical context. The parents' attempt to secure housing for their son and his fiancée through public housing assistance schemes bears a striking resemblance to a widespread practice from an earlier historical era. Just as socialist housing loans for urban housing were diverted to *vikendicas*, return and reconstruction assistance targeting rural returnees was diverted in the post-war era to cover the housing needs of urban residents by changing the status of the *vikendica* from a holiday cottage to that of a permanent pre-war home.

On a discursive level, the Dedič family appropriated a *vikendica* discourse in which the countryside was valorized and distanced from the negative stereotypes associated with peasants and their alleged exploitation of personalized relations. While waiting for her family's application to be processed, Alma frequently recounted to visiting friends and relatives (and to me) her gardening activities on a plot of land near the cottage as pleasurable but also as a valuable distraction from her work duties in Mostar. She repeatedly remarked on the abundance of fresh vegetables and fruit preserves in her household before the war. These nostalgic recollections of the socialist era glossed over and recast the official policy of promoting minority return in a framework of interpretation that played on the normative values of intergenerational solidarity and agricultural subsistence gardening as a morally valuable retirement activity.

During socialism, it was widely known that local authorities and enterprises granted socially owned apartments as political favors (Gantar and Mandič 1991: 124–125). Today, people assume that the same motivations influence the practical implementation of reconstruction and return programs. Alma's case shows that urban dwellers in the post-war period have adapted their housing strategies to new exigencies by drawing on practices known from the socialist period and deploying them in novel contexts. Alma sought to improve her chances for getting state aid by approaching an official, who was also a party member, through personal ties mediated by friendship, party membership, and residential proximity. Rather than resorting to a public platform, the family relied on its network of friends, colleagues, and neighbors. In her interactions with state officials, such as the minister, Alma framed her deservingness by referring to earlier personal sacrifices: having remained in Mostar during the war, the loss of family property and employment, and her contribution to the defense of the city as a volunteer. She thereby portrayed herself as having contributed to the common good, which should make her deserving of assistance.

Notwithstanding the family's favorable spatial position in a neighborhood with strong ethno-nationally defined channels of patronage and their ability to artfully negotiate personal relations, socialist-era discourses and practices, and recent administrative categorizations, the Dedič family's approach to securing housing was initially unsuccessful. They were not among the selected beneficiaries. However, two years later, in the run-up to the municipal elections, I was told during a visit that the Dedič family was reapproaching local party officials for reconstruction funds. When I left Mostar, these negotiations had still not been successful, but it was evident that Alma believed her personal access to, and relationships with, state officials to be the decisive component of her housing strategy.

Alma's strategy could be interpreted as a classic case of dyadic patron-client relations, wherein access to resources and power is asymmetrically distributed and transactions are informal and exclusive, rather than based on the universal criteria of eligibility. Recent studies of clientelism have shifted from these often negatively evaluated characteristics to a closer investigation of the underlying notions of reciprocity, moral obligations for solidarity, and the inclusive potential of patron-client networks and relations of dependence in so-called modern democratic states (cf. Ferguson 2013; Roniger 1994). I, too, argue, that Alma's mode of interacting with state officials not only was aimed at securing instrumental, material gains but also strove to include her family in the post-war political community. Receiving state assistance meant that the state recognized her as a part of that community, much as housing provision during socialism had symbolized recognition of one's political subjectivity as a worker. In this case, the particular state officials she could approach presented themselves as ethno-nationally Bosniak, and Alma accordingly foregrounded the Bosniak solidarity formed during the war for entering into a relationship with them. During her exchanges with the local authorities, her political subjectivity and the political community were consequently constituted as ethno-nationally Bosniak.

"Displaced in Our Own Town": Fighting for the Reconstruction of Inner-City Apartment Blocks

In the second case study of Šantićeva residents, we will again encounter discourses about rurality, as residents appropriate the category of *raseljeni* to claim state assistance for housing. As in the first case, this appropriation goes hand in hand with an attempt to establish a meaningful relationship with city authorities and to be publicly recognized, but both discourse and practice take a different form.

Constraints and Possibilities for Housing Assistance in a Divided City

It was no coincidence that the residents of Šantićeva did not enter public awareness until 2006. These residents lived in a section of the central zone where practical and ideological rationales had come together to prevent reconstruction. As the buildings in the area were so close to the front lines of the war, the damage was tremendous and restoration work prohibitively expensive. Residents of apartment buildings in the central zone had been of mixed ethno-national background,[10] and neither of the two dominant political parties showed much interest in pushing for reconstruction of apartment blocks because benefits could not be restricted to their respective ethno-national electorate. Only after the OHR passed a new municipal charter in 2004, establishing a unified city council, did a citywide public and regulatory space come into being in which the residents of Šantićeva could voice their concerns and hold locally elected representatives accountable.

Discursive and Practical Appropriation of the Raseljeni Category

During their public protests, the residents of Šantićeva had used the slogan "Displaced in our own town" to engage with popular discourses about how rural newcomers to Mostar had become unjustly privileged with housing assistance. In an ironic twist, the slogan emphasized their long-standing belonging in the urban community of Mostar. Šantićeva residents adopted late-socialist discourses on urban civility and deservingness to prioritize their claims over demands from the rural quarters, thereby transforming their seemingly negative position in the destroyed central zone into a discursive resource. They successfully appropriated the category of 'displacement' while simultaneously distancing themselves from the stigma of rurality, which had become intertwined with the image of the IDP. This helped these families to establish the legitimacy of their demands for housing assistance but had not yet brought them into a direct relationship with municipal authorities.

One of the group's leading activists described how earlier attempts to meet the mayor in person and the numerous petitions that they had submitted to various local and national authorities and the OHR had all failed, and how they had begun to look for alternative strategies for approaching state officials. Instead of seeking appointments with city officials in the privacy of their offices, they now confronted local authorities in the public urban space.

Moreover, Šantićeva residents deployed the *raseljeni* category not just metaphorically as a way to garner public attention to their cause. They proceeded to appropriate state recognition as IDPs through regular administrative channels. Šantićeva activists invited a representative from the BiH-wide umbrella organization Council of Refugees and IDPs to one of their early meetings in order to explain the procedure for registering and verifying one's status as an internally displaced person. Many of those in attendance did not consider themselves displaced, and the representative had to spell out clearly the correlation between IDP status and eligibility for reconstruction aid. The following morning at the municipal Office for Social and Housing Affairs, I saw a woman, who had been at the meeting, request verification of her IDP status. Members of the protest group now understood the importance of deploying the category of 'displacement' in their interactions with administrators.

With financial and organizational support from the Council of Refugees and IDPs, the activists then proceeded to form a housing association, registered as an NGO, and organized a donor conference to which they invited local and national functionaries, as well as representatives of the OHR and other international organizations. In an effort to extend the visibility of their cause to local and global audiences, the activists produced a video for screening and distribution at the conference. This video combined the discourses about displacement and belonging with appeals to the global humanitarian community. Several scenes showed residents discussing their hopes of returning to their old homes and deployed the slogan "Displaced in our own town," attesting to their Mostarian roots. But they also directly addressed the "well-meaning people in the world" (*dobrovoljni ljudi iz sveta*) and international organizations such as the UNHCR, asking them to help the citizens of Mostar. By positioning themselves within a globally constructed civil society and supranational structures of governance, the activists were able to strengthen their legitimacy as key figures in local civil society and as rightful partners of the local state.

In 2007, these efforts met with first success: the city council set aside a special fund for reconstruction, co-financed by the statewide Refugee Return Fund, and a reconstruction commission was formed. Three members of the Šantićeva housing association were appointed to the commission as civil society representatives. They had finally gained the recognition of the local authorities and established working relations with them. Constituting themselves as an NGO, they had become eligible to participate in decision-making processes about the distribution of funds. The fact that they had thereby secured a place in the politico-administrative structure of the city sits uneasily with classic notions of civil society, according to which organized public life is distinct from the state and the autonomy of society vis-à-vis the state is emphasized. As in the case of clientelism, such conceptualizations, often normatively charged, have been criticized by anthropologists (Hann 1996; see also Read, chap. 5). Following their lead, I propose an alternative interpretation for the case of Šantićeva residents in the following section.

Emphasizing the active attempts of Šantićeva residents to seek out state categorizations, I suggest that the Šantićeva activists made themselves legible to state authorities as a means to facilitate further communication and interaction (cf. Jansen 2014; Street 2012). As with the Dedič family, they were driven not merely by material interests but by a desire to be 'seen by the state' (Street 2012) in order to secure recognition as citizens and to establish a sense of biographical continuity with their pre-war status as esteemed members of the political community. Far from indicating a wish to gain autonomy from the state, forming a housing association in fact underscores a desire to be incorporated into local governance structures as an expression of a larger political community (cf. Murray Li 2013).

Continuity and Transformation, Representation, and Practice in the Strategies of Šantićeva Residents

The leading Šantićeva activists were all in their late fifties to sixties. They had received apartments on Šantićeva Street before the war through their employment with state companies in the city's utilities and transport sector, with the police or the army. The high social prestige of employment in these sectors was mirrored by the prominent location of their apartments in the inner city's center. The residents of Šantićeva were thus largely from a privileged professional stratum and were well-connected to the pre-war political elites. With the deep changes to the political landscape after the war, these formerly privileged households lost their earlier level of influence, becoming acutely aware of the degradation of their current social situation. Yet these families were still well-equipped with the social and cultural capital necessary to articulate their cause and found discursive and practical means of pursuing it.

What appeared to be a novel and innovative strategy adopted by the residents of Šantićeva can be traced back to the mobilization of socialist organizational patterns. Socialist housing associations, in fact, fulfilled a purpose similar to the Šantićeva housing NGO. They, too, sent delegates to municipal and sub-municipal councils to represent housing interests and to participate in the planning of housing construction and the distribution of funds (Višnjić 1980). In terms of language and visual display, the Šantićeva association combined old and new elements, evoking simultaneously the legitimacy of socialist housing associations and that of a global civil society. The association's logo was clearly socialism-inspired, harking back to Mostar's socialist housing associations. On the other hand, the association's charter described its stance vis-à-vis government authorities in the classic language of a civil society organization: "The association will use legal means to put pressure on local, cantonal, federal, and state institutions of government to speedily realize its founding goal [i.e., reconstruction of housing]."[11] Again, we find a context-specific strategy by which Šantićeva residents aimed to bridge the gap between their past experiences and future expectations and to maintain channels of communication and interaction with local state officials.

As in the case of the Dedič family, the strategy of the Šantićeva residents could barely be termed an overnight success. Rather, it resulted in a prolonged struggle with the city council. The reconstruction came to a premature halt three years after it had begun due to budget shortfalls, and the city offered the residents the option to take over the unfinished apartments themselves or to wait indefinitely for local authorities to resume reconstruction. When renewed public protests were to no avail, the residents of Šantićeva decided to sue the city. This did not mean that they had cut ties with the city council; instead, it merely marked one moment on the relational continuum between the two poles of cooperation and conflict (see also Forbess and James, chap. 4). Šantićeva residents developed a political subjectivity initially based on urban socialist citizenship that was increasingly reformulated in terms of membership in global civil society. In the process, they achieved a sense of recognition and biographical continuity by casting themselves as local representatives of civil society, thus regaining some of their former status, even if this entailed opposing the city council in a lawsuit.

Conclusion: Transformation and Continuity in State-Citizens Relations

The two cases highlight different modalities for relating to particular state officials and institutions. Past state policies, discourses, and practices had in both cases coalesced into a spatially structured imaginary of redistribution. This pre-war imaginary of redistribution was built on a rural-urban dichotomy, which could then be mapped onto the new (post-war) administrative category of *raseljeni*. However, how the protagonists in these two case studies had appropriated the *raseljeni* category and played upon the spatial imaginary of redistribution took different forms, depending on their pre- and post-war social embeddedness and situatedness in different parts of this divided city: The Dedič family had limited resources in terms of education, professional status, pre-war political connections, and ties to socialist state institutions, and they lived in a neighborhood on the eastern bank that was now dominated by the leading nationalist Bosniak Party. The apartments of the Šantićeva activists were located in this divided city's administrative no-man's-land, but they themselves had belonged to privileged pre-war professional strata that were supportive of—and supported by—the socialist state.

Although very much a product of the present, the practical strategies of both parties draw on socialist-era practices and partially reproduce older forms of state-citizens relations. Underlying continuities are masked in the Dedič family's allusions to an idyllic *vikendica* discourse by means of which family members try to distance themselves from the negative connotations of rurality and the stereotypes of backward clientelistic patterns of behavior. In a similar manner, the Šantićeva residents' rationale of civic engagement for a civil society bears striking continuities with some structural features of the Yugoslav socialist self-government, which operated through a system of interest associations and delegates. Both representations and actual practices are the result of the protagonists' attempts to navigate an uncertain and shifting terrain and to find grounds on which they can access and interact with local state officials from their particular positions in the divided city space.

From these embedded positions, the residents of Šantićeva and the Dedič family came to imagine 'the state' as a political formation differently. For the Dedič family, interactions with the state through personalized relations begin in their neighborhood and end at the Federation of Bosnia and Herzegovina. The state here is largely perceived as a Bosniak political formation constituted by a Bosniak political community and based on shared ethno-national solidarity. Accordingly, Alma Dedič presents herself first and foremost as a Bosniak citizen. The residents of Šantićeva interact with the city council, the national-level state, and non-state agencies and international organizations in a manner that is perceived and represented as a transnational, interrelated world of governance. In the course of these encounters, Šantićeva activists learn to present themselves as multi-ethnic citizens of Mostar who stand for a larger civil society. But as shown above, their claims on the state also depend on local notions of urban belonging.

Despite casting themselves as different kinds of citizens with distinctive political subjectivities, in both cases the people involved ultimately aim to foster vital relationships with state representatives. By being formally recognized as agents of civil society or by being recognized for one's contribution to the common good during the war, residents of Mostar try to secure material support from the state while simultaneously seeking recognition and building notions of political belonging. Citizens achieve coherent subjectivities not because of continuities in representations and practices, but by establishing channels of communication and interaction with state officials, which allows for representations and practices to be negotiated, adapted, and changed.

Prevailing politico-administrative structures are transformed during the course of these interactions that are simultaneously constrained and enabled by the actually existing structures. In both cases described here, the source of funding is the Refugee Return Fund, a body set up at the central state level. However, because of the specific funding line (in the Dedič case, a federal program vertically implemented in several municipalities; in the Šantićeva case, a municipal initiative co-funded by the state and locally implemented), different politico-administrative configurations and practices arose. In response to the Šantićeva residents' claims, the city council of Mostar established a committee for reconstruction funds, thus incorporating citizens into a governance structure that became incrementally more diversified and inclusive. One could speculate that the Šantićeva residents' ability to navigate within a multi-level governance structure and to play a local public institution (city council) off against another public body (the cantonal court to which they submitted their claim) might lead to increased pressure on local authorities for accountability. The Dedič family, on the other hand, is incorporated into a structure of governance that has been framed as ethno-nationally Bosniak by party functionaries. Here one might conjecture that the Dedičs' repeated reliance on this frame of representation could potentially reinforce the capacity of party functionaries in government positions to implement welfare policies in ethno-national and exclusive terms. Instead of concluding this chapter with an assessment emphasizing either clientelism or civic engagement as a dominant mode of state-citizens relations in contemporary BiH, I wish to reaffirm the theoretical significance of the contingent nature of these two co-existing relational modalities.

Scholars and policy makers have variously predicted an imminent breakdown of the post-war Bosnian state, prescribed recipes for radical transformation, or blamed the consociational political system, the international community, and ethno-national political leaders for having produced insoluble political stasis. I suggest that bringing the various modalities of citizens' relational work with 'the state' into the picture supplies a much-needed ethnographic counterpoint to such scenarios. It reveals how different relational modalities, based at once on historical continuities and embedded transformative choices, can—for the time being—come together to stabilize and legitimize such a highly disaggregated and fragile state power as the one in Bosnia and Herzegovina. Although the Šantićeva residents and the Dedič family acted in different relational modalities, they each nevertheless created a sense of continuity in their dealings with the state. The significance of clientelistic and civic relational modes therefore lies in the fact that they enable multiple avenues for achieving continuity and coherence in relations with state officials. A stategraphy that documents the interplay of continuity and transformation in citizens' relational modalities, in which state representations and state practices are contingently articulated and negotiated, can make visible this sense of continuity and coherence amid fragmentation and instability and can offer an explanation for the endurance of a seemingly non-functional and inefficient state. Such a relational perspective on the state therefore provides an analytical framework to address the stability or instability of the contemporary Bosnian state and citizens' role in its reshaping in a way that differs from dominant interpretations of state failure, radical transformation, or stasis.[12]

Acknowledgments

This chapter has benefited immeasurably from comments and discussions with the members of the project group "Local State and Social Security in Rural Hungary, Romania, and Serbia." Some of the ideas presented here were first developed during the workshop "Towards an Anthropology of Hope? Comparative Post-Yugoslav Ethnographies" at the University of Manchester in 2007, and the conversations held there continue to inspire me.

Larissa Vetters currently acts as a Research Coordinator of the Law and Society Institute at the Humboldt University of Berlin. She previously worked as a Coordinator of the project "Local State and Social Security in Rural Hungary, Romania and Serbia" carried out at the Max Planck Institute for Social Anthropology (2009–2011) and as a Lecturer at the Institute of Social and Cultural Anthropology of the Martin Luther University of Halle-Wittenberg (2011–2013). Her research focuses on processes of (external) state building in Bosnia and Herzegovina and, more recently, on migrants' encounters with the German state in the frame of administrative court cases.

Notes

1. All names are pseudonyms.
2. Ethnographic fieldwork was carried out between 2004 and 2007, with shorter stretches in the fall of 2004 and of 2007 as well as a 12-month period in 2005 and 2006.
3. Drawing on Hansen and Stepputat (2001) and Trouillot (2001), I introduce the term 'state imaginaries of redistribution' to denote the coming together of the

spatializing effects of housing policies with the discursive and social constructions of space that flow from people's experiences with these policies.
4. I follow Migdal and Schlichte's (2005) call for a dynamic approach to understanding state (trans)formation but emphasize a relational perspective that puts repeated face-to-face interactions between citizens and state officials center stage.
5. 'Socially owned' was the legal designation for collective property in socialist Yugoslavia. Ideologically, it was opposed to private property in capitalist systems but also to Soviet-style state-owned property.
6. The Bosnian state consists of two entities, the Republika Srpska (RS) and the Federacija Bosne i Hercegovine (FBiH). While the RS has only two levels of government, municipal and central, the FBiH is further divided into 10 cantons and thus possesses municipal, cantonal, and federal governing bodies.
7. 'Bosnian' is the term for all citizens of Bosnia and Herzegovina. The term 'Bosniak' has come to stand exclusively for Bosnian Muslims.
8. According to the 1991 census, Mostar had 126,067 inhabitants before the war, of whom 29 percent declared themselves Croats, 34 percent Muslims, 19 percent Serbs, and 15 percent Yugoslavs, while 3 percent chose the category 'Other' (Yarwood 1999: 2). In 2016, results of the first post-war census conducted in 2013 were published. They contained the following figures for Mostar: 105,797 inhabitants of whom 48.4 percent declared themselves Croats, 44.2 percent Bosniaks, and 4.2 percent Serbs; 1.8 percent chose the category 'Other', 1.2 percent chose not declare an identity, and 0.2 percent did not answer (BHAS 2016).
9. For the widespread extent of this discourse, see also Stefansson (2007).
10. Of the 94 households residing on Šantićeva Street and registered with the protest movement in 2006, 29 declared themselves Croats, 42 Bosniaks, and 23 Serbs.
11. Article 5.2.2 of the charter of the Moj Dom Association (Association RIO 'Moj Dom' 2008; my translation).
12. While writing this chapter in the spring of 2014, large-scale public protests against inefficient governments erupted across Bosnia. Initial scholarly evaluations distanced these protests from ethno-nationalist political rhetoric and depicted them as justified civic protest against political elites who have enriched themselves and impoverished the population. See http://www.balkaninsight.com/en/page/bosnia-protests-2014 (accessed 10 May 2017). With hindsight, it is likely that the diversity of relational ties that binds citizens to political elites and state institutions; particular embedded social, political, and economic positions; and contingent transformative choices have shaped the course of these protests and contributed to their fading. See Arsenijević (2014) for testimonies of protesters and a first analysis.

References

Arsenijević, Damir, ed. 2014. *Unbribable Bosnia and Herzegovina: The Fight for the Commons*. Baden-Baden: Nomos.
Association RIO 'Moj Dom'. 2008. Statute of the Association 'Moj Dom'. [In Bosnian.] Mostar.
BHAS (Agency for Statistics of Bosnia and Herzegovina). 2016. *Census of Population, Households, and Dwellings in Bosnia and Herzegovina, 2013: Final Results*. Sarajevo: BHAS.
Bose, Sumantra. 2002. *Bosnia after Dayton: Nationalist Partition and International Intervention*. New York: Oxford University Press.

Ferguson, James. 2013. "Declarations of Dependence: Labour, Personhood, and Welfare in Southern Africa." *Journal of the Royal Anthropological Institute* 19 (2): 223-242.
Fisher, Jack C. 1962. "Planning the City of Socialist Man." *American Journal of the American Planning Association* 28 (4): 251-265.
Gantar, Pavel, and Srna Mandič. 1991. "Social Consequences of Housing Provision: Problems and Perspectives." In *Yugoslavia in Turmoil: After Self-Management?* ed. James Simmie and Jože Dekleva, 119-130. London: Pinter Publishers.
Hann, Chris. 1996. "Introduction: Political Society and Civil Anthropology." In *Civil Society: Challenging Western Models*, ed. Chris Hann and Elizabeth Dunn, 1-26. London: Routledge.
Hansen, Thomas B., and Finn Stepputat, eds. 2001. *States of Imagination: Ethnographic Explorations of the Postcolonial State.* Durham, NC: Duke University Press.
Jansen, Stef. 2014. "Hope For/Against the State: Gridding in a Besieged Sarajevo Suburb." *Ethnos* 79 (2): 238-260.
Kenny, Michael, and David I. Kertzer, eds. 1983. *Urban Life in Mediterranean Europe: Anthropological Perspectives.* Urbana: University of Illinois Press
Mandič, Srna. 1990. "Housing Provision in Yugoslavia: Changing Roles of the State, Market, and Informal Sectors." In *Government and Housing: Developments in Seven Countries*, ed. Willem van Vliet and Jan van Weesep, 259-272. London: Sage.
Migdal, Joel S., and Klaus Schlichte. 2005. "Rethinking the State." In *The Dynamics of States: The Formation and Crises of State Domination*, ed. Klaus Schlichte, 1-40. Aldershot: Ashgate.
Murray Li, Tania. 2013. "Insistently Seeking Social Incorporation." *Journal of the Royal Anthropological Institute* 19 (2): 252-253.
Roniger, Luis. 1994. "The Comparative Study of Clientelism and the Changing Nature of Civil Society in the Contemporary World." In *Democracy, Clientelism, and Civil Society*, ed. Luis Roniger and Ayşe Güneş-Ayata, 1-18. London: Lynne Rienner.
Simić, Andrei. 1973. *The Peasant Urbanites: A Study of Rural-Urban Mobility in Serbia.* New York: Seminar Press.
Simić, Andrei. 1983. "Urbanization and Modernization in Yugoslavia: Adaptive and Maladaptive Aspects of Traditional Culture." In Kenny and Kertzer 1983, 203-222.
Spangler, Michael. 1983. "Urban Research in Yugoslavia: Regional Variation in Urbanization." In Kenny and Kertzer 1983, 76-108.
Street, Alice. 2012. "Seen by the State: Bureaucracy, Visibility and Governmentality in a Papua New Guinean Hospital." *Australian Journal of Anthropology* 23 (1): 1-21.
Stefansson, Anders. 2007. "Urban Exile: Locals, Newcomers and the Cultural Transformation of Sarajevo." In *The New Bosnian Mosaic: Identities, Memories and Moral Claims in a Post-war Society*, ed. Xavier Bougarel, Elissa Helms, and Ger Duijzings, 59-77. Aldershot: Ashgate.
Taylor, Karin. 2010. "My Own *Vikendica*: Holiday Cottages as Idyll and Investment." In *Yugoslavia's Sunny Side: A History of Tourism in Socialism*, ed. Hannes Grandits and Karin Taylor, 171-209. Budapest: Central European University Press.
Trouillot, Michel-Rolph. 2001. "Anthropology of the State in the Age of Globalization." *Current Anthropology* 42 (1): 125-138.
Vetters, Larissa. 2007. "The Power of Administrative Categories: Emerging Notions of Citizenship in the Divided City of Mostar." *Ethnopolitics* 6 (2): 187-209.
Višnjić, Miroslav J. 1980. "Selbstverwaltungsinteressengemeinschaften." In *Die sozialistische Selbstverwaltung in Jugoslawien: Grundbegriffe*, ed. Bogdan Trifunović, trans. Zoran R. Jovanović, 359-362. Belgrade: Sozialistische Theorie und Praxis.
Yarwood, John. 1999. *Rebuilding Mostar: Urban Reconstruction in a War Zone.* Liverpool: Liverpool University Press.

Chapter 2

THE STATE, LEGAL RIGOR, AND THE POOR
The Daily Practice of Welfare Control

Vincent Dubois

In his article advocating a renewal of the anthropology of the state, Trouillot (2001: 126) suggests a research strategy that would "focus on the multiple sites in which state processes and practices are recognizable through their effects." I share the general perspective according to which one of the main purposes of studying the state is to account for its impact on individual lives, material conditions of living, modes of social organization, or representations of the world, but my starting point is slightly different. In my view, it is necessary to grasp and better identify state processes and practices themselves before trying to establish such possible effects.

Accordingly, this chapter focuses on 'state acts' (Bourdieu 2012) by which agents vested with the power of the state define situations, classify people, and control access to resources. State acts are inseparably symbolic and material, relying on abstract categories and on concrete objects—consisting of both discourses

Notes for this chapter begin on page 54.

and bureaucratic routines—that shape the perceptions of the people as well as their material situations. To be performed, such acts require institutional settings and resources accumulated in the socio-historical genesis of the state, such as legal rules, specific organizations, finance, and civil servants. Conversely, if these pre-existing conditions, which define 'the state', are necessary for them to be carried out, it is only through these deeds that the state 'comes into being'. State power, monopolies, and images are realized, and sometimes materialized, by these very concrete acts of authorizing, sanctioning, or providing identity documents. On these occasions, citizens experience the state, which otherwise remains an abstraction to them. To paraphrase Radcliffe-Brown (1955: xxiii), only in the performance of such acts does the state evolve from "a fiction of the philosophers" and begin "to exist in the phenomenal world" (quoted in Trouillot 2001: 126).

Encounters between state agents and citizens are a prime setting in which to observe such acts. Following Lipsky's (1980) foundational theory of street-level bureaucracy, herein I argue that these everyday interactions play a key role in the delivery of public services, in the implementation of state policy, and, consequently, in the definition of what the state actually is. Discretion is the explanatory kernel of street-level bureaucracy to account for this role. It refers to the leeway of officials in the enforcement of rules or implementation of programs. Following this notion, bureaucrats are not neutral in these processes and, under certain conditions, interpret rules and programs following their own preferences or prejudices. In this chapter, I elaborate on the functions and meanings of this discretion as a pattern of governmentality in the contemporary neo-liberal state (Foucault 2010).

To do so, this chapter focuses on what can be regarded as the state act par excellence: control practices. More precisely, I analyze here the daily enforcement of control by street-level bureaucrats in French welfare agencies in the early 2000s. I show that, contrary to the common-sense idea of control as a rote enforcement of rules by a bureaucratic machinery following a strict chain of command, local agents of control have ample room to maneuver and partially define the legal norms that they are supposed to secure 'on the job'.[1] My research is proof that everyday practices and interactions in relatively banal settings serve as the organizational foundation of the state and state policy (Dubois 2009; see also the introduction to this volume). My argument is twofold. First, I posit that the categories of perception and judgment defined at the top of the state apparatus and inscribed in formal rules and those that street-level bureaucrats actually use in their daily practice may differ, but that they are closely intertwined. Individual stereotypes and discretionary interpretations of norms do not necessarily contradict the rationales of official policy and may also serve its goals. In other words, if 'seeing like a state' (Scott 1998) means imposing schematic visions that do violence to complex situations, the state also sees through the eyes of its individual agents, who, facing this complexity, use their own perceptions to master it and to enforce state categories. This inevitably leads to a diversification of how these categories are enforced and to a breaking up of state power and state policy into local inter-individual arrangements. But—and this is my second argument—rather than signal disaggregation of the state, individualization and uncertainty can instead signify a consistent mode of state governance in which the state exerts power over its citizens by affording street-level bureaucrats discretion and leeway.

From Welfare Changes to Individual Interrogations

Controlling the validity of the provision of welfare and the situations of its recipients is as old as welfare itself. But the meaning and form that control takes have recently changed. During the period of 'classic' welfare in Western European countries, control was nothing more than an unimportant bureaucratic routine. It became, however, a key feature of multiple transformations of the welfare state that gained momentum in the 1980s and an increasingly important part of social and employment policies. The rise of managerial rationales emphasizing the monitoring of expenses has resulted in an increase in checks—both internal (within the organizations) and external (of the recipients)—that are aimed at detecting mistakes or cases of abuse. More prosaically, the prevalence of a financial vision of welfare means that expenses have to be cut by all possible means, including reducing the number of benefit recipients by carrying out more stringent checks. As a rule, welfare recipients are encouraged to be more 'responsible'. Their cases are handled individually as part of the promotion of an 'active welfare state' that strives to put people to work. The unemployed are now closely 'monitored'. With unemployment high for the most precarious and least 'employable' members of the lower class, these principles are applied coercively, with increasingly severe checks and penalties.

Although they have much to do with the political and media stigmatization of 'fraudsters', control policies are not merely an effect of circumstantial rigorist discourses: they relate to deeper transformations as well. Control has become an instrument of social policy in the sense that control procedures fulfill a function by achieving the goals assigned to such policies. Targeting the 'bad' poor and the supposed scheming of those accused of choosing welfare over work, the reinforcement of control is part of a broader political rationale that combines paternalistic morals and neo-classical economic rationalism (Cordonnier 2000). Individualized control of the attitudes of welfare clients and of their willingness to improve their situation is currently a policy tool, inspired by neo-classical economics notions such as the 'poverty trap' model, according to which benefits recipients 'choose' whether to remain on welfare or to take a job after the calculation of their financial interest (Dubois 2014a). This amoral rational and technical view is nevertheless associated with practices reviving the pre-welfare moral categories of deservingness. In the classic welfare, controls focus on the legal status of the entitled with no other goals than avoiding errors in benefits payment. In the new programs launched during the past three decades, checks are designed to verify compliance with behavioral criteria and are part of the policy instruments used to 'activate' the non-working poor. Control is therefore both one of the practical means of post-welfare policies and a symbol of them. It is meant to impact welfare recipients by saving them from 'the culture of dependence' and making them 'prefer employment', as official discourses put it, or at the very least by reminding them of the duties that come with their status as being 'useless to the world'. Welfare control is a practical expression of the social expectations that weigh on these categories of the population, now seen as a necessary component of the public treatment of the poor.

Checks may be carried out at all stages of file processing, from verification of the first form to ordinary conversations with the reception agent, counselor, or social worker, the last of whom procures information that the institution previously had no knowledge of. Checks are frequently carried out from a distance, whether traditionally, by requesting supporting documents, or, as is increasingly common, through recourse to computers, making it possible to cross-reference personal data from diverse administrative files. Here I focus on face-to-face control interactions.

These investigations are crucial, as they serve to establish the institutional definitions of individual situations that ultimately determine how would-be recipients fare in seeking assistance. Will they receive all of the requested services? Will they be asked to reimburse the state for benefits that they received but have been retroactively declared ineligible for? When fraud is discovered, will legal prosecution follow? The investigators' interviews with recipients are decisive because of the combination of three factors: (1) the coercive power of welfare institutions is vested in the investigators, (2) this power is exerted over the uncertain situations of the recipients, and (3) the modalities of control themselves remain uncertain. As investigators are mandated to apply rules to cases that by definition do not fit well into existing legal categories (investigations are generally launched in borderline or unstable situations), they derive their institutional necessity from these uncertainties. During these interviews, the investigators' power comes from both their institutional mandate and the ambiguity of the situation, which renders the outcome unpredictable. Far from being mutually exclusive, institutional power and the uncertainty of the recipients' situations are intertwined and mutually reinforcing, imparting a strategic role to interviews with recipients.

In this sense, welfare interviews cannot be seen merely as an enduring, long-established practice of the welfare state; on the contrary, they are very much a part of its contemporary transformations. They attest to the growing role played by direct, physical encounters between welfare recipients and representatives of welfare organizations (in welfare offices or the homes of recipients, due to various appointments or summons), as the provision of benefits on the basis of the administrative recognition of a status gives way to a case-by-case assessment of applicants' situations and behavior (Dubois 2014b). In this new configuration, what used to be a simple bureaucratic practice of file verification has become a key instrument of contemporary social and employment policies that, in practice, increasingly reflect a government over the poor that strives to remake dispositions and behaviors rather than socio-economic structures.

The paradox of a rigorist state policy that is dependent on ambiguous individual interactions thus yields broader insights into how such a government works. It does not revolve around a politically legitimized central authority but rather arises from a multitude of individual relationships, which, although unevenly coordinated, derive from a structural rationale. Fragmentation does not necessarily indicate weakness or dismantlement of the state; in this case, it is a specific way for the state to exert power over its population. While interactions of control are pre-framed in and by the institutional and relational structures that precede them, several conditions keep them relatively indeterminate. The mastery of the situation by the investigators constitutes both the necessary condition for and the means of an institutional control whose practical basis partly escapes the institution's control.

Fieldwork

This chapter is based on a study conducted between 2001 and 2003, which investigated how local representatives of the Caisses d'Allocations Familiales (CAF), the institutions in charge of giving out welfare benefits in France, control their recipients. These institutions distribute a wide range of financial assistance, including housing benefits and non-means-tested family benefits, to around 10 million households of diverse social backgrounds. However, payments mostly focus on two minimum benefits, the Revenu Minimum d'Insertion (RMI), paid to adults over the age of 25, and the Allocation de Parent Isolé (API), the lone parent benefit for single mothers, which was merged into the Revenu de Solidarité Active (RSA) in 2009. In the early 2000s, there were over 1 million recipients of the RMI (about 450 euros monthly for a single person without children) and around 160,000 recipients of the API (with the amount depending on any other sources of income and on the number of children). RMI recipients were equally men and women and were predominantly single. Among API recipients, 98 percent were women, 90 percent of whom were under the age of 40. Most of both RMI and API recipients were long-term unemployed with underprivileged backgrounds and low levels of qualification. I conducted 42 interviews with investigators and 39 with managers of the relevant institutions in five different sites. Additionally, I conducted direct observations of checking procedures for a total of 12 weeks between June 2001 and February 2002.

The Indetermination of an Institutional Injunction

In the name of greater rigor—both in terms of severity and accuracy—control practices have become prevalent in monitoring and applying the rules pertaining to welfare provision. Yet these practices themselves largely escape the strict legal and institutional framework they are meant to guarantee by implementing and enforcing rules against welfare recipients.

The Stringency of Vague Rules

However precise and thorough the legal regulations, their application always entails a degree of uncertainty and leeway with regard to those in charge of enforcing them, even if they are at the bottom of the bureaucratic ladder (Bourdieu 1990; Lipsky 1980). In the administration of social welfare in contemporary France, low-level bureaucrats have come to wield considerable power over members of the lower class. Rather than interpreting the rules in light of novel situations, these grassroots workers tend to translate their interpretations of situations into the language of rules. Bureaucratic work is no longer only about ensuring conformity but, as the administrative jargon aptly puts it, about 'establishing the situation'—that is, exerting what Pierre Bourdieu (1991) calls a power of 'nomination'. This marks an important change in control practices: the verification of objective criteria, such as flat size, number of dependents, professional status, and so forth, has given way to detailed evaluations of lifestyles and living conditions, as regulations now require applicants and recipients to be assessed in terms of individual situations.

Grassroots agents thus have an unprecedented amount of leeway, especially as their task of legal characterization is frequently based on vague criteria. The paradigmatic example of this is the concept of being 'isolated' (or 'single'). This criterion is a precondition for means-tested benefits for single parents and factors into the calculation of other benefits. It features prominently in the control of welfare recipients, but remains largely intangible. The application of these categories still hinges on the statements and performances of recipients in interviews, which are subsequently validated or invalidated by investigators based on a number of different clues they use to "get an idea of the situation," as they say, and which they ultimately assess in light of regulations.

Additionally, the practical conditions of the investigators' work limit the impact of prescriptions from the hierarchy and favor discretion. Previously, investigators received on-the-job training from a senior colleague and mostly learned through individual experience. Only the most recently appointed investigators have received institutional training before taking up their duties. Yet, as we discovered, these training sessions do not ensure inculcation of institutionally defined norms. These norms have little binding power anyway: they are enunciated in the charter of control issued in 1998, which reasserted a number of principles while making few precise prescriptions. Compliance with the charter is left up to the investigator, who may also take into account local norms and expectations.

Investigators view their situation as both a blessing and a curse. Their administrative work is made more interesting by their independence, but they describe themselves as being left on their own. Only the largest offices group investigators into teams. Direct, day-to-day supervision is rare, and the office is not necessarily the primary space of work, as investigators frequently visit organizations and make home visits. Some investigators even process files and draw up reports from their own homes. Investigators can keep in contact with the institution through e-mail or an actual mailbox where they receive files and leave reports. This physical distance creates practical conditions that favor independent judgment: in theory, investigators are subject to the mandates of the institution, but in practice, the institution exerts little control over them. As one investigator explained: "In this job, you can be quite individualistic. We've got the directives, and then the managers give us pointers, but otherwise, we pretty much do what we want."[2]

Deciding the Undecidable

The characteristics of the populations and of the social contexts subject to control further reinforce the importance of the inspectors' appreciation of the situation, as we will now see. While the rules they enforce are vague, the situations in which they apply these rules are for the most part unstable.[3] Indeed, individuals whose living situations are rapidly changing or otherwise unstable are subject to greater levels of scrutiny than others. Investigators meet few recipient families with stable career, family, and housing situations, and they concentrate their efforts on unstable relationships, changing family configurations, intermittent professional activities, and frequent moves. As intermediaries between an institution that needs fixed criteria to work with and the irregular lifestyles of the populations they investigate, the inspectors are well aware that the 'truth' they can ascertain, far from being conclusive, represents a compromise between their diagnosis of the situation and the need to comply with the demands of administrative processing. In an informal conversation, an investigator put it as follows: "You see, we tell them that accommodation is necessarily temporary and that after two months we consider that they are living maritally. But for them, marital life can last only one month or two! One day, they're with someone, and the next day it's over! Why would they want to come in and report 'Oh, by the way, I'm living with someone now' since they might break it off the next day?"

In addition to being unstable, situations subject to control are by definition equivocal. As one investigator explained: "If everything were all black or white, we wouldn't need to go and do checks!" Sometimes those chosen to be inspected are picked at random from a pool of recipients identified as 'at risk' under the so-called targeted control policy. Home investigations can also be initiated after a front desk interaction, such as when a submitted report or letter of denunciation arouses suspicion and, more broadly, when circumstances are too complex to be assessed merely on the basis of documents. Hence, control focuses on situations that escape the standardized application of bureaucratic categories and actually demand the application of principles of judgment that go beyond these categories. A manager in charge of the benefits department (the main department in CAF offices) explained the functional character of the inspectors' autonomy in the following terms: "The fact that the investigators are isolated from the institution has a very positive effect. It allows them to gain perspective on the internal jargon. They're not experts—they're not knee-deep in papers, codes, computers—so they can act as mediators with the recipients. They're translators."

One must step outside or beyond the rules in order to better enforce the rules: such is one of the paradoxes of control. Tenuous and non-formalized factors such as the tidiness of the recipient's homes, the state of their clothes, or the tone of their voices are taken into account. An individual investigator's record of personal case histories comes to serve as a sort of individual jurisprudence, with no basis other than personal experience. Investigators frequently, and visibly, refer to principles other than the legal rules because cases that bureaucratic categories cannot capture also do not fit the social norms on which these rules are based. The recipients' distance from the institution's norms and expectations (individuals lost in paperwork, incapable of cooperating, or unwilling to do so, in structurally indeterminate social situations) comes with a social distance that separates them from the investigators, as these social agents have a vision of the social world that they have forged outside of bureaucratic categories. Investigators apply this vision when they apply bureaucratic rules. This double distance makes the interaction between investigators and recipients decisive, as the latter must try their best to fit the institutional categories through a wide range of practical and cognitive resources mobilized by the investigators.

These conditions create a very distinctive relationship to law that we might sum up as follows: the investigators hold a position that predisposes them to a legal formalism that they cannot uphold in their professional practice, which varies with the differing relationships investigators take on with the institutions that employ them. This relationship to law can be analyzed as a form of 'legal insecurity'. Legal insecurity here refers not to legal loopholes or contradictions in existing law but rather is inspired by and an extension of William Labov's (1976) concept of 'linguistic insecurity'. Linguistic insecurity concerns situations in which agents who, because of their social position and trajectory (as members of the lower middle class who recently experienced upward social mobility and are increasingly confronted with the upper classes), have a strong faith in linguistic standards (linguistic hypersensitivity) but find it impossible to live up to them fully. The linguistic imperfections observed during their interactions with those who embody these standards are a painful reminder of the inadequacies of their efforts to be 'hypercorrect' (ibid.). Likewise, investigators are predisposed to have a strong faith in legal standards. This relates mostly to their place within the institution and more broadly to the fact that their relationships with other categories of agents (from the benefits office and other institutions, as well as the recipients they investigate) lead them to define their function in terms of a formalist conception of the law. In a relational approach, I call 'positional legalism' this formalist conception of the law based on the position of the agents in those relationships. This positional legalism pushes investigators to condemn the slightest deviations from the rules (hypersensitivity) and to enforce them strictly. Yet this tendency toward 'legal hypercorrection' and ideals of 'legal perfection' comes up against a number of obstacles: the limitations of essential practical legal definitions, the complexity of and frequent changes to the rules being enforced, and the very nature of the social situations investigated.

Investigators respond to legal insecurity in different ways. The first factor that explains these differences pertains to the relationships of the investigators to the institutions, which vary according to their career rationales. Some investigators are promoted as a boost at the end of a long career in the benefits office. Others have taught themselves the job and have worked as investigators for a long time but now feel stuck and disillusioned. Still others are recent graduates who will only temporarily work as investigators before transitioning to a more prestigious position. Finally, there are mid-level employees who have become investigators mainly because they were unable to secure positions as managers. Each type takes on a different role and relationship with the institution. Both those who owe everything to the institution and the newcomers whose beliefs have yet to be shaken may be predisposed to legal hypercorrection, regardless of what it takes to achieve it. But the *déclassés*, who see themselves as legally competent enough to favor the spirit over the letter of the law, and the old investigators, often described by their colleagues as solitary cowboys who, having 'seen it all', assert the supremacy of their knowledge of the field over the technical quibbling that goes on in the offices, allow themselves—and sometimes indeed assert their prerogative—to make a few arrangements with the rules.

The second factor has to do with the degree of social distance separating investigators from the populations they investigate. Some investigators are more inclined to understand them as poor people who do what they can to get by. Others are more motivated to seek out and punish frauds who take advantage of the system at the expense of others. When directly faced with great poverty and social tragedies, agents adopt attitudes that vary according to their personal preferences (including religious and political ones) and past employment situations (e.g., having been personally unemployed or having seen relatives or close friends in that situation). Most investigators vacillate to some degree between these two poles. However, neither the frequent assertion of rigor as a value ("I like what's straight") nor the fact that most investigators have not experienced unemployment or precariousness primes them to favor expressions of empathy for situations, such as unemployment, that the people they investigate are facing.

Ultimately, the uncertainty that characterizes control practices cannot be accounted for by imprecise regulations or problems with administrative organization, even though they are factors. More fundamentally, uncertainty stems from singular situations that do not fit neatly within bureaucratic criteria, which themselves are vague. As a result, investigators may summon personal feelings or prejudices, as well as common-sense notions of social life, to produce a definition of these situations that meets the demands of rigorous institutional treatment, as my research reveals.

Controlling the Situation

Investigators usually prepare ahead of home visits. Typically, they have thorough knowledge of the welfare recipient's file. They frequently expand their knowledge of an individual recipient by speaking with neighbors, tax authorities, social workers, or gendarmerie. More broadly, these face-to-face encounters are pre-framed by thinking habits acquired through personal and professional experience. These habits inform the investigation and the investigator's conduct in interviews, with scattered elements from past experience serving as reference points within an ongoing interview. Investigators draw on knowledge of prior, similar cases, a familiar family name, the neighborhood, and other factors in a process of typification that fluctuates between the unconscious activation of pre-existing schemes of perception and the methodical application of an investigative template designed to record systematically anything that might serve as a clue. While the interview is to some extent structured on the basis of the script established during these preliminary phases, it remains an unpredictable process, one that requires the investigator to make an effort to keep the situation under control.

Therefore, the first step in controlling recipients lies in controlling the investigation itself. Keeping the situation under control can be difficult because of the underlying tension of such face-to-face encounters. This is not a routine interaction for recipients, who frequently become stressed or worn out or react aggressively, depending on the perceived intrusiveness of the interview or on concerns about the outcome of the investigation (canceled benefits, obligation to repay, prosecution). During interactions within the benefits office, institutional representatives can rely on the noticeable features of the official space (designated queuing areas, access to paper and digital files) and on assistance from colleagues in navigating the situation (Dubois 2010). But the investigator paying a home visit is alone in the recipient's home, which entails risks, disruptions (a blaring television or child crying), or even the recipient's attempts to sidetrack the investigation by forcing the investigator to wait or by trying to seduce him or her.

Getting Off to a Good Start

The practical skills of the investigator are therefore particularly important, especially in the initial phases of the interaction (Gumperz 1989). This means primarily maintaining a sense of ambiguity regarding the purpose and the status of this visit, especially considering that it has not been announced: uncertainty is thus combined with surprise. Investigators almost never show their professional identification and rarely mention their status, merely announcing that "Mr. [X] from the CAF is here."

Likewise, visits are frequently justified in terms that conceal their investigative dimension. Investigators strive to depict the investigation as routine and wholly benign, omitting that the recipient has been specifically flagged for investigation. They introduce the investigation as a legal obligation, saying that welfare institutions must "ensure that the files are accurate," which enables them to control "any recipient at any time." Maintaining ambiguity involves both tact (not upsetting the recipient) and tactics (encouraging the recipient to speak freely without arousing suspicion).

Another technique consists in having recipients furnish official papers and especially identification. While identity checks may have police undertones, dealing with documents can also have a neutralizing effect, as the first moments of the relationships are fixated on an object and direct confrontation is delayed. Some investigators thus systematically ask for confirmation of the information mentioned on the papers, initiating an exchange that consists in a form of cooperative back-and-forth dialogue. This is, for instance, the case with the family register (*livret de famille*), "a non-conflictual document [that] makes it possible to see who people are, how many children they have, and their marital status and also to check for possible spelling mistakes" (informal conversation with an investigator).

Keeping the Upper Hand

Home visits are initiated and led by investigators. Thus, "although on the surface an air of equality, mutuality, and cordiality prevails, participant roles, i.e., the right to speak and the obligation to answer, are predetermined, or at least strictly constrained" (Gumperz 1982: 9). The investigator asks questions and leads the interaction, while the recipient merely reacts. The interaction is structured by a questionnaire, often materializing in a small sheet with a number of sections to be completed. Investigators use such documents as mnemonic aids, as a pretext for repeating questions, and as a means of reorienting the interview. Some inspectors only jot down notes in a notebook. In such cases, the questionnaire is internalized, and it guides the interview in a way that is invisible to the subject of the investigation. Sometimes this is done on purpose in order to disorient recipients or to lower their vigilance. Indeed, one inspector we talked to had been nicknamed "Columbo" by his colleagues for his superior command of such tactics. As he explained:

> My working method is quite a personal one ... I kind of go all over the place on their situations, their jobs, and then I say, "Oh, I forgot this." But actually, I'm trying to throw them off. Or otherwise I close my briefcase, I pretend like I'm leaving, and then I come back to ask a question that I say I'd forgotten about but that was actually on my mind from the beginning. The thing is, I try to throw them off a bit because some of them are prepared. We've already got three investigations in the file, so they know how it works by heart. I sort of try ... to destabilize them because some of them have ready-made sentences and they've been briefed by a social worker.

Bluffing and dissimulation particularly matter here. Investigators frequently allow themselves to tell small lies in order to uncover recipients' lies. They may exaggerate the consequences of false statements or ask for information they already have as a test of goodwill. More broadly, investigators retain control of the game by controlling themselves: self-control is a condition of control. As one inspector put it: "I find this job difficult because you always have to be careful about what you say, the way you behave ... You can't be too anxious, you can't do this job if you're afraid while you're doing it, and you never know what you're going to find. I've been held against my will once. Lots of things happen in this job, so you shouldn't be scared!"

The relation between self-control and control becomes particularly clear in cases where the recipients' aggressive attitudes or strategies to arouse pity threaten investigators' control of their own attitudes. Investigators can empathize with the suffering they witness, yet they claim that they do not let themselves feel pity for recipients. They resist such feelings because the job requires it. One investigator stated that "you can't last if you allow yourself to be too sensitive." She elaborated as follows:

Some of them tell me [adopting a whiny tone], "Ooh, I'm ill." So they undress to show me their scars. I tell them nicely, "No, no, put your clothes back on. I'm not a doctor." When they say they're ill, they hope they'll be asked fewer questions or for fewer documents. Some of them go, "Oh, I don't know where my head is, you understand, you can't ask me too much, I've been ill," or "I've got cancer." I dread that enormously. Each time I tell them, "Listen, I'm very sorry about that, but …"

Investigators also resist feeling sorry for recipients because they are all too aware that recipients oftentimes intentionally and manipulatively try to inspire such feelings. Suspicion works as an antidote to uncontrolled compassion. One investigator described what happened in an investigation where the recipient "went on and on" about her problems: "By the end, she was playing the pity card. If I'd followed her there, she would have started crying. She's not sure of herself, so in case she had revealed something that wasn't to her advantage, she played the pity card for my benefit."

Legalism and formalism serve to counteract strategies aimed at arousing pity by desensitizing investigators to the recipients' suffering: both are resources that give meaning and justification to their practices by preventing them from letting their feelings 'take over'. As one investigator explained:

> I could say it doesn't affect me, but it actually does. You've got people telling you things like, "You don't care, you're a civil servant, you get paid at the end of the month." That happens often. You shouldn't let it eat you up, either. It doesn't do much good. You shouldn't think about it in the evening, because it kind of gets to you. Once it's been said, that's it. There are people who have reached the end of their rope, they've had enough. But I try to stay technical, full stop. I tell them it's the law and, "If you're not happy, go and see your MP and ask them to change the law," and that's it.

The Uses of Interrogation

Controlling the interview situation is critical because the interview itself plays a central role in the control of welfare recipients. This role is due in part to the so-called declarative system of benefit provision, which (at least theoretically) is based on statements provided by recipients, and particularly because of the sharing of the burden of proof that it entails. Recipients must be able to prove that the facts match up with their statements; however, in the event of discrepancies, the institution must also prove that the situation to which the statement alludes is not the actual one. The interview is thus doubly important: first, because possible contradictions between the recipients' initial statements and the version they give to the investigator can be a way of exposing them; second, because new statements made during the interview (e.g., about "resuming marital life") may effectively put an end to the investigation process. As in police investigations, a confession remains the best evidence. Beyond the imperative of solving the case, the interview is also said to have a pedagogic value. Practices that alternate between sanctioning and advising, threatening and informing are supposed to enable prevention of fraud or errors. These practices are also supposed to help redress the recipients' behaviors, at least those relevant to the administration's activity: making sure they provide information in case of a change of situation or update their file. From an instrument of bureaucratic control, the interview thus turns into an instrument of social control.

Obtaining a Confession

The relationship of control is first and foremost about obtaining the information necessary to rule on a situation. We have seen that investigators use diversion tactics to reduce suspicion and encourage recipients to collaborate as fully as possible. An investigator explained it this way: "I always try to be very easygoing. I always shake people's hands. They like that. It makes them feel at ease. I always find a subject to lighten the mood at first. For instance, if there are kids, I talk about the kids—'He's cute' or 'He's tall for his age'—stuff like that. If there's a dog, I talk about the dog. If there are houseplants, I talk about the houseplants … That way, people will feel more at ease, less guarded. So that during the interview, they'll be less vigilant. That way I get much more information out of them."

In order to rule on a situation, investigators rely crucially on the contrast between documents and statements. Documents are useful not only for the information they directly provide but as reference points to steer the interview, reorient the investigation, and drive the recipient into a corner. As the validation of their statements generally cannot be made in due form with documentary evidence, recipients must resort to the expression of goodwill, both administrative (taking the required steps) and social (making efforts to get by). Conversely, the primary objective of many investigations is the collection of statements from recipients in which they confess to having previously made statements without the ability to back them up with evidence. Investigators stand to benefit from getting recipients to confess to living as a couple, finding employment, or having unreported income. Getting someone to confess is a way to fill the gap between investigators' personal convictions and the formal justification of these convictions that the recipient can provide. Through discussion and exchange, recipients are led to provide missing evidence to the investigator. A written and signed statement matching the investigator's expectations is a key element that makes collecting additional evidence superfluous. Signed statements allow investigators to terminate the investigation, thus avoiding lingering legal ambiguities and the need for further investigative steps. "It's the icing on the cake," as one investigator told us. This explains why interviews with recipients can work as interrogations, aimed at obtaining confessions. The investigators themselves refer to the model of police interrogation, sometimes humorously or in order to distance themselves from it.

Producing an Acceptable Version

Once the relevant pieces of information have been collected, investigators must order and explain the facts in accordance with their own opinion of the situation, the law, and administrative rules, and only secondarily in accordance with the recipient's beliefs and desires (lest the recipient appeal the investigation). Producing an acceptable version means presenting a coherent set of established facts that cannot be contradicted by tenuous elements that would allow uncertainty to remain. The plausibility and coherence of the version presented will be assessed on the basis of criteria that are external to the recipients' experience. The behaviors of recipients are explained in reference to the living standards and the model of rationality that investigators apply, that is to say, in reference to social norms objectivized in administrative rules. Statements by recipients will not be recognized as true if investigators' own systems of values lead them to judge the statements as irrational. For instance, it is impossible to acknowledge the possibility of long-term free accommodation without having in mind the forms of solidarity specific to the most underprivileged classes. Judging such a situation on the basis of the middle-class standards of domestic economy, investigators are more likely to consider it an unreported sublet.

In working to produce an acceptable investigation, inspectors strive not so much to establish the truth as to achieve a 'reasonable outcome', which they judge in terms of feasibility (it is no use reporting something that cannot be proven), cost (the steps taken should be proportionate to the expected result), and pragmatism regarding the possibility of refunds (there is no point in ruling that a benefit provision is unwarranted if the recipient will obviously never be able to pay the money back). This very practical rationale consists not so much in doing what is legally required, but rather in doing what it is socially possible within the bounds of the law, on the basis of considerations of effectiveness and what the investigators deem to be right.

The production of this reasonable outcome can be likened to the technique of 'legal fiction', that is, ruling on a situation in a way that one knows does not exactly fit the reality of things but that is efficient and/or fair (or at least justifiable). This is particularly the case regarding the registration of dates for events like new employment or marriage that affect a recipient's benefits entitlement status. Once these events have been established, the point for the investigator is not to look for the precise date to fill in but to come up with a solution that balances potentially conflicting goals, such as not unduly disadvantaging recipients, or selecting a date that might be the right one but cannot be proven, or reporting what would be considered to be a fair amount of unwarranted benefits.

Regularizing the Situation

As we have seen, rather than an ideal of truth, the investigators' work has a pragmatic objective: regularizing the files. "We're not white knights, but we set the files straight," one investigator explained. Investigators must ensure that the files 'make sense' and encourage recipients to declare relevant elements, demonstrating that they have everything to lose by not complying with the rules and much to gain by being honest. Making a fresh start on 'healthy foundations' allows them to avoid trouble. In practice, as part of their function as so-called advisers, investigators encourage recipients to set the record straight. Incentives relate to the immediate concern of 'clarifying the situation' and to the more distant horizon of an educational and preventive mission, with investigators aiming to remake the habits of recipients. One investigator put it as follows: "I tell them, 'Listen, stop that now. Make the right statements relating to your situation.' So there's a whole educational side to it, you see." Beyond this, regularizing the files is also about regulating the lives they contain: encouraging recipients to take steps to find work, getting them to "pull themselves together" if they are deemed to be too "entitled," as investigators say. By putting paperwork in order, investigators also hope to put some order into the disrupted lives they investigate.

Investigators reward the recipients who cooperate in regularizing their file. They usually spontaneously offer to file an application for cancellation of debt on behalf of recipients whom they find reasonable. This is a way of encouraging goodwill and lightening the burden of the investigation for those recipients deemed to be honest. This is also a way to make the situation seem less unpleasant when investigators make the determination that a recipient has received unwarranted benefits. Finally, it is a way for investigators to keep their conscience clean: while they avoid turning a blind eye, they do not drag down the recipients further. As one investigator explained: "It gives them hope, although there really isn't much hope, and that way we can leave them alone."

Beyond the possible material sanctions they can lead to, these home interviews with welfare recipients have a strong moral dimension. They are tests of morality, not only in the sense that they aim at identifying lies and wrongdoing, but also because those who lie or cheat must *acknowledge* having done so. Those who confess can expect leniency; those who do not are pressured into signing a sworn statement ("I hereby swear to be living alone"). The possibility of providing a false sworn statement comes with the implicit threat of a harsher sanction. The interview also has a moral dimension in the sense that it serves as an opportunity to point out the rules for and the duties of welfare recipients. Indeed, the legal obligations of welfare recipients are quite often merely the bureaucratic translation of social expectations: legal obligations and social expectations merge constantly during investigations. Lastly, these interviews not only serve the functional imperative of regularizing the files. They are also a symbolic form of social regulation. They provide an opportunity to give the institutional representative information on the respondents' lifestyles, which is related to models of behavior (family structure, stability of the couple, education of the children, relationship to work, etc.) and the legitimate canons used to evaluate them.

Conclusion

The control of welfare recipients has both an economic and a moral nature, as is clear in how the interviews are conducted. Justified in the name of a managerial imperative of rigor in social spending, it fits more broadly within the logic of an 'active welfare state' in which 'entitlement' is seen as the enemy of employment, and unemployment and social problems are seen as the responsibility of benefits recipients. Investigations and sanctions serve partly to cut down spending by filtering out beneficiaries, as can be observed in the case of the RMI, for instance. Investigations also serve as levers used to "make work a real option for all," as the Organisation for Economic Co-operation and Development (OECD) puts it, or, in other words, to force people back to work. And while its social effects are less perceptible, control has a very strong moral dimension. Control consists first in making the recipients feel guilty, both to make sure that 'the privileged' who have work should not expect too much, and to remind those who do not work that they can only hope for conditional assistance and not claim rights. Control consists secondly in attempting to reform habituses that fail to conform to the job market and/or the institution's demands. For all these reasons, control is not a simple epiphenomenon but instead is a key instrument in the ongoing transformations of the welfare state.

The observation of the apparently mundane bureaucratic routine of control proves a good viewpoint from which to elaborate on the question of 'the limits of the state' (Mitchell 1991): "[The state] comes to seem something much more than the sum of the everyday activities that constitute it, appearing as a structure containing and giving order and meaning to people's lives … What we call the state, and think of as an intrinsic object existing apart from society, is the sum of these structural effects" (ibid.: 94). Moreover, we have seen that fragmentation in the implementation of 'active' social welfare policies was itself a pattern of their very structure. In the last place, I would argue that the question of the limits of the state pertains to the relationship between state categories and individual habituses. The enforcement of control is itself a not always successful means to rectify the deviant welfare recipient's habituses, according to the social norms promoted by the state. During the course of the daily activities of welfare control, the state and its agents, as individuals of flesh and blood, intertwine, as bureaucratic categories intertwine with the personal modes of agents' perceptions (Dubois 2010: 73–136). Confrontation between state categories and individual habituses based on other grounds, the internalization of these categories, the interference of personal views in the implementation of state bureaucratic norms—in my view, these are the processes that we should explore in order to rethink the question of the limits of the state.

Acknowledgments

This chapter is based on research previously published in French in *Actes de la recherche en sciences sociales* (2009) and translated by Jean-Yves Bart. I want to thank the editors of *Social Analysis* and Jean-Yves for their kind help. A previous version of this chapter has benefited from the comments of participants at the Wenner-Gren Foundation symposium held in Sintra, Portugal, in September 2012, and from the reading seminar organized by Didier Fassin and Joan Scott at the Institute for Advanced Study in Princeton, NJ, in October 2012. Benjamin White and Linda Garat have made useful linguistic revisions. I also wish to thank the editors of this volume—Tatjana Thelen, Larissa Vetters, and Keebet von Benda-Beckmann—and the two anonymous reviewers for their comments.

Vincent Dubois is a Professor at the University of Strasbourg, where he is a member of the SAGE research unit, and was a Fellow at the University of Strasbourg Institute for Advanced Studies (2014–2016). A sociologist and political scientist, he is a former member of the Institute for Advanced Study in Princeton, NJ, and of the Institut Universitaire de France in Paris. His research fields include cultural sociology and policy, language policy, poverty and welfare, and sociological approaches to public policy. Recent works related to the theme of this book include "Towards a Critical Policy Ethnography" (*Critical Policy Studies*, 2009), *The Bureaucrat and the Poor* (2010), "The Economic Vulgate of Welfare Reform" (*Current Anthropology*, 2014), and "Doing Critical Policy Ethnography" (2015, in *Handbook of Critical Policy Studies*).

Notes

1. Since I conducted this fieldwork, the reinforcement of an institutional control policy, through the specification of rules, procedures, and information technologies, has led to the rationalization and standardization of individual checks. However, a closer examination of individual practices reveals that while a standardization process is ongoing, the agents are still able to ground their bureaucratic work in their personal views and preferences, and the analysis presented in this chapter remains relevant in this regard. For a comparison of my empirical findings in the early 2000s with those of a similar research conducted in 2014 and 2015, see Dubois (2015).
2. For reasons of space, I will not specify the characteristics of the investigators quoted or described in this chapter. At the time of our study, around 560 investigators were employed. Their responsibilities and salary range are comparable to those of social workers. Virtually all of them are from the working class or of lower-middle-class origins. Whereas the gender distribution is skewed for other positions in the office (80 percent women, 20 percent men), among investigators, men are better represented (around 50 percent). Lastly, compared to their peers from the same generations, investigators are more educated. All the investigators in our sample held *baccalauréat* degrees, and one-third had acquired degrees beyond the *baccalauréat*, mostly in literature or law.
3. On the translation of complex life circumstances into persuasive cases framed in terms of appropriate legal definitions, see Forbess and James (chap. 4) on the work of legal advisers in the British welfare state.

References

Bourdieu, Pierre. 1990. "Droit et passe-droit." *Actes de la recherche en sciences sociales* 81–82: 86–96.
Bourdieu, Pierre. 1991. *Language and Symbolic Power*. Ed. John Thompson, trans. Gino Raymond. Cambridge, MA: Harvard University Press.
Bourdieu, Pierre. 2012. *Sur l'Etat*. Paris: Raisons d'Agir/Seuil.
Cordonnier, Laurent. 2000. *Pas de pitié pour les gueux*. Paris: Raisons d'Agir.

Dubois, Vincent. 2009. "Towards a Critical Policy Ethnography: Lessons from Fieldwork on Welfare Control in France." *Critical Policy Studies* 3 (2): 221–239.
Dubois, Vincent. 2010. *The Bureaucrat and the Poor: Encounters in French Welfare Offices*. Aldershot: Ashgate.
Dubois, Vincent. 2014a. "The Economic Vulgate of Welfare Reform: Elements for a Socioanthropological Critique." *Current Anthropology* 55 (S9): S138–S146.
Dubois, Vincent. 2014b. "The Functions of Bureaucratic Routines in a Changing Welfare State." In *The End of Welfare as We Know It? Continuity and Change in Western Welfare State Settings and Practices*, ed. Philipp Sandermann, 127–136. Berlin: Barbara Budrich Publishers.
Dubois, Vincent. 2015. "When Rationalization Meets Discretion: Welfare Fraud Control in the Neo-managerial Era." Paper presented at the conference "Street-Level Research in the Employment and Social Policy Area," Aalborg University, Copenhagen, 18–19 November.
Foucault, Michel. 2010. *The Government of Self and Others*. Ed. Arnold I. Davidson, trans. Graham Burchell. New York: Palgrave Macmillan.
Gumperz, John J., ed. 1982. *Language and Social Identity*. Cambridge: Cambridge University Press.
Labov, William. 1964. "Hypercorrection by the Lower Middle Class as a Factor in Linguistic Change." In *Sociolinguistic Patterns*, 122–142. Philadelphia: University of Pennsylvania Press.
Lipsky, Michael. 1980. *Street-Level Bureaucracy: Dilemmas of the Individual in Public Services*. New York: Russell Sage Foundation.
Mitchell, Timothy. 1991. "The Limits of the State: Beyond Statist Approaches and Their Critics." *American Political Science Review* 85 (1): 77–96.
Radcliffe-Brown, Alfred R. 1955. "Preface." In *African Political Systems*, ed. Meyer Fortes and E. E. Evans-Pritchard, xi–xxiii. London: Oxford University Press.
Scott, James C. 1998. *Seeing Like a State: How Certain Schemes to Improve the Human Condition Have Failed*. New Haven, CT: Yale University Press.
Trouillot, Michel-Rolph. 2001. "Anthropology of the State in the Age of Globalization." *Current Anthropology* 42 (1): 125–138.

Chapter 3

RELATIONSHIPS, PRACTICES, AND IMAGES OF THE LOCAL STATE IN RURAL RUSSIA

Rebecca Kay

The literature on welfare and post-socialist transformations has placed considerable emphasis on state withdrawal and absence (Cook 2007; Field and Twigg 2000), with rural contexts seemingly epitomizing processes of abandonment (Lindner 2007; Wegren 2004). Some authors have pointed out that new vulnerabilities brought about by economic reform have in fact necessitated an extension of state activity, for example, in relation to benefits and legal interventions (Read and Thelen 2007), yet rural places have continued to be strongly associated with an image of structural collapse and disintegration of services. It was with some surprise, then, several weeks into fieldwork in Losevo,[1] the central village of a rural district in western Siberia, that I found myself regarding the state-funded social sector as a rather prevalent aspect of village life.

As I came to know staff and specialists in this sector, observing their work practices and interactions with other villagers as well as conducting interviews,

Notes for this chapter begin on page 71.

I was struck by the enthusiasm and creativity with which many of them approached their work. On the one hand, the dilapidated infrastructure, lack of financial resources, and challenge of negotiating frequent changes in policy reflected some of the difficulties commented upon in the literature on Russia's post-socialist welfare. On the other hand, the 'human' factor and 'charismatic leadership' that ethnographers have noted, for example, in relation to the continued functioning of bankrupt farms (Gambold Miller 2003) or in third sector development (Hemment 2007), were clearly evident in this context. One might have expected the substantial material and bureaucratic difficulties confronted on a daily basis to result in a sense of powerlessness or indifference among staff, and certainly many specialists spoke of the enormity of the problems they faced and their inability to resolve them all. Yet local officials and employees, in what was locally referred to as the 'social sector', placed considerable emphasis on maintaining a sense of community and employed great imagination as they sought to support and assist residents using a variety of methods while drawing on a range of resources and, importantly, personalized relationships.

My empirical observations showed the state to be manifest in many ways and at multiple levels (local, regional, federal) in the day-to-day negotiations of social service provision in the village. Increasingly, my attention was drawn to the complex and often contradictory ways in which staff working within these structures related to one another, to the local administration, and to the regional and federal authorities to whom they were often directly subordinated. In particular, I began to see how webs of personalized relationships were crucial in determining the ability of these local social service providers to get things done and meet at least some of the expectations of fellow villagers regarding their responsibilities and functions as part of the local state. A wide range of interactions and connections are explored in this chapter under the heading of personalized relationships. These might have been subdivided and analyzed separately, for instance, as clientelistic exchange and patronage or as forms of social intimacy such as friendship and kinship, and so forth. Indeed, in the empirical sections that follow, I do indicate some of these differences in the relationships studied. Nonetheless, I have deliberately maintained the broader concept of personalized relationships in an attempt to explore and capture the diversity of guises and strategies through which local state actors facilitate state action in the field of welfare beyond recourse to formal procedures and predefined modes of interaction.

In contrast to some of the other contributions to this book, my focus is on relationships between those villagers functioning as employees and/or elected officials within the social sector, as well as on the relationships between them and other villagers, described by Vetters (chap. 1) as 'citizens' and by Dubois (chap. 2) as 'clients'. Like these studies, I also found a variety of modes of interaction (Vetters) and a degree of flexibility and discretion (Dubois) at play, which, rather than contradicting the image of an orderly and effective state, facilitated state actions in the field of welfare. Relationships certainly were not unambiguously positive in terms of either practice or perception. Close, personalized relationships as a basis for action could bring with them particular enactments of local social and moral norms, placing sometimes unwelcome pressure on both local state actors and their clients to behave in certain ways (cf. Gluckman et al. 1949). Absent or strained relationships produced considerable obstacles to professional cooperation and flexible decision making, undermining the ability of local social service providers to fulfill the expectations of their co-villagers and colleagues. This chapter seeks to tease out such ambiguities and, in doing so, to analyze the role of personalized relationships in the day-to-day functioning of the state, not as an imperfection or anomaly, but as a central facet of the system that helps to bridge the gap between state images and practices (see the introduction to this book).

The State as Image and Practice: Anthropological Theorizations and Ethnographic Approaches

As others have noted, in order to understand how the state functions at the local level and as part of day-to-day interactions, it is necessary to explore how "people construct ideas about the state, how they attempt to make such ideas 'come true', and how they relate to state practices, policies and institutions" (Obeid 2010: 332). Yet remarkably few have applied such approaches to the study of the state in post-socialist contexts,[2] perhaps particularly so in the case of Russia. Instead, discussion of the state has tended to focus on the highest levels of policy making and institutional structures and has often been centered on assessments of the strength or weakness of institutions and policies (cf. White et al. 2010). Even studies explicitly seeking to explore the regional or local functions of the state have often focused primarily on processes of decentralization and recentralization (e.g., Gel'man and Ryzhenkov 2011; Young and Wilson 2007).

Yet in other contexts, the very concept of 'the state' and particularly its "assumed ... coherence, integrity, and autonomy" (Migdal and Schlichte 2005: 2) have been called into question (see also Frödin 2010). With increased attention to empirical detail, new theoretical perspectives on the state have emerged. Here the state is viewed as a social construct, brought into being through a combination of ideas or images, on the one hand, and actual practices, actors, institutions, and places, on the other, through which people interact with the state on a day-to-day basis (Gupta 1995; Krohn-Hansen and Nustad 2005; Migdal and Schlichte 2005). Clearly, these two aspects of the state are intertwined and mutually constitutive. As Migdal and Schlichte (2005: 15) have pointed out, it is necessary to interrogate the "ongoing relationship of image to practices, how they reinforce each other and how they undermine each other," in order more fully to understand what they term the 'dynamics of states'. Indeed, where state images and practices are in tension with one another, the dissonance between ideals and realities may of itself offer considerable explanatory potential (Nuijten 2004; Obeid 2010). Such tensions reveal multi-dimensional aspects of how the state is 'seen' and 'done' (Migdal and Schlichte 2005: 14) in a particular time and place and how they relate to imaginings and experiences across time and place. The projection of an 'ideal face of the state' (Obeid 2010) can be found in the future, in nostalgic reminiscences of the 'caring' state of a bygone era, in a transfer of blame and/or faith to a higher state authority (Gupta 1995: 390), or even in a foreign state, where ideal and reality are imagined as more closely aligned.

In attempting to understand the state in these messier, multi-dimensional ways, ethnographers have brought the practices and performances of state actors and local bureaucrats into focus (Gupta 1995). This has involved examining how they interact with citizens who rely on them as gatekeepers to state-controlled resources, information, and power (Benda-Beckmann and Benda-Beckmann 1998; Herzfeld 1993). Where personalized relationships between individuals or groups *within* the state have been discussed, however, these have most often been viewed as problematic, as a means of maintaining questionable (if not illegitimate) forms of power and of 'privatizing' public resources (Gel'man and Ryzhenkov 2011; Verdery 2002). In some contexts, such personalized relationships and the failure to prioritize formal frameworks, structures, and ordinances are framed as evidence of dysfunctional states (Frödin 2010: 278–279).

And yet, as Frödin (2010: 274) points out in calling for greater attention to the "relational characteristics of the state," interactions between state actors follow a range of patterns. Such actors also almost always incorporate "multiple identities and interests (not only that of state officials) and may act on behalf of other rules and interests than those officially sanctioned" (ibid.). In different contexts and situations, "different repertoires of socially acceptable practices and principles of decision-making and exchange exist" (ibid.: 278), and these are couched in both formal and informal interactions. Many of the "mundane actions of officials, clerks, police officers, inspectors, teachers, social workers and doctors" that "give rise to state effects" (Painter 2006: 761) happen in practice *through* relationships. Thus, like Dubois (chap. 2), who argues that government "does not revolve around a politically legitimized central authority but rather arises from a multitude of individual relationships," I suggest that unpicking and scrutinizing relationships and exploring the intersections and interactions between practices, images, and relationships are key to an understanding of the state as it exists at the everyday, micro level of interactions and effects. While what follows is a detailed case study of a particular time and place, I believe that the findings are more widely instructive regarding our understanding of the role played by relationships in the realities of state action and can usefully be brought to bear on case studies taken from very different contexts.

Fieldwork in Losevo: Getting to Know the Local State

Losevo, which has approximately 4,500 residents, is the central settlement of an agricultural district with a total population of 13,000. Significantly larger than the surrounding villages, it is home to a rather extensive set of state structures designed to provide support services to the local population. In Russia, the formal responsibilities of local administrations for the provision of social services have changed repeatedly since the early 1990s. At first, village and district councils, made up of locally elected representatives, took over responsibility for the provision of a range of services relating to childcare, health, and education that had previously been provided by collective and state farms. Although formally subordinated to regional-level administrative structures and departments, in this early period local councils were often left largely to their own devices and struggled to maintain services in the context of profound economic crisis (Gel'man and Ryzhenkov 2011: 450).

In the mid-2000s, however, a new wave of local government reforms, brought about within the recentralizing logic of Russian President Vladimir Putin's 'power vertical', significantly changed the responsibilities and financing of local government. Village and district councils saw their mandate for social service provision significantly reduced as various services became directly financed and controlled by regional administrative structures. In some cases, responsibilities were divided: in education, for example, local administrations retained responsibility for the upkeep of school buildings, while the regional government took over the payment of salaries (Young and Wilson 2007: 1080). In other areas, such as health care and centers for social assistance, the physical infrastructure was also signed over to regional administrations.

While this "pendulum swing of reforms" (Gel'man and Ryzhenkov 2011: 449) made a significant difference to the working practices, job security, and reporting structures of those directly employed within local government and social service provision, it was perhaps of less significance for their co-villagers. Service users were not always aware of (or interested to know) the particular level of state formation that was formally responsible for ensuring that their needs were met; rather, they considered it the duty of locally elected officials and/or those directly employed in service provision. Since local administrations retained an infrastructure of sub-committees and deputy heads in charge of areas such as education and social assistance, this was where villagers were most likely to direct demands or complaints regarding the services available to them.

In Losevo, the District Center for Social Assistance to Families and Children (CSA) was the main locus of my fieldwork. However, villagers who knew of my interest in researching social service provision directed me to several other institutions and services. These included a large primary and secondary school, a hospital, two kindergartens, a newly modernized sports center, creative arts and music schools, a house of culture, a job center, a registry office, a welfare benefits office, a pension fund, a department for guardianship and fostering services, and various offices of the district and village administrations. In other words, it was here that local people perceived the presence of the state as a provider of welfare and social services.

These structures provide access to services, benefits, information, and advice. As such, they represent sites within the village where local people interact with the state on a day-to-day basis and where co-residents perform the identities of state employees and representatives, wielding a certain authority but also being expected to accept certain responsibilities as a result (Benda-Beckmann and Benda-Beckmann 1998). These institutions and services, the local officials responsible for them, and staff members employed within them often collaborate closely in order to provide social support, educational activities, and leisure services within the village and to the wider district. In so doing, they form a rather coherent presence in the village, one within which both personalized and professional relationships have an important role to play.

During fieldwork visits in 2009 and 2010, I interviewed staff and clients at the CSA and other social and cultural structures in Losevo and several outlying villages. I engaged in ethnographic observation at activities and events organized by the CSA, as well as at wider community events and celebrations. I interviewed and interacted more informally with members of the local and district administrations, particularly those responsible for social protection and cultural affairs, as well as with other villagers. I spent a great deal of time listening to people discuss their ideas of the state—what it should be and how it functioned in practice.

Many of the social service structures situated in Losevo are designated to serve the district as a whole, yet inevitably they are accessed more readily by the residents of Losevo. This is in part a result of physical proximity and increasing difficulties of travel caused by poorly maintained roads, canceled bus routes, and rising fuel prices. It is also a consequence of the role played by local state actors as nodal links in overlapping networks of relationships through which state effects are accessed and experienced in the form of social services and assistance. Even within Losevo, not everyone can make the same relational claims on local state actors. The multiple identities and roles held by these individuals come into play here, and those who are kin, former colleagues, classmates, or friends are often able to enjoy privileged access, regardless of where they live. Nonetheless, it is easier for co-villagers to establish direct, personalized relationships with local state actors whom they see on a regular basis and with whom they share other local facilities and community settings. By contrast, those from the outlying villages may seek access to services via formal channels—calling for appointments or simply arriving to wait in line—but also often use intermediaries with personal connections in order to make a request.

Villagers wishing or needing to use state social services thus employ 'modalities' of interaction (Vetters, chap. 1) with state employees or officials in order to optimize their access to these services. Different modes of interaction may be activated directly and simultaneously. For example, villagers who have personalized links to those in positions of authority may use more informal approaches as a way to flag their presence in a formal process of application and/or lining up for services. Alternatively, different modes may be employed consecutively and indirectly, such as when a resident of an outlying village makes a formal approach to the local mayor or teacher who then uses his or her own more personalized relationships to approach service providers in the district center.[3] While it may appear anomalous compared to the supposed effective and impartial functioning of a state welfare system, this combination of modes of interaction in fact assists the social sector to function across the district, as required in its formal designation. Webs of relationships spreading into the smaller, more remote villages provide a relatively effective means of bringing cases in need of assistance to the attention of centralized services in the absence of more extensive resources for outreach, mobile services, or better transport and communications with outlying villages.

The Image of the Local State

In Losevo, people discussed the state rather frequently in response to my questions but also in more casual conversations. Impromptu discussions occurred most frequently when people's ideas about what the state *should* be doing were at odds with what they experienced on a day-to-day basis. As suggested above, these points of tension were particularly useful in shedding light on both images and practices of the state at the local level.

In January 2010, villagers were angry about the problems caused by poorly maintained infrastructure during a prolonged period of extreme cold. The standpipes that many households rely on for their daily water supply had frozen, and elderly pensioners, as well as the home-care workers who assisted them, were frustrated at the lack of response from the local administration. As I accompanied one of the home-care workers on her rounds, we bumped into two others running errands in the village center. Gesticulating angrily toward the buildings of the district administration, one woman exclaimed, "I've already phoned twice to complain. They said it's been fixed, but I went today and it's not working again. I'm going to phone again and write to the paper." The others agreed that the situation was scandalous, but they expressed little confidence that anything would be done because, as they put it, "Nobody cares!"

In a similar vein, Irina, the director of the CSA, was extremely upset that no one had been willing to help when the Center's pipes froze during the New Year holiday period. As the director, she felt caught between the regional authorities, who own the premises and, she feared, would hold her personally accountable for any damage, and the local administrative and emergency services, which she believed should have helped her as a local resident but were either unavailable or indifferent. She expressed her frustration as follows: "Everyone had their phones switched off for a fortnight over New Year. I couldn't get through anywhere. Finally, someone picked up at the fire station, but then they just said, 'It's your problem.' What is the point in having all these *chinovniki*[4] [officials] if they don't do anything to help people?" Irina's final, exasperated comment about local officials is particularly interesting since she was included among them herself. Her switching between registers exposed an interesting complexity in the ways that an ideal image of the state was projected and how the realities of practice and encounter were experienced.

In the role of local residents, villagers with a wide variety of professional backgrounds and levels of engagement in local state structures made demands on the state, complaining bitterly about the "indifference" and "irresponsibility" of local state actors. 'Caring' in this context amounted to taking responsibility for the provision of reliable infrastructure and access to resources. People were particularly frustrated when they found themselves caught between different levels or channels of authority. The ideal image of the state (Obeid 2010) projected by villagers involved a coherent set of structures and actors with clear lines of responsibility who are able and willing to access resources and respond quickly to the needs and problems of local residents. In other words, the image conjured is in many ways that of the monolithic modernist state so critiqued in much contemporary theorizing. Rather than being "the state's own version of itself" (Harvey 2005: 127) or a necessarily externalized and abstracted ideal (ibid.: 130), this version was claimed by villagers in very specific and material terms and with direct reference to the minutiae of everyday life (Gupta 1995). Indeed, where local state actors made such claims, they seemed to shrug off their official roles, identifying instead as local citizens with the right to make particular demands on the state. And yet, as we will see in the following sections, in their roles as representatives of the local state struggling to provide services and forms of social assistance to co-villagers, local officials acknowledged and embodied a more relational, informal, and messy version of the state in practice. As intercalary leaders, they faced familiar problems in terms of the conflicting demands and constraints placed on them 'from above' and 'from below' (Gluckman et al. 1949: 93–94; Kuper 1970: 356) and used personalized relationships in a variety of guises as an effective and accessible resource to overcome these tensions.

Up Close and Personal: How Do Local State Actors Exercise Their Duty of Care?

Local state actors shared many of their fellow villagers' frustrations regarding the realities of limited resources and unclear divisions of responsibility and power. Speaking as co-villagers, they shared an ideal image of a duty of care for the state. When they switched register and spoke in their roles as local state actors, however, rather than evoking the formal structures, chains of command, and material provisions referred to above, they drew out examples of very close and personalized interactions with other villagers grounded in the social intimacies of friendship, good neighborliness, and even kinship as evidence of the proper exercise of this duty of care. Relating how she had worked together with other local state actors to "help difficult families," a former secretary to the village council in one of the district's larger villages commented: "If the problem was that the parents were drunk and didn't get the child up for school in the morning, I would go round on my way to work and get him up and ready for school. If the problem was a material one, say, for example, that they had no shoes to send the child to school in, then we would find shoes from somewhere—from a family with older children or from humanitarian aid, which we got a lot of in the 1990s."

On several occasions I heard of village mayors who intervened personally to deal with issues of drunkenness or family problems in their communities, and villagers generally reflected positively on those who did so. In one of the smaller villages, the mayor spoke of her recent involvement with a young mother whose persistent drinking was putting her children at risk: the local fostering and guardianship services were threatening to take away her custody rights. The mayor discussed the situation with the young woman's mother, and they decided on a joint course of action. Both older women repeatedly remonstrated with the young mother. The grandmother took the children away for a period, while the mayor found temporary employment for the young woman and accompanied her personally—and rather forcibly, it seemed—to a nearby town for a hypnotic 'cure'.

Such interventions were facilitated by the physical proximity and overlapping qualities of informal and formal relationships in the village context (Benda-Beckmann and Benda-Beckmann 1998). On the one hand, the actions of local state actors were prompted by formal regulations (requiring children's attendance at school, or designating children as 'at risk'). They cooperated with other state officials and employees in a professionalized manner, passing on information about 'problem families' and pooling access to resources such as humanitarian aid. Their status as local officials gave them the power and authority to intervene, which may well have been experienced as intrusive by those on the receiving end (cf. Khlinovskaya Rockhill 2010). As such, they incorporated the coercive and redistributive functions of welfare (cf. Dubois, chap. 2), reflecting the ambiguities engendered by relationships where there is an imbalance of power and an element of control. On the other hand, the practices of local state actors overlapped with and reproduced more intimate modes of interaction (e.g., forms of good neighborliness and support among kin), which were also upheld, at least discursively, as part of a local social norm of care and community (Kay 2012): the village council secretary 'popped in' on her way to work, much as a neighbor might, and the mayor worked closely with the young mother's kin, particularly her mother.

In their exercise of care through hybrid practices involving the simultaneous use of diverse modes of interaction, local state officials were able in some way to live up to the villagers' ideal image of the state and its duty of care. There is therefore no straightforward opposition between these apparently "incompatible notions of 'the state'" (Harvey 2005: 131) as provider/enforcer and the much more messy and relational practices that bring them into being. Rather, they co-exist in a dynamic way, providing frameworks, explanations, and legitimation for one another.

Relationships with Higher Authorities: Defending Local Interests via Personal Channels

If helping local residents was an important part of villagers' image of the local state, it was also widely acknowledged that this could be achieved only if local state actors were able to represent the district and its interests at a higher level and thus defend local resources and attract new ones (cf. Gluckman et al. 1949: 92). Here, important interdependencies were revealed between successful state formation at the local level and the maintenance of community through both tangible institutions and more intangible issues of pride and identity. Nobody doubted that defending local resources and attracting new investments were problematic. Since their villages lacked non-agricultural industry and their agricultural sectors were barely solvent, local authorities remained highly dependent on investment and recognition from both the regional and federal state. Local social service institutions provided a useful channel through which this assistance might flow into the district. In both formal interviews and many more informal discussions, members of the district administration, while pessimistic with regard to the prospect of revitalizing agricultural production, were much more positive about their chances of acquiring resources for the social sector. They had, for example, successfully applied for funding from the Russian federal state to repair and refurbish local schools and to install computers and other technology. The CSA had won regional grants for equipment and had been reasonably successful in lobbying to maintain or even increase staffing levels. Such successes were viewed as important in keeping Losevo 'on the map' and as evidence that higher authorities recognized and valued the district and its population's needs. They were also significant in aligning practices and images of the local state by maintaining local services and providing opportunities for community and cultural activities. While funds had been applied for through formal channels, it was no secret that successful applications also depended on the personal qualities, relationships, and communication skills of local officials—that is, their ability to maintain 'personal channels' (*svoi kanaly*) of communication and patronage with those in higher places—but also on their courage and conviction to stand their ground when necessary.

In early 2010, as the district was preparing to elect a new head of administration, a recurring theme in discussions of the virtues and shortcomings of the various candidates was their ability to play a positive role as the 'face of the district'. Candidates who were thought to be "uncouth" or who had little experience beyond the village and district levels were criticized, and people spoke of their fear that they might become an "embarrassment" and would let the village down (*pozorit nas*). Candidates were assessed more positively when people felt that they were "one of us" (*svoi*) and also that they were able to hold their own among the "city folk" and regional authorities. Here the position of local state actors was clear: they were considered both co-villagers (sharing local concerns, priorities, and sometimes defensive positions vis-à-vis outsiders) and external representatives (bearing responsibilities and obligations to act as intermediaries and as a conduit to higher-level authorities) (cf. Benda-Beckmann and Benda-Beckmann 1998; Kuper 1970: 356).

There was strong support for the candidacy of the then deputy head of district administration, Boris, and the CSA staff backed his campaign. The reasons for this—as was explained by everyone at the CSA, from the janitorial staff and home-care workers to the director—included Boris's credentials as a 'son of the village', one with higher education, good manners, and excellent connections as a result of his long history of service (formerly in the Communist Party of the Soviet Union and more recently in administrative structures), and his ability to command respect from a variety of audiences, both local and more distant. In his role as deputy head, for example, Boris had an excellent track record of assisting the local social sector to win additional funds by dint of his 'good relations' with regional authorities and external funding organizations, such as the Altai Fund supported by the German government.

Importantly, while Boris's use of relationships to seek support and resources from above was clientelistic, he was able to conduct himself in ways that were perceived as dignified and commanding respect for both himself and for the district, of which he "symbolise[d] the corporate identity" (Gluckman et al. 1949: 92). Rather than pleading poverty or emphasizing the district's shortcomings and his own powerlessness to resolve difficulties, Boris presented a relentlessly positive approach that projected a genuine love of his native district. Insisting that those who acted as 'friends' should visit in order to enjoy the pristine lakes and fresh air, he proudly showed them the cheerfully decorated premises of the CSA, encouraging them to sample the therapeutic massage and other services available, and hosted lavish yet informal dinners of local produce, often in the CSA's cozy kitchen. In this way, Boris performed clientelism as friendship and hospitality, personalizing the relationships involved and engineering situations that unsettled hierarchies and demanded a reciprocal performance of respect and friendship.

By contrast, the current head of the district, Nikolai, was described as weak, unable to defend the district, and unwilling to stand up for other villagers in the face of attacks from higher authorities. People feared that Nikolai was at best patronized and at worst ridiculed and ignored by the regional authorities. I was told stories about village mayors who had been fined for failing to bring local buildings in line with health and safety standards, the head of the local employment office who had been fired by superiors at the regional level, and problems that the CSA had experienced with auditors and supervisors from the region. In each case, Nikolai was criticized for not having intervened in spite of the fact that it was not within his formal powers to do so, since the various structures and organizations involved are in fact directly subordinated to the regional level. Nevertheless, it was argued that he should have been able to use personal channels and his knowledge of the realities of village life in order to defend local officials. The fact that he had not done so was seen to imply that he had been incapable of cultivating or maintaining the necessary relationships at the regional level.

In discussing their interactions with higher authorities, local state actors projected a dualistic image of the state, particularly at the higher level, as both a welcome source of resource and as a potentially threatening intruder (cf. Obeid 2010: 343). As a result, they were careful to demonstrate not only that they had strong personal relationships, which they were able to mobilize in forms of patronage for the good of the district or village, but also that they were able to stand up to the 'higher-ups'. Direct challenges were not the only way for local actors to demonstrate their ability to stand their ground. They could also use their closer knowledge of the realities of village life, as well as the advantage of being geographically rather far from the center, to avoid or at least mitigate the impact of unwanted interference. Working around the rules, being inventive, and piecing together solutions to problems despite a lack of resources were common features of the practices I observed among local state actors. These might involve both engagements with and disengagements from the higher regional and national authorities, but they almost always entailed a complex web of relational activity within the local context.

Relational Webs, Avoiding the Rules, and Getting Things Done at the Local Level

Relationships between local state actors who were responsible for the different parts of the social sector in the district and village were highly personalized and often based on underlying ties of friendship, kinship, or at least long-term acquaintance, and local officials frequently called on each other for help. For example, while professional cooperation between the benefits office and the CSA was formally required in policy directives emanating from the regional Committee for Social Protection, in practice, collaborations seemed to function best when they were supported by personal affinities and a combination of formal-professional and informal-personalized modes of interaction. When local state actors got on well and supported one another, they were able to act as a set of coherent structures and to develop creative and collaborative solutions by pooling competences and resources to help those in need.

Through their interactions with the social sector, villagers demonstrated their expectation that local state actors would use such personalized ties to provide help and support. When staff at the CSA were presented with a complicated custody case involving a large family of recently orphaned siblings in one of the district's outlying villages, family members came initially to the Center and insisted on speaking personally with Irina because their aunt knew and trusted her. Although the Center could offer counseling to the family and support for the children, the issues of housing, employment, benefits, custodial rights, and health, which the case revolved around, were not within Irina's competences to resolve. Nonetheless, the family expressed their confidence that she would be able to help since, after all, "she knows everyone."

As the details of the case emerged, a range of local state actors became involved: the fostering and guardianship service, medics, social workers, teachers, employment officers, the benefits office, the village mayor, and the deputy head of district administration. A meeting of the district committee for juvenile affairs discussed the case. Everyone agreed that if the higher authorities were presented with the full details, the youngest children would almost certainly be placed in a children's home beyond the district, an outcome that all were keen to avoid. In part, this was due to strong local norms regarding kin relations and an emphasis on family-based care as being most appropriate for children. It was also, however, a reflection of a range of personal, emotional, and more instrumental interests and attachments. Recently bereaved of a parent, the older siblings in the family were distraught at the idea of 'losing' their younger siblings as well. The extremely constrained material circumstances of the family made it quite likely that maintaining regular contact between the separated siblings would become difficult. Retaining custody of the children also brought potential material benefits, as the family would be able to claim a range of regionally funded benefits and subsidies, which would relieve some of the pressure on local resources to support them. Meanwhile, local teachers were keen to keep the children at their school since falling numbers threatened closure. For the fostering and guardianship service, keeping the children in the family, while undesirable in terms of the formal rules that prioritize the material well-being and physical health of children, was in keeping with other normative values inscribed in the service's mission. This emphasizes the family as the best and proper place for childcare and states that children should be removed from families only as a last resort and placed with relatives or in an alternative family environment if at all possible.

Various solutions were proposed, all of which involved working across structures and bending, if not breaking, a number of official rules and requirements regarding the children's custody. The employment office had no available jobs but would register one of the older siblings for community work, meaning that the CSA could offer her a job that would be partially subsidized through the community work program. The district authorities would register the family for municipal housing even though there was none available, allowing the fostering and guardianship service to fudge a report regarding the family's access to housing. Schoolteachers would support the family on a day-to-day basis, allowing the children to remain in the outlying village even if they were officially registered as residing with a relative in Losevo. All of these solutions involved local state actors pooling their competences and means of leveraging resources from beyond the district while avoiding giving up decision-making control or relinquishing valuable human resources to the external authorities. Implementing such solutions relied on a high degree of mutual trust, cooperation among those responsible for the different services, and a willingness to act outside of their formal remit. All of these efforts would be for nothing if even one official was not on board. The head of the local fostering and guardianship service, Svetlana, was visibly nervous about the solutions being proposed. It was she who would have to sign any final decision about the children's living circumstances, and during the meeting she repeatedly referred to her problematic professional relationship with the head of the fostering and guardianship service in a nearby town, who was officially designated to supervise activities at the rural district level: "She will seem to support us to our faces, and then she'll go off behind our backs, telling tales to the regional authorities." The chair of the meeting proposed that the decisions would be recorded in the minutes so that everyone present would take collective responsibility. Svetlana acquiesced, but without seeming completely reassured.

Significantly, as a relative newcomer to the village, Svetlana was not part of the more closely knit group of former classmates, long-term colleagues, and distant relatives to which many of the other local state actors belonged. While her relationship with them incorporated the formal-professional mode, she lacked the more intimate ties underpinning the informal-personalized mode of interactions that the others drew on. Discussing the case later, Irina said that she had been surprised by Svetlana's reaction, implying that it was a lack of courage that led her to resist the flexible, locally based solutions proposed at the meeting: "Svetlana's scared. She isn't brave enough about taking responsibility for things and always wants to check up with the regional authorities before making a decision." Although unacknowledged by Irina, Svetlana's comparative isolation and lack of closer relationships with the group likely contributed to her sense of vulnerability. As others had discovered at their own expense, the higher authorities could intervene to punish local officials when things went wrong, and, despite statements to the contrary, other local state actors did not always stand up for 'their own'.

Yet personalized relationships and intimacies did not always work in favor of greater or more successful collaboration. On the contrary, when relations were antagonistic, they might hinder formal-professionalized modes of interaction. In conversations with CSA staff, I was told that personal jealousies and personality clashes, particularly between those at the head of different structures, were undermining the potential for better-coordinated approaches to service provision. The rather unfriendly relationship between the directors of the CSA and the local benefits office in Losevo was a case in point. Despite formal rules stating that these two structures should work closely together, there was little evidence of such collaboration. The two directors avoided each other whenever possible and worked together rather grudgingly when they had to, leading to delays in decision making and disputes over who should take responsibility for what. Thus, the more negative aspects of personalized relationships—distrust, animosity, or simply personal differences—could undermine professional modes of interaction and in doing so hamper and constrain activities of the local state. Significantly, the mismatch between ideal state images and practices was increased here, not because of corruption or privatization of resources, but because negative personalized relationships resulted in inefficiency and a lack of coherence, reinforcing a perception of uncaring officials who choose to pass the buck instead of providing assistance to those in need.

Conclusions

This chapter began by arguing for the need to consider a three-way interaction between images, practices, and diverse relationships that make up the state, especially as it is encountered and experienced at the local level and in relation to welfare and social service provision. In Losevo, local people project an ideal image of the state that incorporates a strong duty of care, which is envisaged mainly as a kind of paternalistic provision by a state that is imagined as unified and coherent, even though people are aware that this is not the case in practice. Local state actors play an important role as the embodiment of the state within the village. The moral responsibility of the state to find ways of helping local people in spite of constrained material realities is most directly ascribed to them, and they frequently achieve this by drawing on a range of relationships and modes of interaction.

By using personalized relationships and more informal modes of interaction alongside their professional status and responsibilities, local state actors are able to meet some of the expectations of their co-villagers. In doing so, they rework their duty of care into something that, while still carrying the authority and power for intervention of professionalized officials, draws on local moral norms and familiar practices to allow a certain leeway or creativity in the application of formal rules and regulations (cf. Dubois, chap. 2). Personalized relationships based on long-standing ties and forms of social intimacy with other local state actors can result in flexible working conditions, cooperation between structures, and holistic support to those in extreme need. They can bring a degree of mutuality and trust to situations where local state actors have to make difficult decisions and (re)interpret formal rules in ways that could bring them into conflict with higher authorities. By the same token, when personalized relationships are absent or are characterized by more negative attributes of jealousy, mistrust, or mutual animosity, the ability of local state actors to live up to the image of an efficient and caring state is undermined.

In interactions with higher authorities, relationships also matter, although here they tend more often to resemble forms of patronage and clientelism. Local state actors have an important role to play in attracting resources to the district and keeping at bay interventions that might be damaging to local interests or run counter to local moralities and norms. This can require the skillful management of relationships to mitigate power differentials and encourage investment without the loss of face or dignity for either the local state actors in question or the district that they represent.

Several varieties of relationships and modes of interaction (cf. Vetters, chap. 1), both formal-professional and informal-personalized, are thus practiced between local state actors and their co-villagers in the role of clients, between local state actors and officials within the social sector, and between local state actors and higher-level authorities. These different modes of interaction are not separate and distinct but are combined into simultaneous, hybrid modes or used consecutively and in tandem to reinforce one another. Rather than being perceived as imperfections or anomalies, such combined modes of interaction should be recognized as an integral facet of this field of state action, bridging the gap between images and practices of the state.

Acknowledgments

This research was funded by the British Academy Small Research Grant Programme (Grant No. 50447/1). I would like to thank Larissa Vetters, Agnieszka Pasieka, and Mihai Popa for interesting and inspiring discussions about early ideas for this chapter.

Rebecca Kay is Professor of Russian Gender Studies at the University of Glasgow. She previously explored gendered transformations in Russia in the 1990s and early 2000s, but more recently she has researched experiences of social security, welfare, and care in rural Russia. Since 2013, she has been principle investigator of an ESRC-funded project exploring perspectives and experiences of 'social security' among migrants from Central and Eastern Europe and the former Soviet Union to Scotland. Key publications include "Migrants' Experiences of Material and Emotional Security in Rural Scotland" (*Journal of Rural Studies*, 2017) and the edited volume *Gender, Equality and Difference During and After State Socialism* (2007).

Notes

1. The village's name and the names of all respondents have been changed to protect their identities.
2. Notable exceptions include Verdery's (2002) study of local officials and processes of land restitution and Khlinovskaya Rockhill's (2010) study of state interventions in childcare.
3. In doing so, they employ well-established practices from the socialist era of reciprocal favors, often involving indirect reciprocity through complex networks of acquaintance (Ledeneva 1998).
4. The term *chinovnik* (official, functionary) is used pejoratively to refer to bureaucrats and self-serving officials.

References

Benda-Beckmann, Franz von, and Keebet von Benda-Beckmann. 1998. "Where Structures Merge: State and Off-State Involvement in Rural Social Security on Ambon, Indonesia." In *Old World Places, New World Problems: Exploring Resource Management Issues in Eastern Indonesia*, ed. Sandra N. Pannell and Franz von Benda-Beckmann, 143–180. Canberra: Australian National University, Centre for Resource and Environmental Studies.

Cook, Linda J. 2007. *Postcommunist Welfare States: Reform Politics in Russia and Eastern Europe*. Ithaca, NY: Cornell University Press.

Field, Mark G., and Judyth L. Twigg, eds. 2000. *Russia's Torn Safety Nets: Health and Social Welfare during the Transition*. Basingstoke: Macmillan.

Frödin, Olle J. 2010. "Dissecting the State: Towards a Relational Conceptualization of States and State Failure." *Journal of International Development* 24 (3): 271–286. doi: 10.1002/ jid.1743.

Gambold Miller, Liesl. 2003. "Interdependence in Rural Russia: The Postsocialist Mixed Feudal Economy." Working Paper No. 51, Max Planck Institute for Social Anthropology, Halle/Saale, Germany.

Gel'man, Vladimir, and Sergei Ryzhenkov. 2011. "Local Regimes, Sub-national Governance and the 'Power Vertical' in Contemporary Russia." *Europe-Asia Studies* 63 (3): 449–465.

Gluckman, Max, James C. Mitchell, and John A. Barnes. 1949. "The Village Headman in British Central Africa." *Africa: Journal of the International African Institute* 19 (2): 89–106.
Gupta, Akhil. 1995. "Blurred Boundaries: The Discourse of Corruption, the Culture of Politics, and the Imagined State." *American Ethnologist* 22 (2): 375–402.
Harvey, Penelope. 2005. "The Materiality of State-Effects: An Ethnography of a Road in the Peruvian Andes." In Krohn-Hansen and Nustad 2005, 123–141.
Hemment, Julie. 2007. *Empowering Women in Russia: Activism, Aid, and NGOs.* Indianapolis: Indiana University Press.
Herzfeld, Michael. 1993. *The Social Production of Indifference: Exploring the Symbolic Roots of Western Bureaucracy.* Chicago: University of Chicago Press.
Kay, Rebecca. 2012. "Managing Everyday (In)Securities: Normative Values, Emotional Security and Symbolic Recognition in the Lives of Russian Rural Elders." *Journal of Rural Studies* 28 (2): 63–71.
Khlinovskaya Rockhill, Elena. 2010. *Lost to the State: Family Discontinuity, Social Orphanhood and Residential Care in the Russian Far East.* New York: Berghahn Books.
Krohn-Hansen, Christian, and Knut G. Nustad, eds. 2005. *State Formation: Anthropological Perspectives.* London: Pluto Press.
Kuper, Adam. 1970. "Gluckman's Village Headman." *American Anthropologist* 72 (2): 355–358.
Ledeneva, Alena V. 1998. *Russia's Economy of Favours: Blat, Networking and Informal Exchange.* Cambridge: Cambridge University Press.
Lindner, Peter. 2007. "Localising Privatization, Disconnecting Locales: Mechanisms of Disintegration in Post-Socialist Rural Russia." *Geoforum* 38 (3): 494–504.
Migdal, Joel S., and Klaus Schlichte. 2005. "Rethinking the State." In *The Dynamics of States: The Formation and Crises of State Domination*, ed. Klaus Schlichte, 1–40. Aldershot: Ashgate.
Nuijten, Monique. 2004. "Between Fear and Fantasy: Governmentality and the Working of Power in Mexico." *Critique of Anthropology* 24 (2): 209–230.
Obeid, Michelle. 2010. "Searching for the 'Ideal Face of the State' in a Lebanese Border Town." *Journal of the Royal Anthropological Institute* 16 (2): 330–346.
Painter, Joe. 2006. "Prosaic Geographies of Stateness." *Political Geography* 25 (7): 752–774.
Read, Rosie, and Tatjana Thelen. 2007. "Introduction: Social Security and Care after Socialism—Reconfigurations of Public and Private." *Focaal—European Journal of Social Anthropology* 50: 3–18.
Verdery, Katherine. 2002. "Seeing Like a Mayor: Or, How Local Officials Obstructed Romanian Land Restitution." *Ethnography* 3 (1): 5–33.
Wegren, Stephen K. 2004. "Rural Adaptation in Russia: Who Responds and How Do We Measure It?" *Journal of Agrarian Change* 4 (4): 553–578.
White, Stephen, Richard Sakwa, and Henry E. Hale, eds. 2010. *Developments in Russian Politics 7.* Durham, NC: Duke University Press.
Young, John F., and Gary N. Wilson. 2007. "The View from Below: Local Government and Putin's Reforms." *Europe-Asia Studies* 59 (7): 1071–1088.

Chapter 4

ACTS OF ASSISTANCE
Navigating the Interstices of the British State with the Help of Non-profit Legal Advisers

Alice Forbess and Deborah James

The role played by the many officers who staff bureaucracies has recently come into ethnographic focus in the work of anthropologists. In the modern French welfare state, for example, these people are said to play a key role in defining policy. According to Dubois (2009: 222), they make decisions on individual cases, often using "their discretion in the orientation of their practices and the definition of their attitude" and basing their decisions on highly idiosyncratic moral judgments about whether or not welfare beneficiaries are deserving. It is the sum of these decisions, practices, and attitudes—rather than the designs of those higher up in the system—that comprises "concrete public policy" (ibid.). While the actions of such actors should not necessarily be seen as malign, since bureaucracies contain "progressive elements" (Heyman 2004: 491), a critical policy ethnography should be attentive to the importance of their actions (Dubois 2009; see also Dubois, chap. 2).

Notes for this chapter begin on page 88.

The present chapter is written in similar vein: it contributes to the ethnography of policy in a setting where forces of state, society, and market overlap. But instead of exploring the practices of 'street-level bureaucrats' (Lipsky 1980), it considers the work of a different group of actors: the givers of advice, often framed in legal terms but not necessarily so, who staff the many law centers, citizens advice bureaus, and advice charities that proliferate in a modern welfare state—in this case the United Kingdom. The state at the local level provides its services in an uncoordinated manner. Different departments exist to provide diverse resources, and increasing levels of professionalization are required to navigate between them; however, those at the lower levels of each separate bureaucracy are often increasingly inexpert. Advisers have become increasingly essential to help people negotiate the tricky terrains of existence and to interpret, mediate, or challenge the often inappropriate decisions made by the kinds of bureaucrats Dubois describes (see also Eule 2012; Good 2007; Moorhead and Robinson 2006: 27-28, 35). In England and Wales,[1] such assistance is particularly necessary in the closely interrelated areas of indebtedness, housing, employment, social security, and immigration and asylum—matters that often converge to form 'problem clusters' (Moorhead and Robinson 2006; Pleasence et al. 2004).

Although the state is often referred to in the singular, reflecting how citizens experience it as monolithic and indivisible (Abrams 1988), writings on the everyday state also show the divergent and inconsistent ways in which citizens engage with it locally (Fuller and Harriss 2001), producing a relational state. In the English welfare state, social security is administered via a particularly labyrinthine multiplicity of different agencies. People are required to negotiate with an array of institutions, each with its own rules and procedures, in order to actualize their rights. Furthermore, problems arising in one area often have unanticipated effects on others. At the local level, advice-givers attempt, as brokers, to find ways of traversing these gaps and of forcing bureaucrats to communicate with each other, and they sometimes confront inadequate decisions by taking more aggressive steps that may end in litigation. The government's recent attempt to reform these fragmented arrangements and cut the legal aid funding on which they depend through the introduction of a more seamless social security system known as Universal Credit will likely create new disjunctures and fault lines, augmenting the need for advice while simultaneously trimming the funds necessary to pay for its provision.

Contributing to the ethnographic exploration of the relational state as it emerges from the interactions of officials and citizens, our chapter explores the role played by these intermediary advisers in facilitating state-citizen interactions. They expertly shape such interactions by translating complex life circumstances into persuasive cases framed in terms of appropriate legal definitions. It is by highlighting these actors' engagements with officials from various state agencies, on the one hand, and with citizens/clients, on the other, that we shed light on the question of how state formations are continuously recreated and transformed through embedded relations (see the introduction).

The ethnographic examples we present were documented in a context of accelerated change in which the role and means of advice were being rethought and debated by NGO advisers, solicitors, and policy makers. Legal aid is the main source of funding for many advice services in England and Wales, but as of April 2013, with the exception of a handful of services, this legal aid was cut for social welfare law cases—those involving problems such as debt, housing, social security, employment, immigration, and asylum (see Biggs 2011; Moorhead and Robinson 2006). Our fieldwork details how two non-profit legal services organizations grapple with the loss of a significant portion of their funding, how this is reshaping their interactions with clients and various state agencies, and how they attempt to make the state more relational against the background of policies aimed at producing the opposite effect.

Legal Aid, Legal Advice, and the Fieldwork Setting

Simple advice provisioning might appear to have little to do with legal aid: the former is associated with organizations such as the Citizens Advice Bureau (CAB),[2] while the latter is thought of in relation to trials and courtrooms. But in an adversarial common law system like that of England and Wales, where the law is to a significant extent made and administered by judges in ordinary courts and where litigation routinely alters legislation through an accumulation of precedents, access to a legal expert familiar with recent case law is essential to the success of legal action and underpins the most basic advice given in the most lowly settings.[3]

The architects of Britain's welfare state understood, on the eve of its establishment, that funded legal advice would be central to establishing citizen equality before the law. What was less fully grasped was the centrality of such advice in enabling fairness of access to the services that the welfare state was itself to provide. The 1942 Beveridge Report, foundational to the establishment of Britain's welfare system, aspired toward universally available legal aid to pay for professional assistance in a situation where increasing amounts, and the increasing complexity, of legislation were deemed to have made this necessary. The 1949 Legal Aid and Advice Act followed not long afterward (Biggs 2011). Subsequently, eligibility criteria were increasingly tightened, gradually excluding all but the poorest claimants, and—under the 1997 Labour government—restricting the areas of the law covered by legal aid. Finally, departing from Beveridge's vision of legal aid as a guarantee of universal access to justice and establishing the setting of austerity in which our study was conducted, the Conservative–Liberal Democrat coalition, as part of its austerity package, passed the 2012 Legal Aid, Sentencing and Punishment of Offenders (LASPO) Act, which cuts most civil cases out of the scope of legal aid.

Over the years, legal aid has been overseen by a series of administrative bodies. From 1999 to 2013 (and during our study), it was administered by the Legal Services Commission (LSC), a body nominally independent from both the state and from legal professional organizations.[4] Most of the administrative duties of the LSC were subsequently incorporated into the Ministry of Justice. The funding regime, too, has become increasingly circumscribed and bureaucratic. In its early days, legal aid was disbursed through solicitor practices based on hours worked on each case, but in the mid-2000s the LSC introduced a new, fixed fee system of thresholds. This limited the amount of time that could be spent on simpler cases, or at least the pay that could be claimed for this time, and imposed much stricter audits on how money was spent in more complex cases (James and Killick 2012: 438).

While funding has become increasingly restricted, legal advice services have become more diverse. They are delivered by a range of organizations, including statutory providers, voluntary sector organizations, and private businesses. Since the Thatcher era, as a result of state agencies routinely subcontracting public services to the most successful bidder (see Moorhead 2001), the demarcations between legal services providers have undergone continual renegotiation, giving rise to a cross-pollination of values and approaches. Government contracts often force organizations governed by distinct and even opposing logics to work together, thus developing a common ground. For instance, when one advice-giving organization competed against a private company for a government contract and won, it later subcontracted work to its former competitor. The advice-giving organization had become involved in defining how the services were provided, thus influencing the values and ethos of the subcontractor. The separation of such spheres is an aspiration in line with theories of modernity and democracy, but one that flies in the face of the actual tendency of such arenas to overlap (Narotzky and Smith 2006), especially in settings characterized by the outsourcing logics associated with neo-liberalism.

The extent to which advice is 'legal' escalates, depending on the level to which it is referred and—accordingly—the professional qualifications of the adviser. Corresponding more closely to the familiar image of citizen advice, the first tier involves generalists, many of them volunteers, who attend to a client's problems at the initial port of call. More complicated legal problems are then referred to second-tier advice-providing organizations that employ solicitors and other experts specializing in key areas of social welfare law. Finally, the third tier of advice involves representation in court. Generally, advice agencies' approaches to social intervention tend to be framed either as 'legal services' or (less legal in focus) 'social care', although in practice the lines are blurred and some organizations combine approaches.

In the two London non-profit legal services providers in which our fieldwork was conducted—Southwark Law Center (SLC) and the Advice Center at Community Links (CL)—this upward escalation is in evidence, in different ways. CL is an East London charity that aims to fulfill the need for specialist legal advice alongside other more general forms of intervention. Its advice center, employing four solicitors, offers mostly first- and second-tier assistance. An administrator assesses potential clients. If their problem is deemed 'legal' in nature and their income entitles them to legal aid, they are referred to one of these solicitors; if ineligible, they may be sent to another advice-providing agency, may be referred to the volunteer advice arm of CL, or may receive the same assistance as legal aid clients but with funding from another income stream.[5] The SLC, our other field site, is a community-owned and -operated charity dedicated to providing specialist legal services in the areas of immigration, employment, social security, and housing.[6] In contrast to CL, it works by referral only. Clients come by appointment to see a specialist in the relevant area of the law, while non-clients are normally referred to a local first-tier advice organization. The SLC is subject to the Law Society's more stringent regulatory regime, which requires a high proportion of a law center's staff to be fully qualified solicitors. Adviser-client interactions are also subject to a more formal rigor. For these solicitors and their paralegal assistants, the act of giving advice may never be informal because actions taken during the advice encounter have a constitutive and binding effect, shaping the future of a case. Speaking to a person about his or her problems can be taken to constitute a retainer, thereby rendering a solicitor responsible for the case. Accordingly, SLC advisers do not give casual advice to non-clients, but instead contribute to the provision of more informal advice by cultivating close relations with local first-tier agencies and training their staff. Thus, the SLC is an organization of experts that operates as part of a network, receiving referrals for more complicated legal matters from front-line advice providers and educating advisers employed by the latter, as well as local government decision makers, regarding the correct application of the law.

When the coalition government significantly slashed legal aid funding as of April 2013, both organizations secured short-term alternative funding to keep their legal advice services open, but no substantial and sustainable long-term funding stream has yet been secured. Whereas some SLC cases were complex—with adviser-client interactions lasting months or years, and with the resulting relationship often outlasting cases—the interactions in CL cases were more limited. The complexity of the former was due to the SLC's position as a referral-only organization, while the latter took any qualifying cases that came through the door, most of them routine.

Our fieldwork methods in the two organizations included participant observation and semi-structured interviewing, documenting caseworkers' consultations with clients, tracing the progress of cases, analyzing case documents, observing tribunal hearings, and interviewing staff involved in administration and billing. A total of 46 cases were encountered, of which 7 were followed and documented more closely. Four of the caseworkers we shadowed were fully qualified solicitors, including Emma (SLC).[7] Two were paralegals, one of whom, Robert (SLC), was a trainee solicitor while the other, Luka (CL), was not training as a solicitor but had three years of legal training and two years of experience volunteering at a Citizens Advice Bureau. Their clients included people afflicted by the problem clusters mentioned above, which may be brought on by mental or physical illness, the breakdown of relationships, youthful inexperience, poor language skills, or interactions with the system that result in prosecution or pursuit of arrears that clients cannot repay or, in some cases, ought not be required to repay. Others were unable to access benefits to which they were entitled, usually because of officials' ignorance of the legislation or unwillingness to give them a fair hearing.

The state agencies with which such clients routinely interact include local institutions, such as local administrative departments responsible for housing, social services, and council tax collection,[8] and national ones, such as the Home

Office, the Department of Work and Pensions (including its Jobcentre Plus and other agencies), and the Inland Revenue (HMRC). The social security system combined a range of funds: council tax benefit, child tax credits, housing benefit, income support, disability living allowance, jobseeker's allowance, and so forth. These were administered by various agencies in a poorly coordinated manner. In many cases, the temporary suspension of one benefit triggered the retrospective revocation of others. This led to "overpayment demands," with claimants being asked to return money that they had already received—often thousands of pounds—or face benefits fraud charges. This commonly resulted in rent arrears that could easily bring financial ruin and homelessness. Cases typically involved appeals against official decisions that denied a person's eligibility for a fund or challenges to the suspension of a means-tested benefit. In other words, the problems resulting from the failure of a key aspect of the welfare system on which the client has become reliant are as serious as, or more serious than, the elements of the initial problem cluster itself. Much of the advisers' work strove to halt this avalanche of problems by addressing them within the limited time frame for appeals.

Legal Advice and the Local State: Between Litigation and Negotiation

Advisers' relational strategies in dealing with state officials spanned a continuum ranging from litigation, on the one hand, to negotiation and collaboration, on the other, and from a normative approach, calling upon state officials to follow the rules, to more discretionary and personal entreaties. While litigation often entails an adversarial stance toward local state officials, negotiation is built on collaboration, the aim of which is to establish a culture of mutual trust between local authorities and service providers. The two approaches are not mutually exclusive: our study found that different types of legal problems fostered different degrees of adversarialness and/or negotiation. On occasion, one was used to buttress the other. The threat of litigation, for example, was often used as leverage in negotiations. At other times, legal services providers and local authorities joined together in programs aimed at preventing housing evictions, setting aside adversarialness in the name of mutual cooperation. Conversely, in some immigration and housing cases, adversarialness could be exacerbated to the point where solicitors sought a judicial review, in which both sides were obliged to disclose all their evidence before a judge.

Several SLC advisers pointed out in various ways that their work is about actively defining, through their cases, how the law should function in a fair society, thus potentially making legal history. In theory, this involves continually engaging with the latest case law, with the ultimate aim of challenging legislation through the courts and of going beyond the application of the law in order to probe tensions within—and openly drive challenges to—unfair legislation. Each case that comes through the doors of the SLC and CL may go all the way to the Supreme Court. Even if such instances are relatively rare, the fact that they exist, according to SLC employees, reflects a broader commitment by the increasingly embattled legal professionals to ensure that these formal legal channels remain open to all. Another way in which solicitors actualize an ideal of justice is by ensuring that cases are taken to their logical conclusion. In deciding what course of action is best for a client, they claim to be guided by their duty to the client, to the court, and to the LSC and professional standards. Their judgment, however, may be disputed by the clerks at the LSC, who determine which funds are payable. In some cases, the LSC argued, the work done after a certain point (when a temporary solution had been offered by the opposing side) should not have been carried out under a public funding certificate, but under a separate funding regime called "legal help." In the end, the LSC refused to pay for the work undertaken by the Center in such cases.[9]

Adversarialness is a source of ambivalence for advisers like Emma, an SLC solicitor specializing in housing law, who sees it as tactically useful and even ethically necessary but at the same time aspires toward a more reconciliatory approach. She related that in homelessness cases the council sometimes rides roughshod over the vulnerabilities of potential evictees: by routinely ignoring the "nice letter" written by SLC solicitors, council employees "push us into being aggressive and adversarial." She wishes that they would embrace a "culture change." The continual pressure to cut down on expenditures has greatly exacerbated levels of adversarialness—in this case between the SLC and the local authority—since the 1990s, when Emma worked for another organization addressing homelessness. While there, she was encouraged to believe the story of every woman claiming abuse so as to avoid any possibility of returning a victim to her abuser, but now there is a tendency to avoid helping the vulnerable clients she represents. This, as SLC personnel acknowledge, is due to diminishing housing stock. Although local authorities have a legal duty to accommodate such clients, they lack the resources with which to provide accommodation, and this forces them to focus on gatekeeping, turning legitimate housing applicants away whenever possible. As the SLC's housing law expert explained to us, the Housing Authority "will often prevaricate and obfuscate by providing accommodation to a destitute or homeless family for a short period of, say, seven days or even less in some cases, but refuse to comply with [their] duty to provide longer-term accommodation until the very last moment." Aware that the most fruitful approach would combine adversarial elements with aspects of the negotiation that seemed more desirable, Emma and others wished there was a way to move past this "negativity."

In cases concerning citizenship status, the solicitor adviser has the power—for example, with would-be immigrants—to resolve and obliterate an "illegal" past, but this often involves delicate negotiations with different state agencies. Vulnerable people often exist "below the radar" of the authorities, afraid to approach them and claim the assistance to which they may be entitled. As a CL solicitor observed, "Unless you make contact, [the authorities] can't help you." In one case, a woman with housing problems and an uncertain immigration status "was afraid to make contact and ask for emergency housing assistance and immigration advice because she was mentally ill and feared she would be sectioned. Hence, she remained on the streets, and no one knew she needed help." In such cases, the adviser guides the client through the process of approaching the authorities while also trying to deflect any negative repercussions.

Our research revealed that advisers often orchestrated complex interactions intended to secure for the client a range of forms of assistance. This involved contacting various state agencies and drawing them into a complex web of relations. To facilitate these interactions, advisers created diachronic representations of the client's history of contacts with the state, describing them in ways that would be legible to state officials and would enable them to act on the information. By carrying out all these tasks, advisers, in effect, 'conjured up' the state for their clients in a variety of relational guises.

Some of these incarnations were more benevolent than others. One set of officials, for instance, those in the Home Office, might be the hostile party delaying and obstructing a resolution of the case, while other officials, such as those in the local social services, might step in to offer psychiatric care, emergency shelter, and so on. Given the shifting, even contradictory positions of the state in these various guises, the capability of advisers to coordinate claimant interactions with the state was essential. The day-to-day management of a case might involve delicate interactions with officials in various state agencies, sometimes pressing for a decision, at other times biding one's time to increase the likelihood of a positive outcome. In order to do this, the paralegal in one case drew on her grasp of the contingencies under which counterparts in the state departments operated. For instance, she knew the name of the Home Office officer charged with making a decision and asked for updates over the telephone. Possessing knowledge of the targets that structured the work of state officials, the adviser could accurately anticipate the actions of these officials and strategically plan around them.

Advice services can be said to make the state work, putting errors of public administration to rights and policing the way that local agencies fulfill their obligations to citizens. Tempering earlier statements about the adversarial character of relations, one informant pointed out to us that the council had agreed to fund a significant proportion of the SLC's budget after the legal aid cuts. This, in his view, amounted to the local authority making sure that its own low-level employees acted as they should. The extent to which such a role became apparent depended both on the local authority's attitude toward advice services, informed by ideological and political commitments, and on other funding contingencies. For example, between 2004 and 2007, the SLC collaborated extensively with the council and with a local advice center in order to reduce the number of tenants being evicted from council properties. The SLC trained both council employees (to identify and help tenants at risk of eviction) and volunteer advisers from the local community (to give advice to these tenants). The council was also asked to revise its policies, leading to a large drop in evictions. After three years, however, the LSC stopped funding this project, arguing that the SLC should instead concentrate on "acts of assistance" (i.e., narrowly framed legal matters).

While collaborations between legal advice-givers and the state frequently succeeded in resolving serious problems, they also blurred boundaries, hence diluting the adversarial tactics necessary for truly robust legal advice. "If you get pally with the other side," it could lead to conflicts of interest and "muddy the waters ... it becomes harder to completely look out for your client's interest," said Emma, invoking a hypothetical case where a solicitor might advise a tenant under the council's auspices one week, and next week—switching sides—might meet him as a court duty adviser and take his case against the council. The blurring of boundaries can damage the legal expert adviser's neutrality on which his or her power to mediate is founded.

Like the SLC, CL tries to cultivate collaborative interactions with its local authority. Levels of collaboration vary according to the unique characteristics of the case and the state agency under whose jurisdiction it falls. For instance, likewise helping to prevent evictions, CL advises council tenants with the full support of the relevant council office. In the area of welfare benefits claims, however, the council seems more inclined to limit access to advice on the grounds that it keeps people dependent on state welfare: reducing or eliminating it would result in more people getting off benefits and back to work. Yet such rejections could later result in closer synergies, as happened when the council developed its own advice structures to serve these goals. In cases of indebtedness, collaboration held sway. The CL advisers' relationships with council staff enabled them to negotiate lenient repayment plans on behalf of clients.

In their interactions with officials, advisers from both organizations often tried to help by providing advice to both officials and the clients they are supposed to serve. Thus, CL collaborated with local counterparts within the council's employment office to develop a mutually beneficial program suggested by a group of advice staff who understood the needs and pitfalls faced by government employees. The resulting translation and form-filling service operated by volunteers led to a 70 percent reduction in claims rejections arising from mistakes and omissions on forms. The two organizations then worked together to push for the nationwide adoption of this plan, but difficulties in obtaining approval from the head office led to the termination of the service (Barbour 2007: 52). Here, micro-management from the top was a problem shared by both CL advisers and local government employees, generating some solidarity between them. Disjunctures may thus occur between front-line and central tiers of state agencies, enabling advisers to establish a rapport with their official counterparts in the local state, blurring the boundaries between them, and generating solidarity against those higher up the chain.

At CL, such solidarity could provide a basis for negotiation on behalf of clients. Luka, the paralegal mentioned earlier, told us that he first approaches government officials by making it clear that he assumes they are keen to follow the law, thereby implicitly holding them to this assumption. Then he simply proves that they have failed to do so. This technique defuses any personal adversarial element that might otherwise hamper negotiations. "You must always begin negotiations from the other guy's point of view," Luka explains. In a case where a tenant is threatened with eviction, he tells the council official,

"If you accept a small monthly repayment of the rent arrears, at least you'll get something. Otherwise, you will never see any of the money."

The manager of CL's advice center, herself a solicitor, told us that they actively cultivated this negotiation-based approach. When asked why few of CL's cases incur the higher levels of legal aid funding that accompany upward referral, she explained that advisers avoid long, litigious situations, opting instead to prioritize quick settlements, which are thought to be more advantageous to the client.[10] To this end, mutual trust and win-win solutions are promoted in interactions with local officials. CL thus recruited the local state to partake (at least to some extent) in its vision of an integrated and functional community. When negotiating directly on behalf of the vulnerable, caseworkers were particularly effective if they succeeded in combining rule-oriented and more 'relational' logics, professional authority, and long-term access to friendly contacts at government agencies. The organization's symbolic capital ensured that cases would be judged on their individual merits rather than on the plaintiffs' ability to speak for themselves, as happened all too often.

This was illustrated in the case of Mr. Patel, a native Punjabi speaker. Patel's marriage had recently ended, and, adding to his anxieties, HMRC was demanding repayment for a child tax credit he had been erroneously granted. The 'overpayment request' stated that the amount was owed because he had failed to inform the agency of his changed domestic circumstances, but Patel and his wife would have been entitled to the same amount of money had they simply passed on this information as they ought to have done. In effect, there was no overpayment; they were being fined for failing to notify HMRC of their separation. Since Patel lives on jobseeker's allowance (one of a complex array of possible forms of welfare), repaying £360 was well beyond his means. Benefits claims put the burden of proof on the claimant, and claims adjudications carried the force of law unless successfully appealed. As Luka put it, "You're always guilty unless you prove otherwise. It's upside down, not like in court ... In effect they are saying, 'Prove us wrong.'" In the case of HMRC demands, there is no appeal tribunal. To contest them, one must negotiate directly with HMRC. But poor language skills and a lack of basic system literacy render such negotiations impossible for most claimants. Furthermore, when the adviser spoke to HMRC, requesting 'notional offsetting'—a legally established payment option whereby the overpayment is subtracted from the tax credits to which the client is eligible, effectively canceling the debt—the HMRC officer turned out never to have heard of the provision, although after some consultation the option was acknowledged. When even a professional adviser had difficulty actualizing his client's right to offset charges, Patel would have stood little chance on his own. HMRC has its own rules that are distinct from those of other state agencies, but this was obvious neither to Patel, who could barely distinguish between the various state offices with which he came into contact, nor even to an officer of this arm of the state. It was the adviser, with his considerable knowledge and experience of similar cases, who was best able to discern how to resolve the situation in the interests of the client and who carried sufficient weight when addressing his counterparts in the local state.

Legal Advice and Clients: Friendly Objectification and the Creation of Evidence

In the relations between advisers and clients that we observed, friendly encouragement was predominant. However, while mediation and negotiation are central to the practice, providing advice is also a gatekeeping practice and, to this end, can involve unyieldingly strict interactions with clients, since lawyers and paralegals are being called on to monitor access to state resources and to the formal justice system itself. Lawyers and paralegals do so, in part, by creating robust evidence. Evidence is a key object of contestation in transactions between various state organs, advisers, and individuals seeking to actualize their rights. In building a legal case, caseworkers gradually strip away extraneous detail in order to arrive at a persuasive line of argument (Good 2007: 15), performing a work of translation between the man on the street and the culture of a legal system whose logic and rules of evidence are far from obvious. If this work is not carried out expertly before filing a legal case, the right evidence may be unwittingly left out from the witness statement, leading to its exclusion and thus the collapse of the case.

Robert, a trainee solicitor at the SLC, explained that the evidential arrangements in the legal system aim not simply to ensure that each citizen has his or her day in court but also to prevent unnecessary litigation. The advice giving explored in our ethnography was largely aimed at helping people stay *out of* court. People without legal advice are more likely to go to court, but it is often more advantageous to negotiate a settlement before proceeding to a hearing, thus avoiding the possibility of being made to pay the other side's costs. Clients, Robert pointed out, are not always aware of this and tend to get passionate about their cases, building great expectations around the tantalizing promise of justice. In such cases, the adviser's job, as Robert put it, is to provide perspective, to "refocus them on what the tribunal will actually do, because their ideas are often based on complete misconceptions. [The judge] will want to know very specific things … A lot of people are using the word 'discrimination', but they do not mean discrimination in the legal sense, only in the sense of being treated differently. Their understanding of the word and concept is different from that of the judge and the tribunal. People are also ill-equipped to put their evidence in the witness statement. They do not know *what constitutes valid evidence* and *what they need to prove*" (emphasis added). If the right evidence is not included in the witness statement, it may never be admitted. Yet many clients do not respond well to written communication or lack the linguistic or analytical skills to grasp what is required. They may provide the wrong evidence or miss deadlines. Robert continued: "Then the judge [says]: 'Your problem!' And that is right, in a sense. He is not an adviser; he is there to decide on the legal issues. Case law establishes that he is under no obligation to dig things out."

Robert illustrated this with a case that he had encountered during a one-off advice session. People, he said, understandably get emotional about their cases: "When you are wronged you get angry, withdrawn, depressed … People lose all sense of worth because of a loss of purpose." When this happens, "part of the adviser's job is to help people deal with that ... [by acknowledging] that you understand they have been wronged but [also explaining] ... how their obsession is different to the issue of fairness. [The] claimant needs to be told to give up worrying and obsessing about the case, abandoning himself to a spiral of difficulty, relationship breakdown, financial loss, all of it encompassed by this massive thing in their mind—the legal case. I try to stop this happening. I think legal advice can help people to reclaim a bit of their self-esteem and understand how to move on."

In discussing how laypersons' beliefs about the law relate to legal process, anthropologists Conley and O'Barr (1990) observed that some people tend to take a rule-oriented approach to their problems, evaluating them in terms of neutral principles and emphasizing these principles in their accounts. Others tend to display a relational orientation, "characterized by a 'fuzzier' definition of issues whereby rights and responsibilities are predicated on 'a broad notion of social interdependence rather than on the application of rules'" (Good 2007: 21, citing Conley and O'Barr 1990; see also Genn 1999: 256–257). Relationally oriented perspectives are not irrational or unstructured, but they conform to a logic different from that of the legal system, rendering them ineffectual in this context. Advisers, then, are needed to perform a work of logical translation, conveying human expectations into legal context. This sheds light on the relational approach to the state proposed by the editors of this book (see the introduction). Relationality is not limited to personal, face-to-face interactions between citizens and representatives of the state; it is also central to the legalistic approach to the state adopted by legal advisers, who expect—or instruct—officials to know and observe the rules. In the eyes of the law, normatively guided actions are opposed to the exercise of personal discretion, which could be seen as more relational in the sense that officials are called upon to make decisions based on more personal considerations. However, the law incorporates and recognizes the exercise of discretion alongside the application of rules. According to Bingham (2010: 48–54), the legal profession views discretion and rules as complementary: the exercise of discretion in cases where the rules would lead to injustice is necessary, but too much discretionary power would lead to tyranny.

In light of these considerations, one can argue that all state environments involve pragmatic configurations—different relational modalities—that may combine personal/discretionary and impersonal/rule-centered strategies. The ethnographer's task then is to understand exactly what the configuration is in a specific case and why. In our case, the advisers are experts who can strategically play upon the boundary between personal discretion and normative rigor, drawing on a thorough understanding of the latter, including what potential pitfalls are entailed in a rigid application of the rules and which circumstances permit and validate the use of discretion. Needless to say, an unaided client would be far less equal to the task, not knowing how to draw effectively on the relational opportunities (both normative and discretionary) offered and created by interactions with the state (Genn 1999: 256–257).

The act of creating evidence is also an act of objectification (Engelke 2008), carried out by both low-level government officials and caseworkers themselves in the course of their interviews. To an extent, advisers have little choice but to participate in gatekeeping activities in reference to welfare benefits. For instance, when in the course of an interview Luka suspected that a client was misrepresenting his circumstances, he felt that he ought not to take the case. Instead, he said, "It is my job to tell you that you are applying for the wrong benefit." When the client persisted, Luka helped him fill out his appeal form, explained the process, and ended the interview. He intended to close the file because the case was likely to fail. And failure also jeopardized funding.

Advisers aimed to mitigate the disempowering effect of interactions with the state by educating clients about their rights. In one CL case, an adviser helped a client to resist eviction. It was, ironically, the client's attempt to stop depending on welfare benefits that had initiated the chain of events that almost resulted in his eviction from his council flat. David was a 22-year-old Ugandan who had acquired UK citizenship through naturalization. He arrived in the United Kingdom at the age of 13 and was raised in foster care, having no family network of his own. At 17, he was granted a council flat and enrolled in college, in addition to volunteering and being paid to work on National Health Service campaigns. During these stints of temporary employment, David informed the jobseeker's allowance agency, but he was unaware that he was also obliged to liaise with the housing benefits office. Unbeknown to David, this resulted in the temporary suspension of his rent subsidy and the accrual of rent arrears. Funding cuts meant that David no longer had access to the social worker who had formerly advised him, and he tried unsuccessfully to resolve the problem on his own. Overwhelmed by the pressure, he then dropped out of college and for eight months ignored the rent arrears that continued to accrue.

David came to CL having missed his eviction court date and about to be ejected from the flat. Luka negotiated a repayment schedule to clear his rent arrears. He explained that the prospects of retaining the flat were slim and that David would have to challenge the warrant in court. Because of David's youthful inexperience, Luka saw his role as an educational one, aiming to prevent the possible recurrence of such problems. David should have sought advice immediately rather than ignoring the problem or trying to resolve it on his own. The only remaining strategy was to prove to the judge that David was "constant" by having him make small payments toward his debt and asking for another chance. Luka advised, "The judge will give you a chance, but you have to [prove that you know your responsibilities]. You must stay in the present to solve this. Forget about the past, forget about the future."

Here, Luka was further pursuing objectification through his insistence on the need for David to adhere to the rules as a long-term strategy. In the short term, he was also pointing to the importance of presenting facts as evidence acceptable in court. As shown by studies of other law centers, the adviser was, in effect, persuading the client to follow the rules by guiding him in appropriate attitudes toward evidence. This friendly/educative role, occasionally verging on the paternalistic, was combined with a stern "recognition that due process must be followed" (James and Killick 2012: 450), and, if necessary, compliance with it must be enforced.

Conclusion

The welfare state in England was envisioned as executing social interventions through concerted programs implemented by state institutions. Its designers envisioned an equally centralized and universalistic approach to legal aid. Perhaps they did so with prescience, given the extent to which the separate bureaucracies proliferating at the local level—as demonstrated here—have become fragmented, leaving the very people intended as the beneficiaries in sore need of advice. Mediators, lawyers, and paralegals draw on both personalized and formal repertoires to make the state relational in different ways, as well as enabling it to function as they feel it should. Our fieldwork reveals how, despite fragmentation and the outsourcing of state processes, there is a basis for certain paths of communication through mediator advisers, which in turn produces forms of integration.

The position of advisers who mediate between the state and its citizens is, in some ways, not unlike that of brokers and mediators more generally (Lindquist 2015; James 2011). In the well-known discussion of the village headman in British Central Africa (Gluckman et al. 1949), the headman's dilemma arises from his being subject to irreconcilable demands based on conflicting value systems: the expectations of his kin and followers (in our case the advisees) versus the political, legalistic, and impersonal logic of the state. The headman is unable to please the latter without upsetting the former and vice versa. However, his knowledge of the extent of his local support and of its heterogeneous nature allows him some room for maneuver (Kuper 1970). Advisers' success in helping their clients likewise depends on their knowledge of and skill in exploiting the gaps between different state (and supra-state) agencies, sometimes using a relational and at other times a legalistic logic, or, most often, combining the two. Their room for maneuver is enhanced by claims of independence from both their clients and the state; they can be trusted to mediate fairly because they are distinct from both parties.

The assumption of advisers' independence stems from the widely accepted premise of the opposition between state and civil society (see Hann and Dunn 1996)—a premise that serves here as a helpful fiction. In the area of legal aid (but not limited to it), charities have long depended for their survival on funds paid by the state when it commissions them to provide public services. This money has increasingly come with strings attached and the imposition of ever more stringent restrictions that have shaped advice services in crucial ways. It would be inaccurate to claim that legal charities are merely carrying out the directives of state agencies, but their financial dependence on state commissioners has meant that their room for maneuver is frequently far smaller than the ideology of the separation between state and civil society would imply. But this ideology is the cornerstone on which their power leverage vis-à-vis state bureaucracies is founded.

Charities are attempting to shore up their independence by developing alternative forms of social finance that rely on the market and investors as well as the state. Yet that independence is simultaneously being eroded as they become drawn into state bureaucratic projects that seek to reorganize the world in specific ways. The project of addressing and redressing social inequalities through legal advice and legal interventions, an initiative formerly supported by the state, is in danger of obliteration due to lack of funding. However, through constructive struggle, charities enlist some segments of state bureaucracy for assistance against others. The picture is neither one characterized by a separation between state and civil society, nor one in which a monolithic state is ineluctably and progressively eroding the independence of the third sector. Instead, what we are seeing is ever more complex, blurred, and idiosyncratic tangles of state, business, and third sector in the field of public services.

Acknowledgments

We thank the London School of Economics for its award of STICERD and Research Committee Seed Fund grants to carry out this research, and the Leverhulme Trust and ESRC for awarding further grants that made it possible to refine and update this work. We also extend thanks to the paralegals, lawyers, and their clients who participated in the research, to the members of our advisory board for valuable feedback, to the editors of this book for their hard work, and to the anonymous reviewers for their suggestions.

Alice Forbess is an ESRC Research Fellow in the Department of Anthropology at the London School of Economics. Her research interests include the intersection of religious institutions and political life in Romania and former Yugoslavia and, more recently, the politics of restorative justice in Kosovo and the transformation of non-profit legal services in the United Kingdom.

Deborah James is a Professor of Anthropology at the London School of Economics. Her research focuses on im/migration, land and property relations, and economic formality/informality. She is the author of *Money from Nothing: Indebtedness and Aspiration in South Africa* (2015). Along with Alice Forbess and several other researchers, she is currently leading a project entitled "An Ethnography of Advice: Between Market, Society, and the Declining Welfare State."

Notes

1. The administrative division is relevant to our cases. Other parts of the United Kingdom have their own legal systems, parliaments, and advice arrangements.
2. The CAB, which is volunteer-operated but receives some state funding, helps people resolve problems by providing advice and influencing policy makers. See http://www.citizensadvice.org.uk (accessed 10 May 2017).
3. The English legal landscape, which combines European statutes, parliamentary statutes, and common or case law (Bingham 2010: 37–47), is unusually complex and inaccessible to ordinary citizens.
4. In 2013, the LSC was replaced by the Legal Aid Agency (LAA), which is part of the Ministry of Justice (and thus not an independent body).
5. CL innovates by testing and refining procedures and training community members. It envisages shifting from crisis management to prevention and aims to adopt ever more holistic approaches.
6. The SLC, part of a wider UK federation, resembles the US Law Center movement of the 1970s. It seeks to make the law freely available to ordinary people and stresses the provision of high-quality legal services and the promotion of legal education by various means.
7. All names are pseudonyms.
8. In England and Wales, lower-tier local authorities are known as 'councils' and may be either borough, county, or district councils. They are funded through a blend of central government grants, council tax levied by themselves, parking charges, and business rates. Their responsibilities include (but are not limited to) administering housing and council tax benefits, administering social housing, and providing emergency shelter.
9. Although the LSC's denial of funding for work carried out was reversed on appeal, the SLC was nonetheless forced to expend resources on appealing erroneous decisions.
10. See note 5.

References

Abrams, Philip. 1988. "Notes on the Difficulty of Studying the State." *Journal of Historical Sociology* 1 (1): 58–89.

Barbour, Aaron. 2007. "Everyday Innovators: Innovating Public Services." In *Making Links: Fifteen Versions of Community*, ed. Richard McKeever, 49–58. London: Community Links.

Biggs, Joanna. 2011. "Who Will Get Legal Aid Now?" *London Review of Books* 33 (20): 19–22.

Bingham, Tom. 2010. *The Rule of Law*. London: Penguin Books.

Conley, John M., and William M. O'Barr. 1990. *Rules versus Relationships: The Ethnography of Legal Discourse*. Chicago: University of Chicago Press.

Dubois, Vincent. 2009. "Towards a Critical Policy Ethnography: Lessons from Fieldwork." *Policy Studies* 3 (2): 221–239.

Engelke, Matthew. 2008. "The Objects of Evidence." *Journal of the Royal Anthropological Institute* 14 (S1): S1–S21.

Eule, Tobias. 2012. "Inside Immigration Law: Decision-Making and Migration Management in German Immigration Offices." PhD diss., St. Edmunds College, Cambridge University.

Fuller, C. J., and John Harriss. 2001. "For an Anthropology of the Modern Indian State." In *The Everyday State and Society in Modern India*, ed. C. J. Fuller and Véronique Bénéï, 1–30. London: C. Hurst.
Genn, Hazel. 1999. *Paths to Justice: What People Do and Think about Going to Law*. Oxford: Hart Publishing.
Gluckman, Max, James C. Mitchell, and John A. Barnes. 1949. "The Village Headman in British Central Africa." *Africa: Journal of the International African Institute* 19 (2): 89–106.
Good, Anthony. 2007. *Anthropology and Expertise in the Asylum Courts*. London: Routledge-Cavendish.
Hann, Chris, and Elizabeth Dunn. 1996. *Civil Society: Challenging Western Models*. London: Routledge.
Heyman, Josiah McC. 2004. "The Anthropology of Power-Wielding Bureaucracies." *Human Organization* 63 (4): 487–500.
James, Deborah. 2011. "The Return of the Broker: Consensus, Hierarchy, and Choice in South African Land Reform." *Journal of the Royal Anthropological Institute* 17 (2): 318–338.
James, Deborah, and Evan Killick. 2012. "Empathy and Expertise: Case Workers and Immigration/Asylum Applicants in London." *Law & Social Inquiry* 37 (2): 430–455.
Kuper, Adam. 1970. "Gluckman's Village Headman." *American Anthropologist* 72: 355–358.
Lindquist, Johan. 2015. "Of Figures and Types: Brokering Knowledge and Migration in Indonesia and Beyond." *Journal of the Royal Anthropological Institute* 21 (1): 162–177.
Lipsky, Michael. 1980. *Street-Level Bureaucracy: Dilemmas of the Individual in Public Services*. New York: Russell Sage Foundation.
Moorhead, Richard. 2001. "Third Way Regulation? Community Legal Service Partnerships." *Modern Law Review* 64 (4): 543–562.
Moorhead, Richard, and Margaret Robinson. 2006. "A Trouble Shared: Legal Problems Clusters in Solicitors' and Advice Agencies." UK Department for Constitutional Affairs, Research Series No. 8/06.
Narotzky, Susana, and Gavin Smith. 2006. *Immediate Struggles: People, Power, and Place in Rural Spain*. Berkeley: University of California Press.
Pleasence, Pascoe, Alexy Buck, Nigel Balmer, Aoife O'Grady, Hazel Genn, and Marisol Smith. 2004. *Causes of Action: Civil Law and Social Justice*. London: Legal Services Commission.

Chapter 5

IMAGES OF CARE, BOUNDARIES OF THE STATE
Volunteering and Civil Society in Czech Health Care

Rosie Read

In Central and Eastern Europe during the 1990s, a dominant notion of civil society came to prominence. Contained within it was a representation of the state writ large. This was of course the socialist state, which in much civil society discourse was projected as domineering or authoritarian, quashing political and cultural dissent and insisting on society's compliance with official Marxist-Leninist ideology. During the 1980s, civil society had been a key reference point for dissidents in the region registering their opposition to state socialism. In the post-1989 period, civil society became a major project, as former dissidents were elevated to new positions of political power and their perspectives on socialism and civil society were viewed as broadly representative of wider populations. Donor agencies from Western Europe and North America collaborated with new governments in the region to guide, shape, invest in, and implement

Notes for this chapter begin on page 105.

civil society as part of a wider goal of democratization. Non-governmental organizations (NGOs) were taken to be paradigmatic emblems of civil society (Hemment 2007; Sampson 1996; Wedel 2001). As Hann (1996) has argued, this model of civil society was a narrow, liberal-individualist one. It tended to assume that a fundamental boundary—and antagonism—existed between civil society and the state. Earlier, more nuanced post-Enlightenment thinking about civil society and its conception of participation, solidarity, and the relationship between political and economic realms were reduced to a simplistic state-society dichotomy (cf. Alexander 2006; Mamdani 1996: 13–16).

Since the mid-1990s, legislative frameworks for welfare and social security have been substantially reformed in many parts of the region. During the socialist period, state agencies took a fairly exclusive role in providing a range of forms of social protection. Now, the picture is far more mixed, as NGOs, church and community groups, and profit-making companies are involved in providing welfare services funded by a range of government, private, national, and international sources (Caldwell 2004; Hemment 2007; Read and Thelen 2007). These developments broadly mirror those in other regions too, such as Western Europe and parts of the Third World (e.g., see Clarke et al. 2007; cf. Trouillot 2001: 132). This chapter explores the continuing resonance of ideas about civil society and the boundaries of the state in one such altered context of welfare—health care in the Czech Republic.

In institutional terms, the post-1989 period has seen Czech health care substantially decentralized and privatized. As a result, health services are far less directly controlled by central government than during the socialist period. Nonetheless, hospital care continues to be widely imagined as a domain of the state, an expert field that is emblematic of the relationship between the socialist state and its citizens. These images of the state within hospital medicine are central to the rationale for hospital volunteering programs. First developed in the late 1990s, volunteering programs aim to bring citizens into hospital wards to provide company and support for patients. This volunteered care is conceived in terms of civil society as a form of patient care distinct from that provided by medics.

Following Thelen, Vetters, and Benda-Beckmann (introduction, this volume), I approach 'the state' relationally in this chapter. I am not concerned with whether health care provision is or is not 'really' the state, or whether civil society in the form of volunteering can be envisioned as something outside of the state. My interest is in how a boundary between the state and civil society is created in relationships between actors involved in hospital volunteering, and how this boundary becomes productive—how it brings new forms of care into being. As Timothy Mitchell (1991: 90) observes: "The line between state and society is not the perimeter of an intrinsic entity, which can be thought of as a free-standing object or actor. It is a line drawn internally, *within* the network of institutional mechanisms through which a certain social and political order is maintained."

I explore this 'line' ethnographically, focusing on how notions of the state and civil society are mediated within relationships between hospital managers, volunteer coordinators, and local government officials in three urban contexts of hospital volunteering—Prague, Ostrava, and Ústí nad Labem.[1] Through these relationships, hospital volunteering becomes recognizable as civil society by being produced as different from the state. Yet contrary to previous analyses of civil society discourses in the region (e.g., Hann 1996; Hemment 2007; Sampson 1996; Wedel 2001), I argue that this boundary does not mark antagonism or competition between the state and civil society. Instead, it results from a productive cooperation among different actors in NGO and public sector positions who seek to bring into being new forms of 'non-state' care to complement what is seen as state care.

Health Care during Socialism—and After

The universal availability of modern health care provision was a central tenet of state socialism in Czechoslovakia. After the Communist Party took power in 1948, a period of rapid modernization of health care occurred. Health care insurance programs were expanded to include the vast majority of the population by the early 1950s. Hospitals, clinics, and other medical facilities were constructed in rural and industrial areas where pre-war access to health services had been basic and limited. Ownership and control of private and charitable health care facilities were transferred to state authorities. The expansion of health care was projected as integral to the development of socialist modernity, and socialist leaders placed great emphasis on the potential of science and medical research to solve health problems and thereby bring about a healthier and more productive society (Inglot 2008; Štich 1954). Scientific research and its continuous implementation within medical practice for the purpose of health improvement was seen as inherently progressive, provided that this process was rid of its pre-war bourgeois distortions and carried out in a planned manner under the control of the state. Science was also strongly incorporated into how the state identified health problems and acted to address them. Leading medical scientists, doctors, and experts were recruited to work with politicians and officials in central and regional government to direct health policies. Scientific idioms of objectivity, neutrality, and quantification were employed by state officials to inform and engage the public in matters of health. The socialist health care system proved remarkably effective at tackling and eliminating some of the widespread health problems that affected the post-war population, such as high rates of infectious disease and infant mortality. In the two decades after World War II, Czechoslovakia was ranked among the best in the world in internationally compiled health indicators (Štich 1954).

It was in the late socialist period that various problems in the health care system became more publicly visible. The first public opinion survey on perceptions of health care in the 1980s revealed citizens' criticisms of certain aspects of the health care system, such as the hidden system of gifts and bribes to doctors and other medical practitioners, the fact that certain political and social groups (e.g., politicians, the armed forces) were provided privileged access to health care, the inability to choose one's own doctor, the impersonal manner of some medical professionals, and the suppression of health information. It was routine for doctors not to discuss diagnoses and their implications with patients. More generally, state agencies disseminated health statistics data rather selectively, usually releasing them only when they implied positive improvement (Jaroš et al. 2005: 199). Thus, some time before November 1989, there was a growing perception among politicians and the public that the system of health provision was inadequate. Protestors called for health care reform even during the brief Velvet Revolution of 1989,[2] which heralded the end of the socialist government, and many doctors were active participants in pushing for changes in its immediate aftermath. Reform also was high on the agenda of the new post–Velvet Revolution government, which proposed radical and wide-ranging transformations of health care as early as December 1990. Politicians perceived the system of health services as too rigid and inflexible, unable to respond to the country's health needs. They wanted to introduce new forms of resourcing, managing, and ensuring the overall quality of health services that would address contemporary health problems more effectively and respond to public concerns about political interference in health care, inequity of provision, and lack of choice.

What was proposed was consistent with the liberal market principles that had oriented other political and economic reforms at the time. There were several key elements of the reforms, the most radical of which were implemented in the early 1990s. First, health care was to be financed no longer from general taxation, but through a compulsory national insurance system, comprising contributions from employers, employees, and the state. This so-called neo-Bismarckian (e.g., see Jaroš et al. 2005: 212; Marrée and Groenewegen 1997), pluralist model of funding health services was characteristic of Western European states as well as Czechoslovakia during the pre-war years, a period of history that was increasingly being idealized as something of a national golden age. It was intended to depoliticize the process by which health facilities were resourced, enabling the creation of health insurance companies operating at a remove from central government, which would administer the redistribution of finance to health providers on a fee-for-service basis. This model sought to promote the entry of new health care services (run by NGOs, church-based organizations, private companies, etc.) in what politicians hoped would become a more competitive, market-based economy of health provision. The state would continue to guarantee all citizens' access to health care, but it would do so through a new system of financing and legally regulating health facilities and services rather than through monopolistic ownership of them.

Second, regional and district health authorities, to which all hospitals, clinics, and other services had previously been strictly accountable, were abolished. Health providers were given a much greater degree of financial and managerial autonomy within a broad form of regulation created by their contract with health insurance companies. Third, the reforms introduced principles of individual choice and responsibility. Patients were endowed with the freedom to choose their own doctor and health facility, and citizens were to assume greater responsibility for their health. Thus, individual patients, communities, NGOs, charities, and profit-making companies were all to become more active participants in health care (Jaroš et al. 2005).

Enacted in the early 1990s, these reforms were complemented by those in other areas. Reforms to the Civil Code defined civil society organizations in law, while the devolution of central government powers to regional authorities gave the latter greater responsibility for providing health and social care services. The 2006 Social Services Act also facilitated a wider range of social care services and providers. The cumulative effect was momentous in terms of stimulating the creation of new networks and organizations. The 1990s and 2000s saw the emergence of different approaches and new activities within the domains of health and social care. These developments also spurred discussion and criticism of health and social care during the socialist period, and civil society activity was often concentrated in those areas in which such established provision was seen as insufficient. This was the context in which hospital volunteering emerged.

Hospital Volunteering as Civil Society

In 2002, a new Czech law was introduced that provided legal recognition of the category of activity known as volunteering (*dobrovolnictví*). It sought to distinguish this activity from paid work and to define how it could take place in a range of different settings, including health and social care organizations.[3] Prior to this law, a number of civil society organizations had been managing and promoting their own volunteer programs and pushing for legal recognition of volunteering for some years. They particularly wished to dissociate it from voluntary work and other forms of public participation of the socialist period (Read 2010). From the perspective of the emerging NGO sector, as well as some academic researchers in the late 1990s (e.g., Frič 2001), voluntary work during socialism had been 'involuntary volunteering', that is, overly reliant on enforcement by state authorities and a form of coercion. As two prominent leaders of the Prague-based National Volunteer Center wrote: "The tradition of voluntary work was violently disrupted under the totalitarian regime and the activities of all forums of independent organizations were purposefully and systematically reduced or completely subordinated to the leadership of the state and the Communist Party and placed under strict control … those which remained independent were put under surveillance by the state and liquidated. The property of foundations and clubs was confiscated, and the ranks of democratically oriented people were investigated and imprisoned" (Tošner and Sozanská 2006: 30). The notion of volunteering needed to be rehabilitated as NGOs found that it was widely discredited among the Czech population. This entailed endorsing voluntary activity as an expression of individual free will and personal choice, free from state influence. As one leading activist and consultant in the area of hospital volunteering explained, volunteering is "not only about good will, but [also] free will."

This vision of volunteering, embodied within the 2002 law, was more broadly consistent with the arguments of proponents of civil society in the country. Václav Havel, a dissident during the socialist period and the first president of (what became) the Czech Republic in the post-1989 period, had portrayed the socialist state as bent on controlling all aspects of social life, quashing freedom of thought and social and cultural diversity (see, e.g., Havel 1990; cf. Hann and Dunn 1996). Havel further argued that the "various political shifts and upheavals within the communist world all have one thing in common: the undying urge to create a *genuine* civil society" (cited in Wedel 2001: 85; emphasis added). To become 'genuine', civil society had to be separate from the state in ideological and organizational terms.

Such ideas about civil society permeated and oriented hospital volunteering programs from their inception. The first of these began to emerge in the late 1990s, and by the time of my fieldwork in 2008, dozens of volunteering programs were in operation in large and small hospitals across the Czech Republic. Alongside this, volunteering projects were also functioning or being established in old people's homes, children's homes, and residential institutions for the physically disabled and mentally ill. The national reforms to health structures and health and social care provision discussed above were an important factor for encouraging and enabling these developments. But it is also important to highlight here why volunteering programs emerged specifically in health and social care settings. What was it about institutions like hospitals that made them the focus for volunteering? And what representations of the state were implicated in the momentum behind these programs?

In recounting to me how the first volunteer program was established in a large Prague hospital, the director of the Czech National Volunteer Center described the children's oncology ward, which was the initial focus for volunteers' activities. The children, as patients undergoing treatment, inhabited a gray, clinical space. They sat or lay in rooms with no pictures on the walls and few toys to play with. The predominant quiet of the ward was broken only by the clicking sound of medical professionals' shoes as they walked in and out of rooms and up and down corridors, carrying files or medical equipment or pushing trolleys. No hospital staff had time to play with the resident children or to provide respite or comfort to them or their parents. While children in this unit received the highest-quality specialist care, recognized nationally and internationally, this professionalism seemed to generate a gloomy, stifling, and depressing atmosphere for its patients. The volunteering program, the director went on, dramatically changed this. Volunteers brought new toys, paints, musical instruments, and games with them to the oncology department. They engaged children in individual and group activities that were fun and lively. Children's paintings and pictures hung around the ward, and singing, art, and drama activities enlivened the previously colorless and largely silent hospital environment.

During my fieldwork, I encountered many other similar depictions of hospitals from volunteers, volunteer coordinators, and medical practitioners. Czech hospital treatment was very advanced, I was told, at treating the medical problems of the population at large, but it was inadequate at acknowledging and addressing the personal, social, and emotional experience of ill health and treatment. Of course, critiques of non-holistic, depersonalized medical models of patient care are not unique to the Czech Republic (e.g., see Boschma 1997). What was distinctive in this case was how such representations of the problems with medical hospital practice were so directly linked to representations of the socialist state. As the founder of the volunteer program above explained, the Marxist-Leninist underpinnings of state socialism privileged a materialist account of history and society, which profoundly impacted how hospital care was organized. It focused on the material—on the treatment of physical, biological bodies—not on individuals and their social experience of ill health.

This orientation also reinforced the authority of medical professionals (already well-established in the pre-socialist period) as part of a more general ideological commitment to a progressive modern society in which scientific knowledge—as opposed to backward religious ideas, for example—underpinned approaches to caring for the health of citizens. Some comments from a nurse in one of the hospitals in my study illustrate this point: "At the beginning of the last century, the doctor was an authority for patients. What the doctor said—that was true ... After [World War II], the situation changed ... I put it down to the [socialist] regime here, which gave precedence to institutional care. And I think lots of nursing staff got the idea that ... they didn't need to discuss things with patients. This wasn't something completely wrong; there were good intentions [behind it], but people were not informed. [It was rather a case of] 'I'm the doctor and you're the patient. I have declared something, and you will obey.'" The nurse referred here to the tendency for health and care services to be provided through, and concentrated within, large institutions (hospitals, residential homes for mentally and physically disabled, old people's homes) in which medical authority was concentrated. Such institutions were represented as places where residents or patients were directly exposed to state authority in the guise of scientific, medical expertise. Volunteer coordinators often described hospitals as if they were other worlds that cut patients off from 'normal' life and everyday interaction. The project of initiating and establishing volunteer programs was one that aimed to bring together the world of the hospital and the outside world of everyday life, thereby "humanizing" health care (as volunteer coordinators put it).

These images of the state as embodied in authoritative medical practice and health institutions were expressed not only in the accounts of volunteer coordinators, civil society activists, and health professions. They had wider resonance among volunteers, many of whom chose to become involved in the programs following difficult or traumatic personal experiences of hospital care. Volunteers were inspired by the idea that patients undergoing intensive or residential hospital treatment needed additional support—personalized care and attention—that doctors and nurses could not provide but volunteers could.

Thus, the programs aimed to offer a form of care that was distinct from that of medical professionals and the state. Volunteers' approach to care was not expert or scientific; rather, it was based on feelings of altruism and compassion for patients. In promotional literature, written guidance, and discussions with volunteers and hospital staff, coordinators repeatedly presented volunteering as a lay form of personalized, social, or emotional support, quite different from patient care based on specialist medical or nursing knowledge. Volunteers were advised not to encroach on the tasks of medical personnel (e.g., by querying patients' diagnoses or treatment) and to be wary of requests to perform tasks such as feeding, washing, or dressing patients. Volunteers were to be recognized not as an unpaid workforce but as individuals giving up their free time to support patients in a unique, non-medical manner.

Several important observations may be made at this point. The volunteering programs aimed to bring into being a new division of caring labor—the care of civil society (volunteers), which would complement existing expert care expressive of state authority (doctors and nurses). But these two forms of care were not envisaged as antagonistic or constructed as competing with each other. To this extent, the Czech vision of volunteering differed from pervasive discourses of volunteering and welfare found in the United Kingdom or the United States. Volunteering in these other contexts, as recent studies have explored, may often be co-opted or mobilized as part of a wider neo-liberal discourse seeking to 'empower' individual citizens against a 'bloated' state welfare system that has supposedly trapped them in passivity, disengagement, or dependency on state handouts (e.g., Fyfe and Milligan 2003; Hyatt 2001; cf. Fraser and Gordon 2002; Kingfisher 2002). In the Czech case, by contrast, notions of volunteer 'empowerment' against an ineffective, underperforming (welfare) state in the form of health care did not feature in narratives of the benefits of volunteering. Hospital volunteering was not projected as an alternative to the care of doctors and nurses, nor did those promoting it even seek to radically alter hospital care. Although at times critical of hospitals and medical professionals in ways explored above, volunteer coordinators were not aiming to significantly challenge how they worked and most of the time accepted that hospital care could not be other than it was. Justifications for hospital volunteering affirmed the existing representations of hospital care as a professionalized, expert practice of state authority. Thus, despite institutional reforms to health care, which had greatly facilitated the entry of civil society actors into this arena and which had been aimed, in part, at creating an appearance of distance between central government and health services, hospital volunteer programs justified their existence by drawing on an older, more widely recognized and more coherent image of hospital care and medical practice as being inevitably *of* the state (cf. introduction).

Producing hospital volunteering as civil society—that is, *not* the state—entailed the affirmation of difference, of a clear boundary between hospital care (as the state) and volunteered care (as civil society) (Mitchell 1991). The production of this boundary enabled supporters of hospital volunteering to present a coherent narrative of its purpose as independent civil society, rather than a mere appeal to the general public to perform unpaid labor in support of hospital services. This process parallels that described by Thelen, Thiemann, and Roth (chap. 6) in which the care provided by workers in Serbian state-funded elder care programs becomes acceptable when understood through the ideology of kinship, which simultaneously serves to uphold discourses of the state as distant or inadequate.

Nonetheless, making hospital volunteering programs successful as civil society required a great deal of effort, support, and resources. The willingness of citizens to give up their time to volunteer was crucial, but so too were salaries and office space for coordinators, computers, telephone lines, promotional materials (posters, signs, websites), and the support and cooperation of hospital staff. In what follows, I explore more concretely three arenas of hospital volunteering, focusing on how representations of civil society and the state, as well as negotiations over the flow of resources, were produced in relationships between key actors, including volunteer coordinators, hospitals managers, and local government officials.

Gaining the Support of Hospital Management: Prague

The volunteer program within a large university hospital in Prague was in many ways the most successful of the three I studied. It had developed rapidly, beginning with the activities of a group of people attending the Adventist church that lay within the hospital grounds, but it was in other ways unconnected with routine hospital business. This church group ran a charitable bazaar to raise money to buy small presents for hospitalized children on various wards, which were distributed to the children as part of the annual St. Nicholas (Mikuláš, in Czech) festivities in early December. In 2005, the group formed a civil association (*občanské sdružení*) and, with the support of the hospital management, began to run a volunteer program in the hospital in July of that year with 6 trained volunteers. By the end of the year, they had 30 trained volunteers, as well as a website and office space in the hospital. At the end of 2007, the association managed 70 volunteers, who actively visited patients on hospital wards at least once a month, and had trained a total of 80 volunteers during that year.

The key relationship sustaining the volunteer program was that between the hospital's deputy director and Iveta, a member of the church group who wished to develop charitable and civil society activity within the hospital. Iveta initially mobilized her congregation to this end but soon involved a wide range of people with no necessary religious affiliation in her endeavors. Since her activities and future plans required access to patients on hospital wards, she needed the explicit support of the hospital's senior personnel. Prior to meeting Iveta, the deputy director had been seeking to develop non-medical, therapeutic forms of care for long-term hospital patients on the children's neurology and the geriatric wards; however, she had encountered opposition from her senior colleagues and limitations to the budget for hiring therapists. Instead of paid professionals, she perceived that a volunteering program could be another way to potentially improve long-term patients' well-being, but this required a dedicated activist willing to establish and manage such a venture. When they first met, the two women recognized their shared interests and thereafter developed a close working relationship, meeting regularly to discuss the development and expansion of the new volunteer program.

The deputy director assisted Iveta's work in two key ways. First, she insisted that doctors and particularly nurses cooperate with the new volunteering program by allowing volunteers onto their wards. In theory, senior ward staff had a choice of whether to accept volunteers or not. Behind the scenes, the deputy director exerted strong pressure on colleagues managing wards with significant numbers of long-term resident patients to admit and work with volunteers. Thus, the head nurse of the geriatric ward, who had initially been highly skeptical about the purpose and value of volunteering, told me that it had been "impossible to resist the deputy director." Since acquiescing to the presence of volunteers, she had also come to appreciate them, in particular, a volunteer who provided a weekly class for dementia patients aimed at retaining memory and physical skills, as well as others who came to sing for, or with, patients, or took them outside for some fresh air on the hospital grounds. Already overstretched staff could not undertake such activities with patients, the head nurse explained.

Second, the deputy director ensured that, from 2006 onward, the hospital provided a full-time salary for Iveta, as well as office space, desks, telephone lines, and computers for a new volunteer center within the hospital's grounds. In providing this core funding, and later extending it to pay for additional part-time volunteer coordinators, the stability and continuity of the volunteer program was guaranteed. It gave Iveta and her colleagues both paid time and office resources to apply for additional funding, not as hospital employees, but as a civil association, which had already been formed and granted legal status in the previous year. Using this status, Iveta made annual applications to the Ministry of Health and to the Ministry of the Interior under funding schemes set up specifically for civil society organizations. In 2007, her civil association was awarded 270,000 korunas (£10,000) by the Ministry of the Interior.

Since salaries, office space, and other essentials were already covered by the hospital, such grant money (alongside money from commercial sponsors, also relatively successfully obtained) could be spent exclusively on materials and activities that allowed the volunteer center to enhance its own public visibility as a distinctive organization, located within the hospital but also autonomous from it in terms of its function and mode of operation. Grant monies paid for the T-shirts worn by volunteers on visits to wards, which featured the civil association's own logo. It covered the costs of creating and maintaining the center's website, public lectures, workshops, and training for coordinators as well as the furniture for and the refurbishment of the office space in which the center was housed. Here, the spacious, brightly painted rooms with comfortable sofas and places to sit and drink tea and coffee certainly felt quite distinct from the somewhat dilapidated external appearance of the rest of the hospital. Grants to the civil association were used to generate a distinctive physical space for the center and strong visibility for its work throughout the hospital and beyond. This supported volunteers' sense of belonging to a unique project that was in, but not of, the hospital. That the center appeared modern, clean, friendly, and well-organized, with a full and varied program of events and activities, also added to its appeal to volunteers.

As a vibrant and autonomous project of civil society within the Prague hospital, the volunteer program manifested a vision shared by Iveta and the deputy director of the benefits of volunteering for hospital patients. Significantly, this vision affirmed not only that professional hospital care had its limits, but also that civil society could step in to meet the needs for which hospital medicine was ill-equipped. Agreeing on this perception of the state-civil society boundary, the two actors worked together to maximize the possibilities for channeling resources into volunteering. The reformed, decentralized structure of health care, which provided hospital managers with scope to develop new collaborations, and the post-1989 legislative context and funding mechanisms for civil society were key prerequisites that helped this project to come about.

Engaging Local Government: Ostrava

In the industrial city of Ostrava and its surroundings in the northeast of the Czech Republic, I examined a model of hospital volunteering that was rather different from that in Prague. Here, I focused on the local branches of an international humanitarian organization, the Adventist Development and Relief Agency (ADRA).[4] Originally founded in 1956 in Maryland as a non-profit agency providing community development and disaster relief, ADRA now has branches and projects the world over. It began to be active in the Czech Republic in 1992, where it now has 10 volunteer centers, each in a different city. Two of ADRA's key goals are to promote health and to work with vulnerable people. Although providing disaster relief globally is a key aim of the organization, ADRA volunteer centers in the Czech Republic focused on promoting volunteering in health and social care organizations. The ADRA's religious foundations and leadership did not, by and large, permeate locally and regionally focused activities. Most of the ADRA activists in Ostrava and Frýdek were not Adventists (some were not religious at all, others were Catholic), nor did they promote religion or work exclusively with religious clients.

ADRA's local mode of operation was quite different from the Prague case. Rather than seeking exclusive partnerships with particular hospitals, ADRA volunteer coordinators aimed to support the development of volunteer programs across a wide range of different health and social care institutions within a city. They did so on a consultative basis following a prescribed model. Specifically, ADRA volunteer coordinators encouraged contact from any hospital or care home interested in establishing a volunteer program. In initial meetings, ADRA coordinators discussed practical possibilities for volunteering with the hospital/care home management. If these early negotiations progressed, a distinctive partnership would be established between the two parties. ADRA produced publicity to generate interest in the proposed volunteer program, but left it to the hospital/care home to distribute it. Training days for volunteers were attended by representatives from ADRA and the hospital/care home, with ADRA staff running presentations on the purpose and function of volunteering, and hospital/care home personnel providing key information about the nature of their patients or clients and the specific kind of help that was required on different wards. Interested volunteers were then interviewed by a panel consisting of both parties. Once a group had passed the interview and been selected, ADRA ran monthly volunteer supervisions, but otherwise left it to the hospital/care home to coordinate the program on a day-to-day basis. Aside from covering its own expenses in this process, ADRA did not seek money from hospitals in return for its assistance and encouraged hospitals to invest available resources in the program itself.

At the time of my research, activists associated with the ADRA volunteer center in Frýdek-Místek (a town close to Ostrava) were exploring the possibility of opening a new volunteer center in Ostrava itself. Hana was the Ostrava-based ADRA volunteer coordinator, and later in 2009 she became the director of the new ADRA volunteer center in the city. When I met her, she was managing two volunteer programs in two separate hospitals, as well as a number of others in old people's homes and a residential facility for the mentally ill. These programs had a combined total of 80 registered Ostrava-based ADRA volunteers in the year 2007. ADRA therefore already had a strong local presence and visibility and was one of several large global charities operating volunteer programs in the city. Hana nonetheless sought to strengthen and consolidate the ADRA's local influence, not only by expanding contacts with health institutions, but also by nurturing those with local government officials.

Like other regional authorities, the Ostrava City Council had drawn up a Community Social Service Plan (Komunitní Plán Sociálních Služeb) for 2007–2010, which sought to map its population's different needs for care and support and then coordinate and mobilize a range of public, private, and charitable organizations toward meeting those needs (Ostrava Municipal Authority 2007). Recognized within this document, which set budgets against current and future service provision, was the need to expand the range of health and social care services on offer to local people beyond large facilities (such as hospitals, care homes, and old people's homes). Widening care provision alternatives was a local government priority, and promoting volunteer programs that provided such alternative forms of care was of particular interest to city officials. Thus, civil society organizations that already ran volunteer programs were invited to work in partnership with city authorities to achieve the goals of the plan. To this end, a round table for representatives from charitable and non-profit organizations working with volunteers was held monthly. Chaired by a local government official, it was tasked with developing shared strategies for expanding and promoting volunteering.

Hana saw this as an important forum through which ADRA could retain its public reputation and strengthen its influence over the future direction of volunteering programs in the city. She and her colleagues used this forum to emphasize the ADRA's specific experience in working with volunteers, pointing out the ADRA's competence as a leader in the field in comparison with other (competitor) organizations on the committee. For instance, the two largest charities on this committee in terms of both funding and numbers of volunteers were ADRA and Caritas, an international Catholic charity that also ran volunteer programs at hospitals and care homes in Ostrava. Aside from these were smaller organizations working with groups of people who attracted far fewer volunteers, for example, economically disadvantaged families, excluded young people, and Roma. The municipal authorities had given one of these smaller organizations responsibility for acting as an umbrella organization for all volunteer programs in the region. Its remit was to provide interested citizens with information about the full range of volunteering opportunities available and to direct them to the program that matched their interests. During a committee discussion about these arrangements, one of Hana's ADRA colleagues criticized this umbrella organization for being "undemocratic" by advertising its own programs but failing to advertise the ADRA's. He added that the umbrella organization was ineffective at recruiting volunteers and that it seemed inappropriate that it should pose as the body sending ADRA volunteers when ADRA was so successful at its own independent volunteer recruitment. This criticism was aimed at drawing the committee's attention to the ADRA's successes, while also highlighting the ADRA's independence from local state structures, as well as the dependence of the city on large organizations such as ADRA for achieving its community care objectives. In response, the official chairing the meeting emphasized how much others could learn from ADRA and invited written responses to review current arrangements.

Hana also sought out informal routes through which to gain resources from city authorities. These relied on direct appeals to powerful officials and elected representatives within regional government via personal contacts and relationships. For instance, Hana had participated in a meeting with Ostrava's mayor at which she asked for his support in securing an office space for the new volunteer center. She requested either financial help with the rent or the provision of a city-owned office with reduced rent. The mayor was open to this request and inclined to help. The meeting itself had been arranged through another contact who was close to the mayor, and this, Hana explained to me, greatly advanced her chances of getting his support without making ADRA publicly appear too close to (or dependent on) local government. As a global charity with significant internal resources, extensive marketing capability, and publicity materials, and which had also been active in the area for some years, ADRA could project itself as an autonomous civil society organization, while simultaneously retaining significant influence over how the state-civil society boundary was to be drawn and maintained through its relationship with local government.

Lacking Distinction: Ústí nad Labem

The third site of my fieldwork was Ústí nad Labem, a chemical industry town in the northwest of the country. Hospital volunteering here differed significantly from the previous two cases. This hospital was the largest in a recently founded shareholder company, consisting of a total of six regional hospitals in the area. The hospital paid for office space and the salary of a full-time coordinator. Jaromila, the coordinator, had been involved in the promotion of volunteering at the hospital since 2000, formerly as part of her position in the city's volunteer center, then as the hospital's employed volunteer coordinator.

Although the hospital management appeared to support volunteering, at the time of my fieldwork Jaromila was deeply frustrated, disillusioned, and on the verge of quitting her job. Chief among her difficulties was the hospital's lack of infrastructural and promotional support for the volunteer program. The hospital management seemed unwilling to insist that ward-level staff cooperate with the program. Despite her own efforts to persuade staff of the value of volunteering for patient care, Jaromila's volunteers regularly encountered dismissive or indifferent reactions from doctors and nurses. The nurse manager did not require that her staff work with Jaromila and the volunteers (as the deputy director in Prague had done). Indeed, it was unclear to Jaromila whether the hospital management really wanted the volunteer program to grow and prosper; they seemed complacent about the low numbers of active, regular volunteers on the program.

Additionally, volunteering had little visibility within the hospital. There were few notice boards where Jaromila was permitted to attach posters and information about volunteer programs. Although her center had a website, it was buried within the hospital's own larger website and contained little information. Jaromila also had no dedicated budget for her activities. She had to get permission from the hospital director for each piece of expenditure, requests that took days if not weeks to be processed. Jaromila's office was in the main administrative building of the hospital, a place where only hospital employees went (not patients or relatives), access to which required a special swipe card. The office could accommodate only two people, which made it difficult for her to hold meetings with groups of volunteers.

Finally, the legal status of the hospital as part of a shareholder company prevented Jaromila from applying to government ministries for financial support for her volunteer program (as coordinators in Prague and Ostrava regularly did). As a full-time employee of a profit-making hospital, there were also significant obstacles in the way of creating a civil association through which to seek financial support for volunteering in the hospital. Jaromila was almost entirely dependent on the hospital's willingness to support her efforts.

Toward the end of my fieldwork in Ústí, things began to look more optimistic for the volunteering program. The hospital directors initially provided a new, more accessible and larger office space, with furniture and a kitchen. They subsequently hired an additional coordinator and agreed to expand volunteering programs across the other five hospitals in the company. Jaromila became the overall director of this multi-sited volunteer center, in charge of managing a paid volunteer coordinator at each hospital. However, after a couple of years, support for volunteering entirely collapsed, following the sudden appointment of a new board of directors at the hospital that failed to see any value in hospital volunteering. All six programs were closed down, and Jaromila was laid off.

Ultimately, Jaromila lacked relationships that would have provided her with sufficient material and representational resources to create the hospital volunteering program as a distinctive civil society project. The management's faltering belief in the value of volunteering for patients, evident in their unwillingness to insist on staff cooperation with Jaromila, coupled with their reluctance to allow her sufficient control over the resources she needed to build her program, left her isolated. The hospital's legal status as a profit-making company blocked Jaromila from securing civil society status for her program in legal/institutional terms and from seeking resources and support on those grounds. The support that did emerge was relatively short-lived, as the new board of directors favored other priorities. In the absence of relationships enabling her to distinguish her activities from the image of the hospital, either as the state (represented by medical practice and the attitudes of the staff on wards) or as a private company, Jaromila struggled to make volunteering emerge as autonomous civil society.

Conclusion

Over the past 20 years, the Czech health care system has been institutionally distanced from central government. A series of reforms has made hospitals far more legally, financially, and managerially autonomous from government ministries than they were during the socialist period. Yet as this study has shown, hospital care provided by expert medical professionals continues to be widely associated with the socialist state, seen to embody various legacies of how health care was organized and oriented during socialist times. This image of socialist health care was affirmed and reproduced as part of the process of developing new forms of volunteered care under the banner of civil society and was established in distinction from the state care provided by expert professionals.

In this way, the discourses of civil society presented here mirror those of the 1990s in the Central and Eastern European region (Hann 1996; Hemment 2007; Sampson 1996; Wedel 2001) in their emphasis on the necessary autonomy of civil society from the state. Yet in this instance, the process of state-civil society boundary creation did not promote competition or antagonism between these entities. To this extent, my case differs from earlier civil society discourses of the post-socialist region, as well as from neo-liberal experiments in the United States and United Kingdom, which posit volunteering as an 'anti-government' alternative to a bloated state (Fyfe and Milligan 2003; Hyatt 2001).

Instead, the process of making volunteering programs coherent as authentic civil society was negotiated through relationships between personnel located in hospitals, NGOs, and local government. Their success depended on a coordinated, visible projection of volunteering as beneficial, valuable, and distinctive from the state (an implicit affirmation of the limits of state hospital care on the part of all parties), as well as a secure flow of resources in terms of paid time, materials, and managerial support for volunteering. In this way, hospital volunteering programs brought into being a new division of caring labor between expert professionals and lay citizens—one that reproduced widely recognized images of the state but also served as an arena for ongoing negotiations over the resourcing of civil society and the maintenance of the line between civil society and the state.

Acknowledgments

I am grateful to the editors of this book for their helpful feedback on earlier drafts of this chapter. I also thank the anonymous reviewers for their comments.

Rosie Read is a social anthropologist and Senior Lecturer in Sociology and Anthropology at Bournemouth University. She has conducted ethnographic research in the Czech Republic and the United Kingdom. Her research and publications explore issues of gender and care work, volunteering, welfare transformation, and the state.

Notes

1. The ethnographic fieldwork on which this chapter is based was carried out between January and July 2008 and was funded by a British Academy Larger Research Grant (project title, "Volunteering Care: The Gendered Politics of Voluntary Networks in Three Czech Hospitals," Ref. No. 45331). I conducted interviews with volunteers, nurses, doctors, hospital management, and volunteer coordinators at all three sites. In addition, I observed and took part in volunteer training and supervision, volunteers' visits to patients, and public events within the voluntary sector. To maintain research participants' anonymity, all names have been changed.
2. The Velvet Revolution took place from 16 November to 29 December 1989.
3. See http://www.ifrc.org/docs/IDRL/Volunteers/Volunteer%20Services%20Act_Czech%20Republic.pdf (accessed 10 May 2017).
4. There was no direct relationship between ADRA in Ostrava and the members of the Adventist church that founded the Prague volunteer center.

References

Alexander, Jeffrey C. 2006. *The Civil Sphere*. Oxford: Oxford University Press.
Boschma, Geertje. 1997. "Ambivalence about Nursing's Expertise: The Role of a Gendered Holistic Ideology in Nursing, 1890–1990." In *Nursing History and the Politics of Welfare*, ed. Anne Marie Rafferty, Jane Robinson, and Ruth Elkan, 164–176. London: Routledge.
Caldwell, Melissa L. 2004. *Not by Bread Alone: Social Support in the New Russia*. Berkeley: University of California Press.
Clarke, John, Janet Newman, Nick Smith, Elizabeth Vidler, and Louise Westmoreland. 2007. *Creating Citizen-Consumers: Changing Publics and Changing Public Services*. London: Sage.
Fraser, Nancy, and Linda Gordon. 2002. "A Genealogy of *Dependency*: Tracing a Keyword of the U.S. Welfare State." In *The Subject of Care: Feminist Perspectives of Dependency*, ed. Eva F. Kittay, and Ellen K. Feder, 14–39. Lanham, MD: Rowman & Littlefield.
Frič, Pavol. 2001. *Donation and Volunteering in the Czech Republic*. [In Czech.] Prague: NROS, AGNES.

Fyfe, Nicholas R., and Christine Milligan. 2003. "Out of the Shadows: Exploring Contemporary Geographies of Voluntarism." *Progress in Human Geography* 27 (4): 397–413.

Hann, Chris. 1996. "Introduction: Political Society and Civil Anthropology." In Hann and Dunn 1996, 1–26.

Hann, Chris, and Elizabeth Dunn, eds. 1996. *Civil Society: Challenging Western Models.* London: Routledge.

Havel, Václav. 1990. *Disturbing the Peace.* London: Faber & Faber.

Hemment, Julie. 2007. *Empowering Women in Russia: Activism, Aid, and NGOs.* Bloomington: Indiana University Press.

Hyatt, Susan B. 2001. "From Citizen to Volunteer: Neoliberal Governance and the Erasure of Poverty." In *The New Poverty Studies: The Ethnography of Power, Politics and Impoverished People in the United States,* ed. Judith G. Goode and Jeff Maskovsky, 201–235. New York: New York University Press.

Inglot, Tomasz. 2008. *Welfare States in East Central Europe, 1919–2004.* Cambridge: Cambridge University Press.

Jaroš, Jan, Kamil Kalina, Martin Dlouhý, and Antonín Malina. 2005. "Decentralization and Governance of Healthcare in the Czech Republic in the 1990s." In *Decentralization in Healthcare: Analyses and Experiences in Central and Eastern Europe,* ed. George Shakarishvili, 191–271. Budapest: Open Society Institute.

Kingfisher, Catherine, ed. 2002. *Western Welfare in Decline: Globalization and Women's Poverty.* Philadelphia: University of Pennsylvania Press.

Mamdani, Mahmood. 1996. *Citizen and Subject: Contemporary Africa and the Legacy of Late Colonialism.* Princeton, NJ: Princeton University Press.

Marrée, Jörgen, and Peter P. Groenewegen. 1997. *Back to Bismarck: Eastern European Health Care Systems in Transition.* Aldershot: Avebury.

Mitchell, Timothy. 1991. "The Limits of the State: Beyond Statist Approaches and Their Critics." *American Political Science Review* 85 (1): 77–96.

Ostrava Municipal Authority. 2007. *Community Plan of Social Services and Associated Activities in the City of Ostrava to the Year 2010.* [In Czech.] Ostrava: Ostrava Municipal Authority.

Read, Rosie. 2010. "Creating Reflexive Volunteers? Young People's Participation in Czech Hospital Volunteer Programs." *Journal of Youth Studies* 13 (5): 549–563.

Read, Rosie, and Tatjana Thelen. 2007. "Introduction: Social Security and Care after Socialism: Reconfigurations of Public and Private." *Focaal: European Journal of Anthropology* 50: 3–18.

Sampson, Steven. 1996. "The Social Life of Projects: Importing Civil Society to Albania." In Hann and Dunn 1996, 121–142.

Štich, Zdeněk. 1954. *Health Care in Czechoslovakia.* Prague: Orbis.

Tošner, Jiří, and Olga Sozanská. 2006. *Volunteers and Methods of Working with Them in Organizations.* [In Czech.] Prague: Portál.

Trouillot, Michel-Rolph. 2001. "The Anthropology of the State in the Age of Globalization: Close Encounters of the Deceptive Kind." *Current Anthropology* 42 (1): 125–138.

Wedel, Janine R. 2001. *Collision and Collusion: The Strange Case of Western Aid to Eastern Europe.* New York: Palgrave.

Chapter 6

STATE KINNING AND KINNING THE STATE IN SERBIAN ELDER CARE PROGRAMS

Tatjana Thelen, Andre Thiemann, and Duška Roth

"You become kin [*srodiš se*] with these people."

In her remark, Ljilja, a state-paid home care worker in central Serbia, reflected on the relations with her elderly clients in February 2010. The intimacy expressed in Ljilja's statement stood in stark contrast to the images of an absent or uncaring state that we encountered in other instances during our fieldwork.

In July 2010, in a village in Vojvodina (northern Serbia), Thelen asked her host about who takes care of the elderly in the village. Emese (43) replied that old people would be cared for solely by their families as there were no locally available state services. On different occasions, she also recounted how she herself had cared for her mother-in-law.

Notes for this chapter begin on page 121.

Emese's emphasis on family norms coincides almost perfectly with a professional ethnographic view.

In August of the same year, Thelen and Thiemann spent a long day with a Serbian colleague, visiting his field sites. Asked if there were any lonely old people in the village they were just leaving, the colleague emphatically rejected the possibility on the grounds that it would be too shameful according to local norms.

In the last two encounters in different regions of Serbia, intergenerational bonds were presented as effectively functioning according to kinship norms, while the state seemed mostly absent.

Two facets of these accounts attracted our attention. First, there is an apparent tension between state images and practices. While state practices and images rarely overlap entirely, the state's actual involvement in our cases surpassed citizens' expectations. This contrasts with many recent studies that show how citizens try to make the state see them or comply with their wishes for more state presence (Jansen 2014; Obeid 2010; Street 2012). The second fascinating point is the intimate, affective nature of relations between state-funded caregivers, or state carers, and their elderly clients. As we will show, its representation (and practice) as kinship goes far beyond the instrumental use described in other studies (e.g., Yang 2005).

Instead of taking comparative welfare studies or national policy making as our analytical point of departure, we pursue the relational approach to the state proposed in the introduction to this book in order to emphasize concrete relations and their significance in the reproduction of the state-kin boundary. Thus, following Timothy Mitchell (1991), we put processes of state boundary production at the center of our analysis by studying processes of kin making in state projects. Our work is thereby positioned at the intersection of the anthropology of the state and the anthropology of kinship.

Although more recent studies since the 1990s on both kinship and the state have stressed flexibility and processuality, they seldom are integrated into one framework of analysis (Thelen and Alber 2017). Some new kinship studies have emphasized the linkages between the state, power, and kinship, but most have confined their purview to considering the state only insofar as it enables or limits the processes of kin making within pre-established families. Signe Howell (2006) introduced the term 'kinning' to denote such processes of establishing and (re)producing significant, intimate relations in the context of international adoptions. She defines kinning as "the process by which a foetus or newborn child is brought into a significant and permanent relationship with a group of people, and the connection is expressed in a conventional kin idiom" (ibid.: 8). Although Howell states that kinning can refer not only to newborns but also to "any previously unconnected person" (ibid.), she and other scholars in the field of kinship have focused predominately on the formation of parent-child relations (Thelen 2010). We take up and expand on Howell's notion of kinning to encompass lasting relations between hitherto non-related adults and, more specifically, in the context of our work, to describe situations in which state carers come to be counted as kin while working with senior citizens, and vice versa.

Recent anthropological works on the state, on the other hand, consider the link between state and kinship in relation either to national identity (Borneman 1992; Herzfeld 1992) or to marginalized groups who strategically deploy kinship idioms to better position themselves in relation to state authorities (Yang 2005). Unlike studies depicting how boundaries of the state are blurred by actors' imaginative strategies of integration despite markedly exclusionary state practices, we show how citizens reproduce exclusive boundaries between state and kinship through the inclusive process of kinning. Moreover, while recent anthropological perspectives on the state have mostly concentrated on representational strategies within bureaucratic settings (Gupta 1995; Gupta and Sharma 2006; see also the introduction to this book), we couple this focus on state images with an emphasis on everyday practices of kinning outside bureaucratic settings. We regard the processes through which state workers become kin to care recipients as the point of intersection between kinship and state. Kinning provides the conceptual link to study kinship in tandem with the state by allowing us to track how representations of kinship and state function as mirror images of one another and how kinning practices contribute to their reproduction and transformation.

Societal aging—the combined result of a decline in the birth rate and an increase in life expectancy among old people—has far-reaching consequences for local communities and family relations in Europe and elsewhere.[1] Different state layers are involved in responding to these new challenges, thereby not only transforming central welfare structures but also extending their reach to the local level and to the supposedly private sphere of families. Viewed from the perspective of carers of elderly kin, state responses to increasing care obligations within families might either solidify or challenge state images on the ground. These processes maker elder care central to kin-state boundary work.

Therefore, before describing the kinning practices in more detail, we give some background information about the images and practices of state and family care in our field sites. Data presented in this chapter were gathered during fieldwork between 2009 and 2012 in the village of Čantavir (located in northern Serbia, with the majority of its 7,000 inhabitants locally identified as Hungarian) and in the municipality of Gornji Milanovac (located in central Serbia, where the majority of the 47,000 inhabitants recognize themselves as Serbian).[2] Although we initially expected ethnic differences to matter in state-citizen relations, it turned out that ethnicity did not play a critical role in elder care.

Images and Practices of State and Family Care for the Aging

We first outline some of the most important state policies and structures with regard to elder care on the central and local state level before turning to images of state and kin care for the elderly.

Welfare Policies and Structures

During the past few decades, societal aging generally has provoked increased state involvement in the field of care. Conversely, there have been strong calls for state retreat, a trend that has far-reaching, highly ambiguous implications for the field of welfare (see Read, Dubois, and Forbess and James, this book). New policies in the field of elder care, while building on existing models and images, are therefore often contested. For instance, the establishment of different versions of state monetary support for kin care or (migrant) care workers has initiated heated debates within various European states (Ungerson 2003; see also Anderson 2000).

An entry point to understanding the dominant values governing policy development in this field is Esping-Andersen's (1990) now classic book, *The Three Worlds of Welfare Capitalism*. According to this classification, citizens of Scandinavian social democratic states place a high premium on social equality and exhibit a clear preference for the state as welfare provider (cf. Bruun 2011; Olwig 2011). In contrast, liberal countries like the United States and Great Britain are described as exhibiting greater distrust toward the state coupled with an emphasis on market relations. Conservative welfare states like Germany and Austria would generally place high emphasis on family obligations with state aid intended to support them. Despite such clear models, in practice, policies are subject to layered interpretations and translation processes in different national contexts. Local implementations then serve more than one goal and often yield different outcomes even among seemingly similar institutions (e.g., Schwarcz and Szőke, chap. 8).[3]

Such transnational entanglements and translation processes could also be observed in socialist Yugoslavia, which developed "a rather generous welfare system upon the principles of solidarity and equality" (Stambolieva 2011: 350), with a combination of liberal, social democratic, and conservative elements. Besides some former Soviet principles such as provision through the workplace (Read and Thelen 2007; Standing 1996), social work curricula and the establishment of Centers for Social Work (CSWs) were supported by American advisers and influenced by trips to Sweden and UN exchange programs in the 1950s (Zaviršek 2008: 738). Investments in the development of Gerontological Centers since the 1970s have allowed CSWs to become the largest state institution in the field of elderly care on the municipal level.[4]

Besides the CSW, the local pensioners clubs have a rather long history as a (semi-)state form of support for the elderly in our field sites. Originally established after World War II, these clubs provide services such as legal advice, subsidized food and fuel, recreational activities, and limited medical treatment (e.g., subsidized visits to health spas). In addition, the so-called baby ladies from the local health care center have begun to make regular visits to the elderly in Čantavir. Their primary tasks are home visits after childbirth, but recently they have begun to take care of elderly in need, measuring their blood pressure and blood sugar. Most elderly also receive minimal state-guaranteed pensions and partially subsidized health care.

After the ousting of Serbian President Slobodan Milošević, international cooperative efforts in the field of welfare were re-established, with British and Norwegian agencies assuming a prominent role among Western donors.[5] Especially interesting is the Norwegian support for the establishment of home care projects for the elderly in Serbia since the mid-2000s; it included funded training seminars as well as trips to Norway so that social workers could get acquainted with the Norwegian practice. Besides generating organizational and professional structures, these different welfare traditions, exchanges, and models also affect how professionals understand their roles. Thus, social workers in our field sites would often describe the 'Scandinavian model' as their aim. Collectively, they expressed a preference for state involvement, but with the emotional intimacy of private homes, aspects described in the literature as salient to Scandinavian welfare (Højlund 2011).[6]

Recently, social workers initiated home care programs for the elderly in both our field sites. In both cases, jobs within the programs are low-paid and—as described for other European societies (Ungerson 2003)—contribute to the formation of a feminized, low-paid labor market segment of care work. Thus, they could be apprehended within the framework of neo-liberal policies as cost-cutting measures. On the other hand, the programs also involve new services that previously had been unavailable, and therefore could likewise be seen as an expansion of state activity in the care sector. More important for our purpose here is how the relations of the elderly to their state carers contradict the hegemonic images of a distant state and caring kin.

Images of State and Kin Care

Welfare policies are inevitably linked to dominant discourses on need, deservingness, and often the nation itself. For example, in some contexts, crisis discourses on national health and family values have legitimated neo-liberal downsizing and the privatization of state services in the field of care.[7] In Serbia, the undertone of alarm in many discourses on aging, in which the elderly are represented as needy, is exacerbated by a constant iteration of 'family values' in public discourse. The latter is supported by a perceived national crisis over low fertility rates called the 'white plague'. This combination feeds into—largely unsuccessful—pro-natalist policies (Jansen and Helms 2009: 223), but also paves the way for the development of elder care projects. The continuous underscoring of family values thereby informs the practices of kinning by enhancing the importance of presenting 'good' family relations, as we discuss below.

While professionals in our field sites readily admitted to the need for new forms of state elder care, other interlocutors in the field—as demonstrated in the vignettes at the outset of this chapter—were more ambivalent. Most of them not only assumed that the elderly would be taken care of by their relatives, but also presented it as the ideal solution wished for by the elderly themselves. When Roth asked in a group interview who should take care of old people, several middle-aged persons answered at once, "The young ones!" In an effort to explain this general wisdom, a father of two sons in their twenties stated: "Because they [the older ones] cared for them when they were little!" Notwithstanding the usual emphasis on the 'proper functioning' of kin care as deferred reciprocity, there were some cases of elderly who were not taken care of by their relatives. These elderly were usually pitied, and state care in an old people's home was seen as the least beneficial alternative.

The image of superior kin care almost presupposed a complementary image of an uncaring state. Describing the annoyances they encountered in seeking out diverse forms of state support, our interlocutors drew a generalized image of the typical state representative as greedy, irresponsible, and/or uninterested, which could extend to the field of elder care. While such complaints usually did not differentiate between varying levels of government, in everyday practice our interlocutors discriminated between concrete local state actors and the central state, seen as located in the capital or in regional centers. For example, commenting on eligibility criteria for support programs, the head of the local pensioners club situated the disinterest of the state a hundred miles away: "He [the imagined bureaucrat] sits in Novi Sad and has his list on the computer. How should he know?" In contrast to the complaints about the distant state actor, the head of the club lauded the local social worker, whom he meets every week, for being aware of the "injustice" and for her familiarity with the family histories of the local people. In his account, if she perceived someone as needy, she used tricks to secure aid against the challenging backdrop of the central state's criteria for eligibility. Local state actors can thus gain a more positive status as members of the local community if they are seen to share the same ideas, values, and experiences.[8]

While the efforts of local state actors to enhance the lives of elderly citizens may not always be successful, they nevertheless undermine prevalent discourses that depict the Serbian state as completely aloof. Similar to the account offered by Rosie Read (chap. 5), wherein heavily state-supported volunteering in the health care system is understood as a civil society activity and distinguished from state practice, in our case, such contradiction seems to be reconciled by viewing local state actors in the welfare sector as non-state community members. But what happens to state actors in the intimate environment of the home? Here we find the same contradiction, and, as we argue in the following, this tension is resolved by kinning, which—similar to discourses on local state actors—de-emphasizes the role of the state within the relation. We now turn to these kinning practices in two specific elder care programs.

State Kinning and Kinning the State: New Home Care Programs

In our field sites, two distinct state-initiated programs of elder care build on the notion of superior kin care at home, which was emphasized in the local and policy discourses outlined above. The first case concerns a program that places the elderly in new families in Čantavir, and the second discusses a home care service in the Gornji Milanovac municipality.

State Kinning in Čantavir

In 2009, with financing from the Serbian Ministry for Work and Social Policy, the municipality of Subotica initiated a pilot project for elderly placement in new families. The program is called locally Porodični Smeštaj (Family Placement) and is modeled on foster care for children (*porodični smeštaj dece*). Carer families take in elderly individuals and receive a regular payment as well as a stipend to cover the direct costs of care.[9]

At the time of our fieldwork, Mila, the social worker who supervised this program, told us that 10 women provided such foster arrangements or were preparing to do so. The requirements were that a separate room and kitchen be made available for the elderly person and that the carer should have a medical certificate attesting to her health. No professional training was needed, which is indicative of the underlying assumption that 'normal' women in 'normal' families are 'natural' experts at caring for the elderly. Only Mila was somewhat ambivalent about what she perceived from her professional perspective as under-professionalization. "There are still some things lacking, like education for the families," she said. Mila's view may have been influenced by the knowledge that a considerable number of care recipients in this program are 'problem cases'. Mila explained: "At the [Gerontological] Center there is a home for old people. But these people cannot live there. They would intimidate the other inhabitants. The staff is scared of endangering the other old people living in the home. This is why the Center tries to find alternative solutions for these people, like the family placement project."

Even if the program was oriented toward 'problematic' elderly, Mila described its aim as encouraging intergenerational cohabitation: "This [foster care program] means that old people move in together with younger ones, who take care of them." Nonetheless, in the cases that we observed, the elderly were in fact housed in a building separate from their host families. Despite actual split living arrangements, social and care workers maintained that the project aimed at providing a 'warm' family environment. Marta, one of the carers, stated: "There are some people who do not want to go to a nursing home. They prefer to go to a family so they won't be alone. Because nursing homes are different. There, they feel like they can't come and go as they please, to the village or—I don't know—to have a walk, to go to the shop to buy oranges." As opposed to the nursing home milieu, the family environment is appreciated for guarding against loneliness and allowing the elderly individual to retain a higher degree of autonomy in day-to-day life.

However, the combination of a problematic target group and idealized images of family care proved to be a challenge for the newly evolving relations. Marta and Viktoria, another carer, complained about being insufficiently prepared for and informed about their role in this new program. Neither was told beforehand that it primarily catered to 'problem cases', and both women were entrusted with caring for alcohol-addicted elder persons who sometimes vanished for days on end.

Besides this exceptional situation of the clients, work conditions comparable to 'real' kin care put stress on the evolving relations. As in a 'normal' family, carers were on duty 24 hours a day, seven days a week, without free time or holidays. Especially Viktoria complained about the heavy burden. She suspected that the three elderly residents in her care deliberately created extra work for her. Interestingly, although she was state-paid for providing care, she placed 'the state' on the side of the elderly. Recalling a recent visit, she tellingly referred to the social workers as "the state" unfairly controlling her: "And the state [asked the elderly man]: 'Where did she put the fire? Was it warm in the winter? Did you catch a cold?' That's what they asked the man! And: 'What is it like in the room? Is it kept decent? Is everything okay?' And he replies that he's not satisfied with the food! Fuck your mother! There is the fridge [waving with her arm in the direction]—he can eat what and when he wants!" Viktoria faulted the state for supporting an 'undeserving' man when it should have been supporting her. She was not alone in this opinion, which her sister—who entered the room during the conversation—echoed:

> Viktoria: And that is really awful, you know, how the state doesn't mind spending money on such [undeserving persons].
>
> Viktoria's sister: Yes, and who would ever support me?
>
> Viktoria: They [the elderly] live like a king. They have no work and they get everything—breakfast, coffee—and they don't do anything!

Later, Viktoria speculated that the elderly man she cared for had been neglected by his family because he had not properly cared for them in the past: "And now he gets it back ... That is why he ended up on the streets, certainly, like a drunken pig. He didn't care for his family, and then they divorced. The kids went with the mother, and now who the hell needs him in his old age?"

In the meantime the interview had developed into a small group discussion between Viktoria, her sister, our host Emese (quoted above), and Emese's daughter. All signaled their approval of what Viktoria was saying. State kinning—as a way to create new kinship relations—had in this case clearly failed. The elderly did not conform to the local norms, and the carer blamed "the state" for the conflicts and the overly demanding working conditions. Yet, while precisely such conditions make 'real' kin care such a difficult experience, 'good family' discourses limit open criticism of kin care. In instances of failed state-initiated family care, this erasure makes it possible to blame the state as disinterested and unsupportive without changing the image of good family care.

Nevertheless, we also encountered cases in which this form of state kinning enabled state carers and the elderly to develop lasting and affective relations. At the time of the research, Marta was caring for two men, Zoltán and Iván, who, she told us, were welcome to stay with her for the remainder of their lives. She recounted how Zoltán once expressed his fear that she would get rid of him and that she had responded as follows: "Listen, we have already talked about this! As long as you do not want to leave this place, I will not allow anyone to carry you away. Only in a box!" Explaining her relationship with Zoltán, Marta described how kinship terms began to be used, albeit one-sidedly: "I continue to address him formally, but since [that conversation], he calls me 'daughter.'" While Marta stressed a degree of formality in her relationships with the two men, she had also developed strong emotional bonds with them. Both appeared at times to serve as father substitutes: "I do not have a father because he died, but now I feel somehow like I have two. It is not the same as it was with my own, but when I have problems, like when I quarrel with the old one [her mother], they say: 'Well, you see, girl, stay here for a little while. We will make you a coffee.'" In addition to the use of kinship terms, Marta's relationship with these two men thus entailed emotional reciprocity, usually viewed as a characteristic of kin care. As Liebelt (2011) argues in the case of Filipina carers in Israel, such mutual emotional relations were clearly the preferred arrangements in Serbia as well.

On the side of the elderly, Iván expressed the reciprocity in their relationship, but also his surprise about the benevolent side of the state:

> I think that this [the project] is a pretty good move. At least something that is good in this state [pause]. I see no other way [pause]. A nursing home? No, I think I like this version better [pause]. We should be conscious enough to understand our [poor] material situation. The entire society, not just the elderly and helpless, [are impoverished]. So it's not a hard choice. The food here is pretty good [he points at his plate]. I can't complain. Well, I cannot and, no, I do not complain. And the relationship is good as it is. Well, we talk. If I need something, I go to them.

In this quote, Iván situates his circumstances within the wider national context. On the one hand, he acknowledges the quality of the relations with his foster family, which also entails sociality and problem solving. He is grateful for being with Marta instead of in a nursing home of the Gerontological Center, where he had lived for some months before he became a part of the project. On the other hand, he hints at Serbia being a relatively poor country, so he is also thankful to the state. More importantly, he judges the care project as "something that is good in this state," thus offering a counterpoint to his otherwise negative image of the Serbian state. In our next case study, the boundaries between state and family get even blurrier in practices of kinning the state.

Kinning the State in Gornji Milanovac

Like the project in Čantavir, the Help at Home for Elderly and Handicapped Persons (HHEHP) project in Gornji Milanovac was premised on the ideal of superior home care. Since March 2008, seven so-called *gerontodomaćice* (home care givers for elder persons) have performed small household tasks, such as cleaning and shopping for the elderly. Unlike the program in Čantavir, eligibility criteria to receive the care were rather inclusive. Any person past retirement age was eligible, although the project sought to target individuals suffering from chronic health problems. Caregivers were paid small salaries and worked with six to eight households, visiting each two or three times weekly for approximately two hours at a time.

HHEHP was initiated with a Public Works grant covering six months. Immediately, social workers tried to secure year-round financing. The "Work

Program for 2008," a document sent to the CSW's immediate superiors—the municipality and the Ministry of Labor and Social Work—stated:

> It can be expected in real terms that the social problematic will manifest itself in the current year as a result of growing mutual dependency and disorder in interpersonal relationships; the services of social work will proportionately shift from predominantly material ones—which are actually expected to rise lineally—toward the psychosocial sphere, involving psychological problems, conflicts, and mental imbalances ...
> The Center, with the aim to improve and implement social policy, has planned and started to implement several crucial projects. Here we think primarily about the project Help at Home, which is intended for elder and disabled persons on the territory of the municipality. (CSW 2008: 3, 4; our translation)

Social workers herein emphasized the importance of immaterial help, and the municipality decided to permanently 'budget' HHEHP. As HHEHP was initially restricted to urban areas, social workers attempted to expand its scope to include villages, but this effort has been running on and off since.[10] An excerpt from Thiemann's field diary shows a typical workday of one urban *gerontodomaćica*, Ljilja (40),[11] and demonstrates that everyday practices within HHEHP are indeed characterized by more than small instrumental help:

> 8 AM, on a freezing winter day I meet caregiver Ljilja at the hospital pharmacy. Together we walk uphill to Maja (79), who is confined to a wheelchair, and her husband Velja (76). We drink coffee while Ljilja does some cleaning and chats about various events and people. It's Ljilja's birthday today, and Velja congratulates her with an improvised mock speech while presenting a box of chocolates.
> We leave after 9 AM for the Polyclinic, where Ljilja obtains medical prescriptions for several elderly. At 11 AM, we climb uphill again and reach Rajka's (83) house. Ljilja delivers Rajka her medicine and then busies herself fetching firewood.
> Shortly after 1 PM, we leave for Milica (80). Passing through the city market, we look for things Milica requested. Upon arrival, we drink yet another cup of coffee, talk, and look at family photo albums. Milica gives Ljilja a small sum of money and instructs her to buy herself a rose for her birthday. We stay until 3 PM.

Different relational aspects become obvious from these notes. First, aside from benefiting from the delivery of food, prescriptions, medication, and firewood, most elderly enjoyed the sociability and gossip they shared with Ljilja. On her birthday, two of the three visited households gave Ljilja a small gift. These gift exchanges are evidence of a growing acceptance of the state actor in the personal circle. Accepting gifts and other kinning offers often resulted in affectionate relationships, in which the state initiative and payment for the services were ignored.

Like Marta's 'new fathers' in Čantavir, the elderly in Gornji Milanovac often employed kinship terminology to describe their relationship with their state carers. Similar to Iván, they expressed gratitude for the care they received, but they went further in stressing the personal quality of their relationship, thereby again de-emphasizing the state element. As Ljilja's client Marija once expounded: "And so I became kin to the child as though she were my own."[12] Like Marija, Ljilja—although indicating asymmetrical use of kin terms—used the reflexive verb *sroditi se* (roughly translatable as 'to kin') in describing her reciprocal relationships: "I can phone on Saturday and Sunday, Aunt Milica maybe most of all, to see how she is doing, if she has high blood pressure ... or Rajka when she fell, or Maja, to see what she needs me to pick up for her. What do I know—you become kin [*srodiš se*] with these people. These people also help you when you need something." In this extended version of our vignette quotation, Ljilja's account entails advanced reciprocal obligations. She describes how, beyond her work obligations, she personally cares about the elderly even in her spare time, but claims also to receive help from them.

The state thus is not always a barrier to new kinship relations, as is often stressed in kinship studies (e.g., Borneman 2001), but may actually initiate and maintain them and even become integral to these relationships through the state carer. This affects the specific ways in which the boundaries between state and kinship are blurred and negotiated. The idiom of kinship is not limited to an imagined kinned state or a strategy for positioning oneself vis-à-vis an unreachable or potentially hostile central state (e.g., Street 2012; Yang 2005). Embedded in sociability, the use of kinship terminology reflects and deepens reciprocal obligations over long periods of time that extend beyond the prescribed confines of a work relation. For instance, Ljilja related how the hospital staff had treated her as Dušan's child when she visited Milica's husband in the summer of 2009: "One morning I come [to the hospital] and the [medical] sister says, 'You know, your father doesn't want to take his medicine. He's waiting for you.' I tell her, 'Sister, excuse me, my father died half a year ago, and I don't have a father.' She says, 'But [Dušan] says that you are his daughter and that he will not take his medicine so we can't poison him.' I said, 'OK.'" Dušan publicly referred to Ljilja as his daughter, thereby attributing certain rights and obligations to her. These go far beyond Ljilja's contractual responsibilities, and while Dušan did not trust the hospital staff, he trusted his new daughter. In the end, not only the medical staff but also Ljilja accepted his kinning decision, and Ljilja persuaded him to follow the medical staff's advice. Once again, in an ambivalent move, both sides ignored the role of the state in their relationship by attributing it to a solely positive family image.

Both projects presented in this section contradict the commonplace images of an absent, or even a hostile, Serbian state. In fact, the state fulfills care duties usually associated with a loving family. The state-client relation is pushed into the realm of kinship, thus negating the state component so that the conceptual opposition between state and family remains intact. In these contexts, kinning as boundary work perpetuates the dichotomy between state and family by reproducing an ideology of superior kin care, on the one hand, and an absent state, on the other. This leads us to the other side of the dichotomy—namely, the family—to consider, in a context in which the family is presumably responsible for the elderly, why care recipients choose to kin state actors and how the rest of the family deals with the new relatives.

Negotiating State Kin

Howell (2006: 9) contends that kinning presupposes a prior de-kinning process, which occurs "when a previously kinned person is thrown out of the kin-community for some reason or another, or when a newborn child is never kinned." State imaginings of elderly care in Serbia and the setup of the described programs clearly build on the idea of de-kinning prior to state care. According to the law on social protection, a "pensioner and other old person who is, due to unfavorable health, social, housing, and family conditions, not in a position to live with his/her family and respectively in his/her household" has a right to accommodation in an "institution of social protection" or in "another family" (MINRZS 2001, Art. 37, 40; our translation). Thus, the law framed the elderly state care recipients as close to 'socially naked' persons, bereft of social relations (like the adoptees in Howell's case), before state carers stepped in to create new kinship ties. This provision as such contradicts discourses on infallible family care, but the extent to which the elderly in both programs were actually de-kinned varied, clearly more so in the case of the elderly fostered into new families in Čantavir. Even though most of them had living relatives, often their children, relations between them were not good, or the relatives worked abroad.

If 'good' children care for their parents in old age, the fact that some elderly people receive state care can easily cast moral doubt not only on the family but also on the receiver, as illustrated above in the case of the 'undeserving' elderly in Čantavir. The risk of moral condemnation of the family became obvious during the initial stages of registering the elderly in the HHEHP project in Gornji Milanovac. For instance, one elderly woman refused to take part in the project, proclaiming that she would not "undervalue her family." To remove concerns about family stigma, state actors desisted from demanding proof of de-kinning before letting them sign up for the service. Instead, they applied loose age requirements. Thus, before the program became a success story with a waiting list, state actors had to make some effort to reach out to the elderly, which again contradicts the image of an absent and disinterested Serbian state. Once elderly individuals in HHEHP were receiving care, they preferred to view their relationships with care givers in kinship terms, hiding the fact that they were receiving help from the state.

New kin can simply mean adding an additional significant tie, but it might also be seen as threatening existing kinship relations, as can be seen in the case of Dušan's family. After several weeks in the hospital, Dušan had passed away, and Ljilja—not for the first time—was involved in the funeral services for one of her clients. In the process, her kinship role was renegotiated. In Serbia, one family member should stay at the house of the deceased during the funeral. Although Ljilja would have preferred to cry at the graveside—a customary practice for close female relatives—upon Milica's wishes she "guarded" Dušan's and Milica's flat. This participation indicates not only the intensity and stability of these relations evolving into kinship; it also shows the ongoing negotiation of that status, since Ljilja was relegated to an extended kinship position.

The process went on, when in late 2009, early 2010, Milica, now widowed, fell several times and had to visit the doctor regularly with Ljilja's help. Milica's son, a doctor, who lives a few hours' drive away, repeatedly invited his mother to come and live with him, insisting: "I don't want them to say, 'The son is there, and the mother died alone in the house.'" Despite his cooperation with Ljilja during his father's illness and funeral, he still did not regard her as a family member. However, instead of succumbing to the ideal of kin care and moving in with her son, Milica preferred to rely on her relationship with Ljilja. As she continued to maintain spatial distance from her 'natural' kin, she explained the situation by pointing to her son's responsibility toward his children.

Like Milica, most of the elderly in HHEHP were not de-kinned and maintained good relations with their children. But even then the ideal of kin care was not always the preferred option for the elderly, and kinning a state employee proved to be a way out without openly calling into question the dominant image of the caring family. Counter-intuitively, kinning the state—like some cases of state kinning in Čantavir—promised greater individual autonomy to the elderly.

Conclusion

Current demographic developments have put governments under pressure to assume new responsibilities for citizens' welfare, while at the same time neo-liberal discourses call for a retreat from responsibility. Discourses on kin as the ideal caregiver come to be reflected in welfare policies, which focus on family homes as the ideal setting for elder care. In this situation, the relations within state programs of elder care constitute an important field for renegotiating state-family boundaries. In this chapter we have analyzed everyday practices of kinning enacted in care relations between state carers and their elderly clients. Concentrating on kinning as (re)producing state boundaries, we conceptually link kinship studies with the anthropology of the state.

Building on structures of social work formed after the US model in the 1960s, and aiming for a Scandinavian model of the welfare state, social workers in both settlements developed home-based care services for the elderly that presuppose an ideal image of kinship care being located in a private home. In the case of Čantavir, the state attempts to create new kin for the elderly, while in Gornji Milanovac, care is delivered to private homes. Although the projects could be seen as part of a neo-liberal policy of state retreat, our examples show instead a gradual enlargement of services. In both cases the state surpasses citizens' expectations, much different from situations in which actors try to gain greater visibility to be 'seen by the state' (Street 2012), or processes in which actors mimic or want to become the state (Jansen 2014; Nielsen 2010). Meanwhile, local perceptions of the state as being distant and hostile remain surprisingly stable (Thiemann 2016).

We have argued that this apparent contradiction is solved by differential practices of kinning. In the case of the problematic elderly care recipients in Čantavir, state-supported care was subject to the same inconveniences as usual family-based care. In order to uphold the image of a 'good' family and a 'bad' state here, participants tended to attribute negative characteristics to the state that had chosen to care for the 'wrong' people, namely, the elderly people with drinking habits and/or those who had failed to maintain kinship relations when they were younger. According to this view, the state remained solely an employer and controller, unconcerned with the well-being of its caregivers.

In more successful cases, kinning goes beyond an instrumental use of kinship idioms. Instead, state carers come to play an intimate and significant role in the lives of the elderly people they care for, participating in the joys and obligations of everyday family life, sharing life-cycle events such as birthdays and funerals, and lending an ear in times of emotional difficulties, as well as being helped themselves in times of hardship. Following in particular the examples in Gornji Milanovac, de-kinning was not a sine qua non for creating new kin that would serve as a kind of last recourse or emergency option sought in a situation of social isolation. In fact, kinning the state helps to maintain existing kin relations by minimizing potential tensions that family-based care might create. While all this points to the blurred boundaries between state and kinship, kinning practices counter-intuitively reproduce the dichotomy by reinforcing images of loving kin and a distant state. The deployment of kinship terminology serves to erase the state from these relationships, despite the fact that state agents were acting beyond their call of duty.

It would be interesting to follow up on these elder care programs to see whether and how the contradictions may be resolved in the long run and what that would mean for the dominant image of the absent state. The examples we have presented highlight the benefits of rethinking the interconnections between kinship and the state with a relational focus. In Serbia, as in many other contexts, family and state are imagined as different, if not opposed, realms. Since these representations work as mirror images of one another, the reproduction and transformation of one must also be understood in relation to the other.

Acknowledgments

We would like to thank the Volkswagen Foundation and the Max Planck Institute for Social Anthropology for funding our research. We are grateful to Larissa Vetters and Keebet von Benda-Beckmann for their helpful comments on earlier drafts of this chapter. We also thank the editors of *Social Analysis* and the two anonymous reviewers for their suggestions.

Tatjana Thelen is a Full Professor in the Department of Social and Cultural Anthropology, University of Vienna. In 2016–2017, she was a Fellow at the Center for Interdisciplinary Research, Bielefeld University, leading the research group on "Kinship and Politics." Her areas of interest include the state, property, welfare and care, and kinship and family. She is the co-editor of a special section of *Focaal* entitled "Social Security and Care after Socialism" (2007) and of *Reconnecting State and Kinship* (2017).

Andre Thiemann received his PhD in social anthropology from the Martin Luther University in Halle, Germany. His research interests include political economy, relational theory, and social security, and he has carried out field research in Nigeria and Serbia. He is currently a Fellow at the Center for Interdisciplinary Research at the University of Bielefeld and an IAS Junior Fellow at Central European University in Budapest (2017–2018).

Duška Roth studied social anthropology at the University of Tübingen, Germany. Her research interests include (post-)socialist states, political anthropology, kinship, and migration. She worked as a Researcher and Coordinator of the project "Local State and Social Security in Hungary, Romania, and Serbia," funded by the Volkswagen Foundation, and has worked in Azerbaijan.

Notes

1. Literature on the topic of societal aging abounds (cf. Öberg et al. 2004). Between 1950 and 2012, the number of people aged over 60 rose from 205 million to 810 million (cf. UNFPA and HelpAge International 2012: 19–23).
2. Thiemann conducted fieldwork in central Serbia, Roth in Čantavir. Thelen made shorter visits to both field sites and has known her host family in Čantavir for 15 years. All personal names are pseudonyms and reflect either Hungarian or Serbian background.
3. See Shimada and Tagsold (2006) on the translation of German care insurance into the Japanese context.
4. The Gerontological Center in Subotica, the municipal center for Čantavir, provides a nursing home facility as well as assisted living services. Gornji Milanovac has a CSW but no Gerontological Center.
5. In 2002, the Ministry of Work, Employment, and Social Policy (MINRZS) introduced the Social Innovation Fund (SIF) in cooperation with the UNDP, Great Britain, and Norway. SIF financed decentralized public-private welfare projects throughout Serbia (Vetta 2009: 37–38). Between 2005 and 2012, the 'case work' system was gradually adopted, with support from Great Britain's Department for International Development, Norway's Foreign Ministry, and the British consultancy Oxford Policy Management (Čeperković 2007). See also Stubbs (2015) on the translation of liberal welfare and care concepts into the Bosnian and the larger Southeast European context.
6. Højlund (2011: 118) investigates the value of "hominess" incorporated into Denmark's state-run children's homes designed to counter a supposedly impersonal state bureaucracy.

7. For health care in Canada, see Stan (2009). For family values in Turkey, see Yazıcı (2012).
8. For a similar adaption of central programs to local perceptions of need, but also a situation in which the local state actors are blamed, see Dorondel and Popa (chap. 7).
9. In 2012, the monthly payment included health care and old age insurance and amounted to 690 RSD (ca. 69 euros), while the stipend constituted 1300 RSD.
10. HHEHP in the village was never budgeted because by 2009 the financial crisis had reportedly depleted the Serbian municipal funds. Already in 2008, CSW resources had been restricted following a stand-by agreement between Serbia and the IMF.
11. Thiemann accompanied Ljilja in February and April 2010, September 2011, May 2012, and September 2013. Vignettes and direct quotes in the text stem from participant observation and semi-structured interviews, which were recorded in February 2010 with Ljilja and her clients at their respective homes.
12. Marija used the word *čeljade*, translated here as 'own'. It can mean child, family, kin, or housemate.

References

Anderson, Bridget. 2000. *Doing the Dirty Work? The Global Politics of Domestic Labour*. London: Zed Books.

Borneman, John. 1992. *Belonging in the Two Berlins: Kin, State, Nation*. Cambridge: Cambridge University Press.

Borneman, John. 2001. "Caring and Being Cared For: Displacing Marriage, Kinship, Gender, and Sexuality." In *The Ethics of Kinship: Ethnographic Inquiries*, ed. James D. Faubion, 29–46. Lanham, MD: Rowman & Littlefield.

Bruun, Maja H. 2011. "Egalitarianism and Community in Danish Housing Cooperatives: Proper Forms of Sharing and Being Together." *Social Analysis* 55 (2): 62–83.

Čeperković, Rade. 2007. "Iz OPM Tima." *GLAS Centara* 17: 6.

CSW (Center for Social Work). 2008. "Work Program for 2008." [In Serbian.] Gornji Milanovac. Unpublished.

Esping-Andersen, Gøsta. 1990. *The Three Worlds of Welfare Capitalism*. Cambridge: Polity Press.

Gupta, Akhil. 1995. "Blurred Boundaries: The Discourse of Corruption, the Culture of Politics, and the Imagined State." *American Ethnologist* 22 (2): 375–402.

Gupta, Akhil, and Aradhana Sharma. 2006. "Globalization and Postcolonial States." *Current Anthropology* 47 (2): 277–307.

Herzfeld, Michael. 1992. *The Social Production of Indifference: Exploring the Symbolic Roots of Western Bureaucracy*. Chicago: University of Chicago Press.

Højlund, Susanne. 2011. "Home as a Model for Sociality in Danish Children's Homes: A Question of Authenticity." *Social Analysis* 55 (2): 106–120.

Howell, Signe. 2006. *The Kinning of Foreigners: Transnational Adoption in a Global Perspective*. New York: Berghahn Books.

Jansen, Stef. 2014. "Hope For/Against the State: Gridding in a Besieged Sarajevo Suburb." *Ethnos* 79 (2): 238–260.

Jansen, Stef, and Elissa Helms. 2009. "The 'White Plague': National-Demographic Rhetoric and Its Gendered Resonance after the Post-Yugoslav Wars." In *Gender Dynamics and Post-Conflict Reconstruction*, ed. Christine Eifler and Ruth Seifert, 219–243. Frankfurt: Peter Lang.

Liebelt, Claudia. 2011. *Caring for the 'Holy Land': Transnational Filipina Domestic Workers in the Israeli Migration Regime*. New York: Berghahn Books.

MINRZS (Ministry of Work, Employment, and Social Policy). 2001. *Law on the Social Protection and Safeguarding of the Social Security of Citizens*. [In Serbian.] Belgrade: Službeni Glasnik Republike Srbije.
Mitchell, Timothy. 1991. "The Limits of the State: Beyond Statist Approaches and Their Critics." *American Political Science Review* 85 (1): 77–96.
Nielsen, Morten. 2010. "Mimesis of the State: From Natural Disaster to Urban Citizenship on the Outskirts of Maputo, Mozambique." *Social Analysis* 54 (3): 153–173.
Obeid, Michelle. 2010. "Searching for the 'Ideal Face of the State' in a Lebanese Border Town." *Journal of the Royal Anthropological Institute* 16 (2): 330–346.
Öberg, Britt-Marie, Anna-Liisa Närvänen, Elisabet Näsman, and Erik Olsson. 2004. *Changing Worlds and the Ageing Subject: Dimensions in the Study of Ageing and Later Life*. Aldershot: Ashgate.
Olwig, Karen F. 2011. "'Integration': Migrants and Refugees between Scandinavian Welfare Societies and Family Relations." *Journal of Ethnic and Migration Studies* 37 (2): 179–196.
Read, Rosie, and Tatjana Thelen. 2007. "Introduction: Social Security and Care after Socialism—Reconfigurations of Public and Private." *Focaal* 50: 3–18.
Stambolieva, Marija. 2011. "Conclusion: The Post-Yugoslav Welfare States—from Legacies to Actor Shaped Transformations." In *Welfare States in Transition*, ed. Marija Stambolieva and Stefan Dehnert, 345–363. Sofia: Friedrich-Ebert-Stiftung.
Stan, Sabina. 2009. "The Discourse on the 'Crisis of the Health Care System' and the New Governance Model of Health Care in Quebec." *Suvremene Teme: Contemporary Issues* 2 (1): 18–31.
Standing, Guy. 1996. "Social Protection in Central and Eastern Europe: A Tale of Slipping Anchors and Torn Safety Nets." In *Welfare States in Transition: National Adaptations in Global Economies*, ed. Gøsta Esping-Anderson, 225–255. London: Sage.
Street, Alice. 2012. "Seen by the State: Bureaucracy, Visibility and Governmentality in a Papua New Guinean Hospital." *Australian Journal of Anthropology* 23 (1): 1–21.
Stubbs, Paul. 2015. "Performing Reform in South East Europe: Consultancy, Translation and Flexible Agency." In John Clarke, Dave Bainton, Noémi Lendvai, and Paul Stubbs, *Making Policy Move*, 65–93. Bristol: Policy Press.
Thelen, Tatjana. 2010. "Kinning im Alter: Verbundenheit und Sorgebeziehungen ostdeutscher Senior/Innen." In *Verwandtschaft heute*, ed. Erdmute Alber, Bettina Beer, Julia Pauli, and Michael Schnegg, 225–248. Berlin: Reimer.
Thelen, Tatjana, and Erdmute Alber. 2017. "Reconnecting State and Kinship: Temporalities, Scales, Classifications." In *Reconnecting State and Kinship*, ed. Tatjana Thelen and Erdmute Alber, 1–35. Philadelphia: University of Pennsylvania Press.
Thiemann, Andre. 2016. "State Relations: Local State and Social Security in Central Serbia." PhD thesis, Martin Luther University Halle-Wittenberg.
UNFPA (United Nations Population Fund) and HelpAge International. 2012. *Ageing in the Twenty-First Century: A Celebration and a Challenge*. New York: UNFPA.
Ungerson, Clare. 2003. "Commodified Care Work in European Labour Markets." *European Societies* 5 (4): 377–396.
Vetta, Théodora. 2009. "'Democracy Building' in Serbia: The NGO Effect." *Southeastern Europe* 33 (1): 26–47.
Yang, Shu-Yuan. 2005. "Imagining the State: An Ethnographic Study." *Ethnography* 6 (4): 487–516.
Yazıcı, Berna. 2012. "The Return to the Family: Welfare, State, and Politics of the Family in Turkey." *Anthropological Quarterly* 85 (1): 103–140.
Zaviršek, Darja. 2008. "Engendering Social Work Education under State Socialism in Yugoslavia." *British Journal of Social Work* 38 (4): 734–750.

Chapter 7

WORKINGS OF THE STATE
Administrative Lists, European Union Food Aid, and the Local Practices of Distribution in Rural Romania

Ştefan Dorondel and Mihai Popa

"I understand that the food aid comes from the European Union, but how does the European Union know who has a small pension, or that I no longer have unemployment benefits? The local government employees do all the shit."

This complaint, uttered by a villager and reproduced from field notes, contains *in nuce* the argument that local bureaucrats play a prominent role in distributing state resources. It also suggests that the relations existing between state officials and recipients of state welfare shape the workings of the state in locally specific ways. How exactly this comes about is the topic of our study.

Since 1987, the European Union (at the time, the European Economic Community) has implemented an annual food aid program designed to help "the Most Deprived Persons of the Community."[1] Predicated on the notions of respect for human dignity and solidarity, this EU program is the only one of its kind. Every year, funds and products from intervention stocks are directed to member states participating in the scheme. According to EU regulations, each member

Notes for this chapter begin on page 138.

state formulates its criteria for establishing categories of beneficiaries and designates national institutions to manage the scheme.[2] According to the regulations issued by the central government in Romania (in force at the time of our fieldwork), the categories of beneficiaries targeted within the program were welfare recipients, the unemployed, low-income pensioners, and the disabled.[3]

As the woman quoted above correctly suspected, the EU is not invested in determining the identities of the beneficiaries of the food aid in Romania. This is the task of the Romanian government, which sets the implementation norms. According to these norms, county-level offices are responsible for identifying eligible recipients. Unemployment, pension, and social assistance agencies, together with the County Councils, are entrusted with the task of compiling lists of beneficiaries. These administrative lists are to be transmitted to the local governments, which carry out the distribution of the food.

This chapter analyzes the implementation of this EU scheme in two village settings in order to contribute to a better understanding of the workings of the state. We follow state officials' practices of distribution in two Romanian administrative units, called 'communes', and show how historically shaped local institutions and hierarchies influence a centralized scheme of social support.[4] To some extent, local state officials circulate resources made available through the support program in accordance with local distributive models. The use of such distributive models both serves diverse political ends and fosters community building.[5] In one of our field sites, the commune of Dragomirești, the EU humanitarian program contributes to community building, albeit by perpetuating long-standing ethnic hierarchies.[6] In Selo, the second field site, a portion of the EU food resources is directed to a community ritual while another portion is individually allocated according to local evaluations of need. Community building is a highly negotiated and contested process, full of contradictions and tensions among different social groups within each of the two field sites. By exploring foodstuff distribution, we show how it is possible for local state practices to differ even within the context of the same centralized social support program. We make two connected arguments: first, through the use of governmental technologies (exemplified here by administrative lists), discretion is unwittingly bestowed upon local officials; second, these officials, in turn, exercise discretion following local logics of distribution, in essence embedding the EU food support program in local power relations.

In this chapter, following Elias ([1984] 2005), we refer to power as the capacity of an individual or a group to withhold or monopolize what others need, ranging from food and love to security and knowledge. As Elias suggested, we need to focus our attention on power balances and power ratios in order to emphasize the relational aspect of power. As we point out throughout our analysis, our concern is with power imbalances: between different state offices located in Bucharest, in the county capitals, and in the villages; between the local bureaucrats and the villagers targeted by the program; and between villagers more generally, structured along ethnic lines.

Our analysis of the EU program's implementation demonstrates how the distribution practices of local state officials give a 'local flavor' to a centralized policy that originates outside Romanian national boundaries and how these practices ultimately shape it. For the purposes of this study, policy established at higher levels of government, the laws and formal norms concerning food distribution, and the distribution practices of local officials are all encompassed under the heading 'workings of the state'. We thus analyze the state 'at work' (Bierschenk and Olivier de Sardan 2014) by bringing to the fore relations between state officials at different administrative levels and between state officials and citizens—in effect, relations mediated by knowledge, governmental technologies, and valuable resources. The remainder of this chapter unfolds as follows. First, we provide the theoretical background for our case studies. Then, we introduce the fieldwork sites and outline the formal criteria of food distribution. Next, we describe distribution practices and point to the significance of observed similarities and differences between the two field sites. Finally, we reflect on the implications of our research for an anthropological analysis of the state.

Bureaucratic Discretion, (Il)legibility, and Lists as Governmental Technology

Our analysis focuses on distributive practices of Romanian village officials, or what Lipsky (1980) calls 'street-level bureaucrats'. We describe the actions of both appointed and elected officials and, following the relational approach suggested in the introduction to this book and specifically Franz and Keebet von Benda-Beckmann (1998), analyze them from the perspective of their 'double embeddedness' in both hierarchical administrative structures and local face-to-face communities. We locate our disciplinary antecedents in the anthropological studies of inter-hierarchical agents, as we examine the practices of local state officials whose structural position resembles that of village headmen in Africa (Gluckman et al. 1949). In our analysis, nonetheless, we focus not so much on the fragility characteristic of village officials' position of double embeddedness, but on the ways in which these village officials manage to garner room for maneuver to broker resources—a point made by Kuper (1970) in relation to Gluckman et al.'s study. We first offer a more general explanation of the work conditions of Romanian rural bureaucrats, both elected and appointed, whose actions we analyze in this chapter.

In Romania, some state officials are appointed as part of various hierarchical administrative chains and are considered public servants. In rural areas, actors appointed in this capacity are, for instance, the local governments' secretaries, accountants, and agricultural officers. These bureaucrats are responsible solely for the administration of the commune and are prohibited from any direct involvement in politics. Other officials, such as the mayor and vice mayor, are elected, and their authority and position derive from the votes of the villagers. Weber (1978) clearly distinguished between these two types of state officials and pointed out that the technical administrative efficiency of elected officials is not very high, given their primary interest in votes rather than in obtaining approval from superiors. In rural Romania, nevertheless, the distinction between the practices of elected and appointed officials is not as clear-cut as in the Weberian definition, and public servants become involved in political struggles as well. Dorondel (2007a) has shown how appointed bureaucrats actively participate in village-level political campaigns, supporting one candidate while opposing others despite existing legal interdictions. Such involvement of local state officials in politics renders the power balance with citizens virtually unstable: the plebiscitary dimension of their office tenure makes local officials also 'servants' of those under their authority (Weber 1978: 268). As we show in our analysis, the power balance between villagers and local officials tilts toward the latter, but symbolic reversals of power imbalances (the 'servant' status) are performed situationally by the officials.

In present-day rural Romania, many local state officials, both elected and appointed, live and work in the village of their birth. This can be traced back to late socialism when locals were privileged for administrative tasks because of their presumed capacity to mobilize the local population for implementing state projects (Sampson 1984).[7] The officials we depict here were born in the localities featured in our analysis and continue living there. As a result, they operate simultaneously as officials and as village dwellers belonging to different local social groups. Das's (2004: 236) remark about state actors in India being "members of local worlds with their own customs and habits" applies also to the cases we discuss here. As community members, local Romanian state officials share the ideas and values of their co-villagers and are embedded in local social networks. This condition is akin to Kay's analysis (chap. 3) in which state actors' physical proximity to village inhabitants and their involvement in village life beyond the formal limits of their job is of crucial importance to how state policies are enacted at the village level.

According to Lipsky's (1980) seminal analysis, 'discretion' is one of the key terms for studying street-level bureaucracies. Discretion can have at least two sources: on the one hand, discretion is delegated by superiors to lower-level bureaucrats by virtue of their professional competence; on the other hand, street-level bureaucrats manifest discretion in their everyday activities because of the impossibility of a strict regulation of their work (ibid.). Building on Lipsky's insights, we show that one important source for local bureaucratic discretion is the inability of central state offices to govern remotely, which renders them dependent on local actors.

Scott (1998) has argued that modern centralized states use grids in order to simplify the complex realities that they want and need to 'see' in order to govern. More recently, authors such as Street (2012) and Jansen (2014) have shown that people themselves want to be 'seen' by the state and seek incorporation into state grids on their own terms as this serves their interests. Also, in our case, those villagers who are not legible to higher state offices try to make themselves visible to local bureaucrats and use the bureaucrats' discretion to access in-kind benefits. Our empirical examples, together with those presented by Street and Jansen, clearly show that people pro-actively engage with state agencies that represent the benevolent side of the state.

In the case of the program we analyze here, the Romanian government established eligibility criteria for European food aid and standardized categories of beneficiaries. While specialized central and regional agencies 'read' the social landscape by employing bounded categories (e.g., unemployed, disabled, pensioner), local bureaucrats read the local social landscape based on direct knowledge of individual people. Even when local officials resort to the same categories as those at county or central governmental levels, they are better able to calibrate them to local and individual circumstances. Our examples show that legibility is lost when different state agencies overviewing distinct but overlapping sections of the social landscape collaborate. Like Forbess and James (chap. 4), we also observe that actions of different state agencies are not always coordinated, and it is the task of actors located at an intermediary level to fit together partial perspectives. In our case, administrative lists generated by state agencies at one governmental level had to be harmonized by local bureaucrats at another.

In the case of the policy we analyze, higher state offices materialize their standardized perspective in lists of names, an archetype of state administrative technology. As records of things that have been removed from their context and written down as facts (Rottenburg 2009), administrative lists and files are instruments of governmental technology (Hull 2008). Lists have a representational function in that they are meant to enable regional and central state offices to read local social realities. As powerful tools of government, lists can paradoxically work against their original purpose and render society illegible when they are modified and forged (ibid.), or when state agencies do not communicate effectively (Hoag 2010). For those who compile the lists, names are devoid of substance, standing as proof for abstract individuals. It is local state officials who have to identify the persons whose names are on the lists. As we show below, local officials do not operate merely as law enforcers or benevolent facilitators. They implement eligibility criteria, distribute or deny resources, and control information that induces and channels policies in multiple ways (Heyman 2004), thereby interfering with central state offices and affecting their ability to decipher the social landscape. Thus, when some of the needy remain beneath the central state's radar and are not identified as eligible for receiving the EU foodstuff, local bureaucrats 'fix' the problem by distributing food according to their own appraisal of the circumstances. On the one hand, in this way they can 'correct' a social policy. On the other hand, such instances of policy shaping are counterbalanced by situations in which local officials take direct advantage of the resources.

The Field Sites

In this section we introduce the two administrative communes where we carried out fieldwork. Dragomirești is located in the hilly region of Wallachia, the southern province of Romania.[8] It is composed of three villages (Dragomirești, the center of the commune, Vâlceni, and Costești) and is mainly inhabited by three ethnic groups: Romanians, Roma, and Rudari.[9] Out of 2,852 inhabitants, 658 are Roma or Rudari.[10] Most of the Roma live in the village of Costești, situated about five kilometers away from Dragomirești. The Rudari live in a segregated settlement located on the outskirts of Costești.

Dragomirești is a highly stratified community with the Romanian population at the top. Most Romanians work at the Dacia car plant in the vicinity of the commune. They own agricultural land and forest, obtained through post-socialist land reform, and rely on subsistence agriculture and industrial wages (Dorondel 2007b). The next social layer comprises the Roma, who mostly are fiddlers. The Roma never owned land or forest before socialism and have not benefited from the land restitution policy. They used to work at Dacia, but after the privatization of the car manufacturer in 1999, they were laid off or they quit. At present, most of the Roma earn an income by playing music, either at local parties and weddings or on the streets of Western European countries. Finally, the Rudari are the most socially and economically disadvantaged. They also worked at Dacia during socialism. Generally illiterate and lacking technical skills, the Rudari were also laid off from the car plant after privatization. Like the Roma, the Rudari never owned land and forest and were also excluded from the benefits of land reform.

At the time of our fieldwork, most members of the Rudari community relied on social aid, a means-tested benefit that they received from the local government.[11] The difference in economic opportunities was visible in the commune: while Romanian and Roma houses had more than two or three large rooms and a kitchen, Rudari homes usually had two small rooms that accommodated up to 15 family members. Under these circumstances, the Rudari population was the principal target for state social assistance. Out of 306 people enrolled for social aid at the local government, only 12 were Romanians and 67 Roma, while the rest were Rudari.[12] For the European food aid program, the Rudari represented the most significant group of beneficiaries.

The commune of Selo is located in southeastern Romania, in the Dobruja region. Its three component villages—Selo (the administrative center), Brătieni, and Livada—counted a total of 5,184 inhabitants in the 2002 census.[13] Historically, the villages of the commune have been inhabited mainly by ethnic Lipovans (Old Believers),[14] Romanians, and Bulgarians. At the time of our fieldwork, the population of Selo was predominantly Lipovan, whereas the other two villages were largely inhabited by Romanians.

In the past, most villagers were involved in fishing or agriculture. The majority of the Lipovans have historically been involved in fishing. During socialism, Selo benefited economically from having a state fishing enterprise. The fact that most of the Lipovans worked in this enterprise created a clear difference between them and the Romanians living in the commune. Historically, the latter were predominantly agriculturists, and during socialism they worked mainly at the two local collective farms. At the time of our fieldwork, fishing had increasingly been taken over by the Romanians, but it was generating reduced incomes when compared with the socialist era. Most of the agricultural land that the villagers from the commune had received after decollectivization was cultivated by a handful of local agricultural entrepreneurs in exchange for annual rent (most often paid in kind). Many people of employable age were relocating to the nearby urban centers of Tulcea (the county capital) and the seaport city Constanța or were migrating abroad for work.

The most fortunate inhabitants of the commune were probably the pensioners, who had secure access to a monthly income. In contrast, many people in their late adulthood were without a job and thus without a stable income prior to receiving their pensions. For some of the poorer villagers (especially the elderly and the disabled), taking part in religious rituals facilitated access to livelihood means. In the village of Selo, money and food were regularly given to those who took part in funerals and in the ceremonies for the commemoration of the dead. Moreover, the annual celebration of the village church's dedication day represented an occasion for the poor to partake of festivities prepared communally with contributions (food and funds) from both modestly well-off villagers and well-to-do local sponsors.

The socio-economic stratification of the two communes and the overlap of economic inequalities and ethnic boundaries are important in explaining the differences in the implementation of the EU food aid program. Also important in this respect is the ethnic composition of the two local governments. Nearly all the officials in the Selo mayor's office were Lipovans. The most notable exception was the mayor, a Romanian from the village of Brătieni, who was on his fourth mandate. In contrast, all of the officials in the Dragomirești mayor's office were ethnic Romanians. Of the three ethnic groups in Dragomirești, only the Rudari had no political representation at the regional or national level (Thelen et al. 2011). In contrast, Lipovans were politically represented at the local, regional, and national level.

Our analysis emphasizes how the implementation of policy is shaped by the differential political representation and participation of the Rudari and Lipovans and by the historically established relations and inequalities between these groups and the Romanians. As will become clear, local distribution was much more tense in Dragomirești than in Selo. In Dragomirești, when the food aid program takes on community-building characteristics, it is primarily used to perpetuate historical hierarchies, an aspect that is absent in the case of Selo. Food distribution stokes existing tensions between the Romanian forest-owning population and Rudari forest poachers, reinforcing the argument that the Rudari are lazy and to be blamed for their poverty. Like the 'bad' poor in France described by Dubois (chap. 2), Rudari are accused of parasitism and of encroaching on state resources. On the other hand, ethnicity plays a diametrically opposite role in Selo, where the feast of the dedication day of the local Orthodox Old-Rite Church is sponsored in part by EU resources. In the next section, we provide a detailed account of these distinct local implementations and outcomes of the EU food aid program in Romania.

Distribution Practices of Local State Officials in Dragomirești and Selo

Formal Distribution Schemes

As previously mentioned, the European Union allocates national-level funding for food aid, with national governments in turn determining how this aid will be distributed. At the time of our fieldwork, the administrative process in Romania went as follows. Adminstrative lists of beneficiaries were compiled by the County Labor Agencies, County Pension Agencies, and the General Social Assistance Agencies from their own electronic databases.[15] Local governments provided the County Councils with data about social aid recipients. All lists were gathered at the County Councils, where they were processed in order to draw up a schedule for the transportation of food from the county-level warehouses to each locality. While county officials knew that these lists contained overlapping entries, as some people straddled several beneficiary categories simultaneously, cross-verification was a task left to local state officials. These officials were responsible for keeping the County Councils informed of the status of distribution in each locality and for reporting possible overlapping entries found on the lists.

The Practices of Distribution in Dragomireşti and Selo

One important point must be made before describing the practices of distribution in the two villages. The Romanian presidential elections took place in November 2009, one month after the annual food aid was distributed. During campaigns, political party activists customarily distribute various goods, such as pens, lighters, hats, aprons, T-shirts, or plastic buckets, as well as food items, such as sugar, cooking oil, or wheat flour (Flonta 2005). It is against this background that local officials could regard the distribution of EU foodstuff as an opportunity for promoting their political interests.[16]

In practice, foodstuff distribution during our research largely followed governmental provisions. The actual distribution process in both localities was arranged so that recipients would take the foodstuff from the local governments' offices. The process, as observed in both localities, largely followed the script of an orderly bureaucratic ritual (Herzfeld 1992): recipients presented themselves to the offices, waited in line for their turn, showed their identification documents to the officials, and signed the distribution list next to their names after receiving the foodstuffs. 'Orderliness' is analytically interesting, but as we choose to start from a point of resistance that "as a chemical catalyst" can "bring to light power relations" (Foucault [1983] 2000: 211), we focus primarily on 'disorderly' events deviating from the bureaucratic norm and on events ensuing from conflict, as described in our ethnography below.

In the late afternoon on 21 October 2009, the vice mayor of Dragomireşti phoned some Romanian social aid recipients and asked them to unload a truck carrying nearly 10 tons of wheat flour coming from the county capital.[17] Two weeks later, nearly 3 tons of sugar was deposited in a storage room at the mayor's office. Local officials knew their role well: they had to mobilize people to unload the trucks, make sure that the packages of foodstuff were safely stored, and inform recipients about the delivery. Although the Rudari were the largest group of beneficiaries for EU flour and sugar, the vice mayor decided that no Rudari would be involved in unloading foodstuffs. "They would steal from the packages. You can't trust them," the vice mayor assured Dorondel.

Because social aid recipients work for their monthly aid at the mayor's office, a few Romanians who received this aid were asked to help unload the flour and sugar. After the work was completed, the vice mayor asked the men to spread the word among villagers, family, and neighbors that the goods had arrived.

The morning after the foodstuffs were unloaded, the vice mayor of Dragomirești informed the Rudari social aid recipients that they should come to the mayor's office with their horse carts and chainsaws. A few days before, the local government had bought large quantities of wood for heating the commune's offices, schools, library, and clinic. These logs were stored behind the local government's main building, and after a few rainy days, they were soaking in a large puddle. The vice mayor explained to the Rudari that they would receive the wheat flour immediately after they finished cutting the logs and storing the wood.[18]

Upon hearing these preconditions, the Rudari protested loudly, raising their voices as they argued. The mayor came to the scene and promised them some good-quality homemade plum brandy from his own stock. To show the men that he meant it, he phoned his wife and asked her to send five liters of brandy. He then asked the janitor to buy some soft drinks, biscuits, and cigarettes "for the workers." This relaxed the atmosphere, and the mayor promised he would stay there with the vice mayor and drink with the men while they worked. This event was significant. Given that the two categories of villagers belong to two different social strata, by drinking with the Rudari, the officials had performed a boundary transgression (Gefou-Madianou 1992).

Only after finishing their work were the Rudari allowed to collect their food packages. The other beneficiaries, Romanians and Roma, were allowed to pick up foodstuffs after the Rudari. This ordering says as much about how local officials perceive the Rudari as about the role of negotiation and conflict in community building. Rudari, by virtue of their low status and their dependency on social benefits, are relatively powerless in relation to local bureaucrats. While local officials control administrative information and know the legislation, Rudari are unfamiliar with the legal norms of EU food distribution or with welfare legislation. Nevertheless, taking into account their protest, the fact that the mayor had personally served them plum brandy, and especially the fact that Romanian and Roma food aid recipients had to wait until the Rudari finished their task, it is clear that the Rudari were able to negotiate certain aspects of their status. By exploiting the ambivalent position of the mayor and the vice mayor—implementers of the governmental programs but also politicians who need villagers' votes—the Rudari received something in return that they otherwise would have not obtained: drinks, cigarettes, and a modicum of symbolic capital. This event also illustrates how local officials manage tensions arising from the incongruencies between job demands and the demands of their fragmented constituencies. As bureaucrats, they had to distribute food aid to persons on the lists sent from the county capital. But as politicians, they had to show their Romanian constituents that the Rudari worked for their benefits and to show their Rudari constituents that they were not outright exploited in exchange for each welfare transfer. Making Rudari work for their EU aid was consistent with the attitudes of the local Romanian class of landowners, who criticized the Rudari (and other poor Romanians) for putatively preferring to receive social assistance instead of working the land.[19] In such a context, striking a balance between different interests was crucial to maximizing political support.

In Selo, EU food aid packages arrived at the beginning of autumn. In contrast to Dragomirești, the program's lists of beneficiaries were on public display at the entrance of the Selo mayor's office building. This observed difference in the transparency of the administrative process can be explained in terms of a distinctive professional ethos in the two local governments, but it can also be related to the different composition of the groups of beneficiaries and to the different ways in which state officials were embedded in the two communities. In Dragomirești, mostly Rudari, Roma, and a few elderly Romanians were among those entitled to food aid, whereas in Selo both Romanians and Lipovans were included in the program. The potential for protest from representatives of these groups of beneficiaries clearly differed in the two localities, and it may explain the lax attitude of officials in Dragomirești. Moreover, Lipovan and Romanian officials in Selo were much more careful to avoid criticism from villagers for outcomes in food distribution than the officials in Dragomirești. While for elected officials this attitude toward villagers can be explained in terms of their dependence on votes, for the appointed officials it can be explained as having resulted from their embeddedness in local social networks that contained many actual and potential beneficiaries, as we explain below.

In Selo, the atmosphere during distribution days was generally relaxed. One local government employee, always a good-spirited man, at times said jokingly to the women taking their flour: "Bring me doughnuts!" It is through such casual banter that the official could frame the distribution process as gift-giving and position himself on the side of benevolence. The good mood was once interrupted by a man who complained about not receiving any flour. Unperturbed, the employee asked him how big his pension was. Upon hearing that his pension was way above the eligibility threshold, the official retorted jokingly that the man should donate rather than collect flour, alluding to the fact that this was a redistributive process targeting the needy. Others complained that they had been expecting food aid only to learn they were ineligible. "The lists are from them [i.e., the County Council], not from us," was the general response of the social worker, who would assign the blame for the outcome of distribution to the county-level bureaucrats, but at other times would explain the intricate process of list drafting. Similar events took place in Dragomirești. Some villagers, confident that they would receive aid, hired a horse cart or a car from a neighbor to carry their flour. To their disappointment, they found out at the mayor's office that they were ineligible. Some were wholeheartedly convinced that the vice mayor had "screwed" them. They pointed to his two-story tall house as evidence that he was manipulating the distribution of flour and sugar to further his own interests. When a woman who thought her aunt was entitled to receive aid found out she was not on the list, she told Dorondel that the vice mayor "most probably takes the lion's share from these staple foods. Otherwise, he would not spend time distributing foodstuff for weeks."

As it turned out, such suspicions were not unfounded. Local officials in Dragomirești took home some of the flour that was sent in excess by higher authorities due to list redundancies and that had remained in the local government's stock after the list-based distribution. They even offered some to Dorondel. Looked on as almost an insider in the local government, Dorondel was considered by the local officials as potentially a more important critic (if left out of the backstage sharing of surplus food) than were the members of the local constituency. Although such sharing of flour among members of the local government was actively covered up, some villagers nevertheless discovered it. Those who thought they should be eligible but were not on the lists were the most virulent critics of such practices. They said that the remaining quantity of flour should have been distributed among those poor enough to make good use of it. Villagers thought that the people who worked for the local government were too well off to need 10 to 20 kilograms of wheat flour and sugar. In contrast, local officials in Selo were preoccupied with avoiding criticism and mentioned to Popa that if he took part in the distribution, villagers would no longer accuse them of not wanting to grant the aid. Popa did not hear about any instances of officials appropriating EU foodstuffs for personal use in Selo. There, the excess foodstuff resulting from list redundancies was used in different ways.

In Selo, an ineligible pensioned widow received flour from her cousin who coordinated the unloading of the food. A mentally disabled man was not listed for food aid because he did not have a formal certificate attesting to his disability. Nonetheless, his sister, in whose household the man was living, was called upon by one bureaucrat-cum-political activist of the mayor and was given flour from the stocks. As Heyman (2004) stresses, files are records used to track people, allowing high-level bureaucrats to make references to impersonal standards when conducting their work. Citizens who lack files or are not listed under appropriate categories do not exist from the perspective of higher-level offices, for which reason villagers like the mentally disabled man described above could not be officially counted among the 'most deprived' persons in the EU. This is the kind of situation that Jansen (2014) and Street (2012) present, in which people actually want to be 'seen' by the state. To a limited extent, street-level bureaucrats, as we observed during our fieldwork, were able to use their discretion to negotiate more satisfying arrangements. The inability of higher state offices to 'see' all the possible beneficiaries was to a certain extent counteracted through the actions of local bureaucrats.

In Selo, the distribution of the EU aid preceded not only the national presidential elections but also the annual village feast. It was in this context that the village's Orthodox Old-Rite Church received a portion of EU foodstuff, which was used in preparing the upcoming communal meal for the celebration of the church's dedication day.[20] With presidential elections on the horizon, the good-spirited worker of the mayor's office presented above, one of the mayor's key 'vote gatherers' in previous campaigns, delivered EU wheat flour to the church.[21] The quantity had an almost insignificant value in terms of market price, but what was important was the local meaning of the act. By giving food to the church, the mayor had responded to the expectation that his office should support local church events, an expectation otherwise difficult to fulfill under the conditions of harsh budget constraints. The mayor could thus maintain the legitimacy of his office tenure and strengthen his claim for support for his party's candidate in the national presidential elections. Such acts were made possible by the discretion that the local state officials had in implementing the policy—a discretion that was not granted but seized. The distributive practices of local bureaucrats ignored national regulations but responded to villagers' expectations. As Thelen, Vetters, and Benda-Beckmann point out in the introduction to this book, a relational approach to the state that views "relations as decisive in shaping state formations, images, and practices" would explain how local officials navigate between national policy and local needs. People's expectations (and pressures) shaped local practices of distribution and changed the official requirements of national agencies' programs.

The food cooked at the church in Selo was consumed in a communal meal by all those attending the Mass on the church's dedication day. While most of the well-to-do participants were Lipovans visiting from other villages, some villagers from Selo in need of assistance attended the meal as well. Thus, even those not officially targeted for food aid nevertheless benefited from the program. In Dragomirești, too, elected officials went beyond the provisions of the law and invested resources into actions that furthered their political agenda. The vice mayor decided to use a vehicle owned by the local government to deliver the food to the listed beneficiaries, mostly the elderly Romanians who were unable to come to the distribution center. On his various stops, the official sometimes jokingly said, "The vice mayor is your servant and brings the flour and sugar to your home." This was an ironic remark that pointed to the ambivalent position of the official, who held a powerful administrative position yet still depended on the benevolence of his constituency. Leaving humor aside, he told Dorondel that for the elderly who cannot come to the mayor's office themselves, or who have no relatives to help them, this was the only way they would receive the food. Such a statement proves that the vice mayor acted not only as a bureaucrat on a mission to distribute the EU food or as a politician seeking votes, but also as a member of the community who knew the people well and offered his help to those in need.

It is clear from our examples that in both localities the local officials attempted to benefit symbolically from their role as distributors. By jokingly asking for a counter-gift from the recipients (in the case of the Selo official) or setting oneself up as a benefactor by taking packages of food to the homes of recipients (in the case of the Dragomirești vice mayor), local officials tried to secure some symbolic capital from the mere act of giving (distinct from granting, which was in large measure controlled by higher state agencies). At the same time, the acts of the local officials in both communes contributed in two different ways to building community relations. In Dragomirești, where community relations are plagued by tensions between the Romanians and the Rudari, the actions of local officials tended to reinforce historically established inequalities between these two groups. In Selo, local officials built community relations in accordance with the local configuration of ethnic relations. The communal meal was a major component of an annual event important to all ethnic Lipovans. The poor, even those beneath the radar of national agencies, were able to take advantage of the EU food indirectly by attending the event.

Conclusion

What do the local implementations of the EU food aid program tell us about the workings of the state in present-day Romania, and how could our analysis enhance a relational anthropology of the state? We have shown how a transnational policy was 'transformed', at least partially, at the local level. Although the standards, rules of implementation, and beneficiary lists of the transnational program were created at a higher level, the discretion of local bureaucrats allowed them to allocate these resources in ways they deemed more relevant for local relations. Rural bureaucrats in Romania did have discretion in implementing the policy articulated in higher offices, as Lipsky (1980) found for US street-level bureaucrats, but the source of their discretion was different in the cases analyzed here. The ambivalent political and administrative position of the Romanian street-level bureaucrats, their embeddedness in village social life, and the inability of higher state offices to discern the local social landscape combined to endow the local state officials with room for maneuver. Their double embeddedness as representatives of the state and as members of their local community has to be acknowledged as a major source of discretion and power. In order to understand the workings of the state, we need to pay attention to the multiple relations entertained by local officials in their roles as elected officials, state bureaucrats, and members of the community. As we have shown, citizens who could not be 'seen' by upper state offices were visible to local bureaucrats. Discretion could be used to correct the 'illegibility' of village settings at higher-level offices. Officials deployed local notions of entitlement in granting EU food aid to the 'invisible' needy.

The germ of the idea of a relational analysis of the state can be grasped in Weber's ([1959] 2009: 78) definition of the state as "a relation of men dominating men." In our analysis, we have demonstrated the need to look beyond relations of domination through state authority and to take into account larger configurations of power relations in order to understand the actual workings of the state. In the cases discussed, power differences in the process of distribution contributed to local social dynamics of inclusion and exclusion. These dynamics were historical and partly independent of the power relations between bureaucratic agencies and between these agencies and citizens. As we have shown, power differences structured along ethnic lines influenced the local workings of the state. At the same time, actions of local officials also contributed to community building, namely, the structuration of wider balances of power within local communities.

Understanding the everyday workings of the state requires understanding power relations between actors embedded simultaneously in the state administrative apparatus and in society. Social relations and the power balances that characterize them have to be analyzed not in static terms but in processual terms. We did this by looking at the circulation of information and goods (i.e., administrative lists and food packages) between different state agencies and between differently positioned social actors. In line with other analyses of the workings of state bureaucracies (e.g., Benda-Beckmann and Benda-Beckmann 1998; Heyman 2004), we have drawn attention to the fact that the practices of local bureaucracies cannot be separated from the society in which they are embedded. In addition, we have pointed toward a more inclusive perspective that takes into account the use of technologies of government of which administrative lists are just one example.

Acknowledgments

We thank Keebet von Benda-Beckmann, Tatjana Thelen, and Larissa Vetters for their helpful comments. We also thank Larissa Buru, Amy Field, Valentin Nicolescu, and Isabel Ströhle for their comments. The chapter would not have existed without the generous support of the Volkswagen Foundation. All remaining shortcomings are the responsibility of the authors alone.

Ştefan Dorondel holds a PhD in history and ethnology from the Lucian Blaga University, Sibiu, Romania, and a PhD in agricultural economics from the Humboldt University of Berlin. He is a Researcher at the Francisc I. Rainer Institute of Anthropology in Bucharest. His research focuses on changes in the post-socialist state and the agrarian landscape. His publications include *Disrupted Landscapes: State, Peasants and the Politics of Land in Postsocialist Romania* (2016) and (with Thomas Sikor, Johannes Stahl, and Phuc To Xuan) *When Things Become Property: Land Reform, Authority and Value in Postsocialist Europe and Asia* (2017).

Mihai Popa received his PhD in social anthropology from the Martin Luther University Halle-Wittenberg. He is currently an Associate Researcher in the Department of Law and Anthropology at the Max Planck Institute for Social Anthropology, a Research Fellow at the Hellenic Foundation for European and Foreign Policy (ELIAMEP) in Athens, and a Visiting Researcher at the Centre for Citizenship, Social Pluralism and Religious Diversity at the University of Potsdam. His ongoing research scrutinizes the relations between religion, politics, and citizenship in Romania and at the level of the European Union.

Notes

1. See http://ec.europa.eu/agriculture/most-deprived-persons_en (accessed 11 May 2017).
2. See http://eur-lex.europa.eu/legal-content/EN/TXT/PDF/?uri = CELEX:31992R3149 &rid = 9 (accessed 11 May 2017).
3. Romanian Government Decision 600/2009, http://www.apia.org.ro/files/pages_files /Hot%C4%83r%C3%A2rea_nr._600_din_2009.pdf (accessed 11 May 2017).
4. Romania's public administration is organized into three governmental tiers located at the central, county, and town/commune level. A 'commune' (*comună* in Romanian) is a rural administrative unit comprising one or more villages. Mayors and local councilors are elected for mandates of four years. The mayor is assisted by one or more elected vice mayors and by an executive staff comprising secretaries, agricultural agents, social workers, and other employees in charge of rendering public amenities functional.
5. We will use here the term 'community' for lack of better alternatives, despite the problems associated with its use. Throughout the analysis, 'community' will not refer to romantic notions of belongingness, relational warmth, and harmony—connotations eloquently criticized by Creed (2006)—but to dynamics of inclusion and exclusion and to social processes revolving around and resulting in power differentials. The term 'community building' will thus refer to structuration processes of power relations at the local level.
6. The names of the field sites are pseudonymous.
7. Katherine Verdery (2002) has shown how local officials were able to obstruct land restitution after the fall of socialism. Part of our analysis speaks directly to Verdery's, in the sense that we also point to how local officials can interfere with the implementation of centrally planned policy.
8. Dorondel carried out fieldwork in Dragomirești (2004–2010), while Popa carried out fieldwork in Selo (2009–2010).
9. None of the censuses present Roma and Rudari as separate ethnic groups. This is an emic distinction, and this chapter will not address the question as to whether or not the Rudari are of Roma origin. The Rudari population refuses to be considered Roma; instead, it defines itself as "people working the wood, living in or close to the forest and speaking the Romanian language" (Chelcea 1940). The Roma population also denies any ethnic relation with the Rudari.
10. Data from the 2002 census were obtained from the County Department of Statistics, Pitesti.
11. The benefit is formally called 'minimum income guarantee'. For an overview of the scheme's implementation, see Rat (2009).
12. The Dragomirești mayor's office provided these figures.
13. Data were obtained from the County Department of Statistics, Tulcea.
14. Selo was founded by Old Believers (*starovery*, in Russian) fleeing persecution in the Russian Empire after having rejected the liturgical reforms introduced in the mid-seventeenth century by Patriarch Nikon of the Russian Orthodox Church (see, e.g., Robson 1995). *Lipoveni* (Lipovans) and *ruși-lipoveni* (Lipovan-Russians) are ethnonyms with which Old Believers are designated and also designate themselves in Romania (Ipatiov 2002).
15. This information comes from interviews conducted by Popa with county officials in Tulcea.
16. For recipients' deep dependency on local officials in rural Romania, see also Mungiu-Pippidi (2010).

17. The vice mayor is charged in this commune with the supervision of social programs.
18. For a detailed account of the mandatory work that social aid recipients have to perform, see Thelen et al. (2011).
19. Verdery (2003: 217) presents a similar configuration of ethnic tensions overlapping with emergent class differences in a Transylvanian village.
20. Religious ritual is central to the Old Believers' history and identity (see, e.g., Naumescu 2010).
21. The EU foodstuff was not recorded officially as being donated to the church.

References

Benda-Beckmann, Franz von, and Keebet von Benda-Beckmann. 1998. "Where Structures Merge: State and Off-State Involvement in Rural Social Security on Ambon, Indonesia." In *Old World Places, New World Problems: Exploring Resource Management Issues in Eastern Indonesia*, ed. Sandra N. Pannell and Franz von Benda-Beckmann, 143–180. Canberra: Australian National University, Centre for Resource and Environmental Studies.
Bierschenk, Thomas, and Jean-Pierre Olivier de Sardan, eds. 2014. *States at Work: Dynamics of African Bureaucracies*. Leiden: Brill.
Chelcea, Ion. 1940. *The Origin of the Rudari: Pages of Ethnography and Folklore.* [In Romanian.] Bucharest: Atelierele Imprimeria S.A.
Creed, Gerald W. 2006. "Community as Modern Pastoral." In *The Seductions of Community: Emancipations, Oppressions, Quandaries*, ed. Gerald W. Creed, 23–48. Santa Fe, NM: School of American Research Press.
Das, Veena. 2004. "The Signature of the State: The Paradox of Illegibility." In *Anthropology in the Margins of the State*, ed. Veena Das and Deborah Poole, 225–252. Santa Fe, NM: School of American Research Press.
Dorondel, Ștefan. 2007a. "Agrarian Transformation, Social Differentiation, and Land Use Change in Postsocialist Romania." PhD diss., Humboldt University of Berlin.
Dorondel, Ștefan. 2007b. "Ethnicity, State, and Natural Resources in the Southeastern Europe: The Rudari Case." In *Transborder Identities: The Romanian-Speaking Population in Bulgaria*, ed. Stelu Șerban, 215–240. Bucharest: Paideia.
Elias, Norbert. (1984) 2005. "Knowledge and Power: An Interview by Peter Ludes." In *Society and Knowledge: Contemporary Perspectives in the Sociology of Knowledge and Science*, ed. Nico Stehr and Volker Meja, 203–242. New Brunswick, NJ: Transaction Publishers.
Flonta, Florin. 2005. "The Third Romania." [In Romanian.] *Sfera Politicii* 115. http://www.sferapoliticii.ro/sfera/115/art2-flonta.html (accessed 11 May 2017).
Foucault, Michel. (1983) 2000. "Afterword: The Subject and Power." In Hubert L. Dreyfus and Paul Rabinow, *Michel Foucault: Beyond Structuralism and Hermeneutics*, 208–226. Chicago: University of Chicago Press.
Gefou-Madianou, Dimitra. 1992. "Introduction: Alcohol Commensality, Identity Transformations and Transcendence." In *Alcohol, Gender and Culture*, ed. Dimitra Gefou-Madianou, 1–34. London: Routledge.
Gluckman, Max, James C. Mitchell, and John A. Barnes. 1949. "The Village Headman in British Central Africa." *Africa: Journal of the International African Institute* 19 (2): 89–106.
Herzfeld, Michael. 1992. *The Social Production of Indifference: Exploring the Symbolic Roots of Western Bureaucracy*. Chicago: University of Chicago Press.

Heyman, Josiah McC. 2004. "The Anthropology of Power-Wielding Bureaucracies." *Human Organization* 63 (4): 487–500.
Hoag, Colin. 2010. "The Magic of the Populace: An Ethnography of Illegibility in the South African Immigration Bureaucracy." *PoLAR: Political and Legal Anthropology Review* 33 (1): 6–25.
Hull, Matthew S. 2008. "Ruled by Records: The Expropriation of Land and the Misappropriation of Lists in Islamabad." *American Ethnologist* 35 (4): 501–518.
Ipatiov, Filip. 2002. *The Lipovan-Russians from Romania: A Study of Human Geography*. [In Romanian.] Cluj-Napoca: Presa Universitară Clujeană.
Jansen, Stef. 2014. "Hope For/Against the State: Gridding in a Besieged Sarajevo Suburb." *Ethnos* 79 (2): 238–260.
Kuper, Adam. 1970. "Gluckman's Village Headman." *American Anthropologist* 72 (2): 355–358.
Lipsky, Michael. 1980. *Street-Level Bureaucracy: Dilemmas of the Individual in Public Services*. New York: Russell Sage Foundation.
Mungiu-Pippidi, Alina. 2010. *A Tale of Two Villages: Coerced Modernization in the East European Countryside*. Budapest: Central European University Press.
Naumescu, Vlad. 2010. "Le vieil homme et le livre: La crise de la transmission chez les vieux-croyants (Roumanie)." *Terrain* 55: 72–89.
Rat, Cristina. 2009. "The Impact of Minimum Income Guarantee Schemes in Central and Eastern Europe." In *Post-Communist Welfare Pathways: Theorizing Social Policy in Central and Eastern Europe*, ed. Alfio Cerami and Pieter Vanhuysse, 164–180. Basingstoke: Palgrave Macmillan.
Robson, Roy R. 1995. *Old Believers in Modern Russia*. DeKalb: Northern Illinois University Press.
Rottenburg, Richard. 2009. *Far-Fetched Facts: A Parable of Development Aid*. Trans. Allison Brown and Tom Lampert. Cambridge, MA: MIT Press.
Sampson, Steven L. 1984. *National Integration through Socialist Planning: An Anthropological Study of a Romanian New Town*. Boulder, CO: East European Monographs.
Scott, James C. 1998. *Seeing Like a State: How Certain Schemes to Improve the Human Condition Have Failed*. New Haven, CT: Yale University Press.
Street, Alice. 2012. "Seen by the State: Bureaucracy, Visibility and Governmentality in a Papua New Guinean Hospital." *Australian Journal of Anthropology* 23 (1): 1–21.
Thelen, Tatjana, Ștefan Dorondel, Alexandra Szőke, and Larissa Vetters. 2011. "'The Sleep Has Been Rubbed from Their Eyes': Social Citizenship and the Reproduction of Local Hierarchies in Rural Hungary and Romania." *Citizenship Studies* 15 (3–4): 513–527.
Verdery, Katherine. 2002. "Seeing Like a Mayor: Or, How Local Officials Obstructed Romanian Land Restitution." *Ethnography* 3 (1): 5–33.
Verdery, Katherine. 2003. *The Vanishing Hectare: Property and Value in Postsocialist Transylvania*. Ithaca, NY: Cornell University Press.
Weber, Max. (1959) 2009. *From Max Weber: Essays in Sociology*. Trans. and ed. H. H. Gerth and C. Wright Mills. London: Routledge.
Weber, Max. 1978. *Economy and Society: An Outline of Interpretive Sociology*. Ed. Guenther Roth and Claus Wittich. Berkeley: University of California Press.

Chapter 8

CREATING THE STATE LOCALLY THROUGH WELFARE PROVISION
Two Mayors, Two Welfare Regimes in Rural Hungary

Gyöngyi Schwarcz and Alexandra Szőke

"I got poor, and I got no bread, I lost my work, now tell me what to do." The words ring out as the keyboard player of the village band starts to play a popular local pop song. Over a hundred women—all local government employees—have gathered in the cultural house of Tiszacseke to celebrate International Women's Day.[1] All the female workers—teachers, nurses, officials, and above all public workers—are invited to the celebration, where the mayor discusses the importance of women's contribution to the village and the achievements of the public workers in particular. As the attendees finish dinner, officials gradually begin to leave the reception, while a group of public workers, accompanied by the mayor, start dancing to the chorus: "Mayor, mayor, I don't ask for nothing but some aid, so I can get some booze at the pub and forget my pain." Marika, the

Notes for this chapter begin on page 155.

mayor's dance partner, a Roma woman in her late forties, is one of the numerous workers who has been continuously employed in the program for the past 15 years.[2] Later, she explains that the salary from the program, albeit only minimum wage, helped her support the education of her children, who are now among the few from the village to have made it to the university.

In Sziroda—another of Hungary's villages—public workers have gathered for a different celebration and are sitting around wooden tables on the grounds of the village museum on a Monday afternoon. After the ceremonial opening of the new decorative sidewalk completed by the public works brigade, the mayor's office begins celebrating with the public workers, in the presence of a few other curious villagers. The 20 or so workers sit and stare at the mayor, who explains the value, achievements, and importance of public works for the village. After the mayor's speech, in the middle of an upbeat conversation, Péter, a skilled mason, a respected member of the sidewalk construction brigade, and a public worker for over a year, comments on the minimum wage most public workers received. The mayor placidly starts to explain that even a small increase in the rate of the minimum wage would cause a radical decrease in the number of jobs. But the head of the maintenance department in the mayor's office, who along with the mayor is in charge of selecting public workers, reacts to Péter's remark with a definite undertone of resentment in his voice. He states that being a public worker is not compulsory and that Péter can choose to stay at home and receive even less money as a social beneficiary.

What links both gatherings, in Tiszacseke and Sziroda, is that both mayors openly recognized public workers employed within a state program. However, these two ethnographic vignettes reveal the very different attitudes of the leading officials—the two mayors in particular—toward the public workers. The two villages we discuss here were subject to the same regulatory and financial framework, yet they organized provisions quite differently.[3] As a result of postsocialist decentralization, various regulatory capacities were delegated to the local level, making mayors particularly influential actors in local governments established after 1989 (Pálné Kovács 2008).

The central regulations of welfare convey certain dominant values about deservingness and undeservingness, but just before we began our research in 2009, the effects of certain measures empowering local authorities to establish and expand eligibility criteria for mandatory benefits had begun to appear, allowing local officials to survey and modify local needs and norms. The measures implemented thereafter constituted an expression of the different ways in which the two mayors imagined the state and had distinct practical and economic effects on the residents of the two villages. Therefore, it is of particular interest to investigate how decentralized welfare provision both shapes and is shaped by the local relations they are embedded in as well as the state images they endorse, that is, ideas about what the state represents, whom it should care for, and in what manner.

By examining how the mayors translated the different images of the state into regulatory practice, we delineate some of the factors that influence this translation process. These include the mayors' embeddedness in local social relations, their specific position in the administrative structures, and the particularities of their respective localities, that is, the socio-spatial character of places. By identifying these specificities, we show how welfare devolution in Hungary has enabled these actors to (re)create local grounds of belonging in line with locally rooted norms.

Decentralized Welfare Provision and Scattered Images of the State

As a result of decentralization at the start of the 1990s, local governments were established in even the smallest settlements in Hungary. They were given control over their own budget and had greater power to influence local matters. Significant responsibilities were delegated to local authorities, most visibly and strongly in the realm of social service provisioning.[4] Thus, the reorganization of social provisions led to a greater involvement of local authorities—especially mayors—in the arrangement of social services and the distribution of social provisions (Ferge and Tausz 2002; Gyulavári and Krémer 2006).

The regulatory framework set up as a part of this process determines a set of compulsory elements for local social protection, in addition to other forms of benefits provided by local governments (hereinafter LGs) from their own budgets. While the central regulation defines eligibility criteria based on categories such as family income, in the case of some benefits it allows LGs to widen the scope of entitlements, in terms of both the number of beneficiaries and the possible benefits. Although the responsibilities of local authorities are extensive, they are not matched with comparable financial funding from the central budget. Over the past 20 years, central authorities have increasingly ceded responsibilities to local authorities, but without rechanneling central state resources to the LGs.[5] In this context, LGs have become increasingly concerned with the 'efficient' arrangement of welfare services.

The national law makes a clear distinction between different forms of benefits for two main local actors competent to decide on entitlements: the appointed notary and the elected body of the LG. Where the notary is responsible for welfare provisioning, the central state delegates only executive tasks to the local level. In all other instances, the central law delegates power to the local level to widen entitlements, and the decision-making power is transferred to the LG. However, in the two discussed villages, each local council delegated its power to its respective mayor, further increasing the mayor's role in the local welfare.

In the Hungarian context of extreme welfare decentralization—with no intermediary levels[6] between the central and local state to organize social provision—LGs and mayors may form their own little 'social regimes'. Gyulavári and Krémer (2006: 43) argue that responsibilities were partly delegated to the local level because central authorities feared that central institutions would not be able to handle large social crises, such as widespread unemployment, poverty, and accompanying social and ethnic tensions that might come about during the political and economic transformation after 1990. As such, our examples further contribute to recent arguments about the devolution of welfare provision, showing that local actors enjoy much discretion in determining and implementing eligibility criteria, thus potentially contributing to social exclusion and dependency (cf. Milbourne 2010a; Pickering et al. 2006; Tickamyer and Henderson 2010). In fact, our empirical analysis shows that what you can expect from the state greatly depends on where you live and on the state images that abound in your respective locality.

Recent studies argue that the state is a multi-layered and multi-actor entity, a trans-local ensemble of institutions, practices, and people that exists in a globalized context (Ferguson and Gupta 2002; Sharma and Gupta 2006). Furthermore, following the introduction to this book, relational processes constitute the state, as individuals (both inhabitants and officials) act and make decisions according to the logics of the different institutional contexts in which they interact (cf. Frödin 2012). Discretionary power, formally delegated by necessity to ease the strict regulation of official work, can be exercised according to different norms, principles, and interests (de Koning 1988; Heyman 2004; Lipsky 1980), sometimes in order to fulfill electoral considerations (Nuijten and Lorenzo 2009; see also Dorondel and Popa, chap. 7).

As pointed out, the variegated embeddedness of local state actors within the webs of local social relations affects how they interact with other local inhabitants in their capacities as state representatives and influences how service provision is conceptualized and practiced (Benda-Beckmann and Benda-Beckmann 1998; Heyman 2004). In their exercise of authority, local officials, however, take into account the social composition of local inhabitants, as well as other officials, legislations, and administrative levels. Their position allows and/or inhibits certain actions, gives access to particular resources they can use, and connects them to other levels and officials in particular ways. As such, the position of actors in the administrative structures and the power and other specificities that yield from this position are of great relevance. Thus, in addition to the discretionary power of local state actors, it is also worth investigating the regulatory power of local state actors in relation to their embeddedness in multiple webs of relations.

In this chapter, we focus on mayors to investigate how state images and practices dynamically interact (cf. Migdal and Schlichte 2005). The mayor's position is reminiscent of the position of the village headman as he also "interlocks two distinct systems of social relations" (Gluckman et al. 1949: 93), namely, the social composition of the locality and the administrative system in which the mayor is embedded. Investigating the double embeddedness of appointed and elected local state actors, Dorondel and Popa (chap. 7) use a similar argument in their study, but they focus on the officials' discretionary power. In comparison, we emphasize the considerable power of the mayors not only to practice discretion but also to establish new local regulations by overwriting central policies and translating local images of the state to very different ends. Other local state representatives in Hungary can alter the course of policy implementation solely through discretionary practices but not by issuing new regulations. Therefore, we underline the importance of the local relations and embeddedness of the mayors as elected officials, the specificities of their regulatory power, and the socio-spatial position of their locality. Last but not least, we also show the results of these practices for local belonging along the lines of deservingness. We argue that such a complex form of embeddedness influences how state officials, particularly mayors, imagine the state and translate it into specific practices. In the Hungarian context of extreme decentralization, this results in disrupted, scattered, and multi-layered local state formations.

The Villages of Sziroda and Tiszacseke

Between 2009 and 2010, we conducted fieldwork in the villages of Sziroda and Tiszacseke.[7] Sziroda has 2,403 inhabitants and is situated in the southwestern, hilly region of Hungary. Tiszacseke, with 1,538 inhabitants, is located in the northeastern border region of the Great Plain. During socialism, the main occupation in both villages was agriculture, while a smaller segment of villagers worked for local industrial firms or commuted to larger towns. Both villages are situated in so-called disadvantaged areas, an official designation that applies to areas with negative population growth, aging populations, poor infrastructure and accessibility, low income, high unemployment, and/or unfavorable economic conditions. However, there are also significant differences within these 'disadvantages'. Whereas Sziroda lies at an important junction and serves as a hub for the surrounding settlements, Tiszacseke is much more peripheral, and its remoteness within the national borders restricts access to services, jobs, and other productive resources. Yet the vicinity of the Hungarian-Ukrainian border also provides Tiszacseke villagers with some trading possibilities and access to cheap goods.

The distinct geographical positions of these two villages are reflected in migration and economic patterns. In Sziroda, waves of in- and out-migration since the 1960s have significantly weakened local social ties. After the restitution of private property, large-scale land cultivation of private companies became dominant while land ownership remained scattered. Aside from the many non-contiguous smaller properties, a handful of families control almost half the agricultural lands, much of which they lease out. In Sziroda, there are two large (1,000 + hectares) agricultural farms, each with around 40 employees, and one electro-technical factory that employs around 80 people. Average income in Sziroda is 80 percent of the national average, and unemployment stands at 12.1 percent.[8] Owing to low incomes, high unemployment, and the growing number of pensioners, social transfers have come to play an important role in supplementing incomes. Occasionally, agricultural and forestry-related jobs become available, but these positions remain in the informal economy.

In comparison, Tiszacseke is less affected by migration or other population changes. Unemployment, however, constitutes a far greater problem in this village. According to the LG, 90 percent of employable citizens are without permanent employment.[9] With little in the way of enterprises or employment options, the LG is the largest local employer, employing people in numerous local institutions and a large public works program. Accordingly, most people share a similar position in the social framework, living mostly from state benefits. Many villagers supplement this assistance with day labor or seasonal work, selling fruits and vegetables or working in the tourism sector. There are a few families with larger farms (100+ hectares), and between 20 and 30 families maintain small agricultural or other private enterprises.

These general patterns are also visible within our data on family income. In Sziroda, two-thirds of families reported incomes of 350 to 600 euros per month, and only one-third got by on 105 to 350 euros per month. In Tiszacseke, 54 percent of respondent families reported falling in the lower-income category, while only 25 percent reported monthly incomes in the 350 to 600 euros range.

Local Welfare Regimes

Public Works

Since 2009,[10] public works in Hungary have become a significant constituent of state-guaranteed, means-tested monetary assistance for unemployed people.[11] Prior to the Road to Work program, income level was the sole eligibility criteria for social assistance. The new program, however, bound social assistance to public works, and local authorities were authorized to implement other considerations of deservingness when deciding on the chosen participants. As such, the program is interpreted as strengthening workfare measures and has been widely criticized for reproducing local socio-power relations in the realm of social assistance (see Schwarcz 2012; Váradi 2010; Virág 2010). Under the new government program, the long-term unemployed can receive regular support from the state (called 'availability benefit') only if they fulfill eligibility criteria for family income and accept employment at a public works project, if offered by their respective LGs.[12] This form of unemployment support is financially more advantageous for LGs, which has contributed to its widespread introduction.[13] The program also delegated further responsibilities to local authorities in order to deal with the problems of large-scale unemployment. Consequently, LGs and/or mayors had the power to decide who would be granted opportunities locally.

The vignettes at the beginning of this chapter are indicative of the crucial differences in the organization of social welfare in the two villages. In Sziroda, the mayor employs only a small number (between 30 and 50) of the local unemployed, favoring skilled workers who, from his perspective, are trying and able to 'advance' on their own.[14] As he put it, "I want to create responsible, hard-working citizens who try to make a living by relying on their own efforts, inhabitants who are concerned with and do something for their village." He translates his educative aim into the public works program by using it for visible infrastructural development projects that he has prioritized for the village. For such work, he employs skilled workers instead of using the work program for basic tasks of cleaning public spaces, as in many other villages.

Accordingly, public works employment is conceived as a regular job, not only by the mayor but also by the public workers themselves. Therefore, in Sziroda, such employment is viewed as a rare opportunity that must elicit gratitude. This was apparent during the event described above.

In contrast, in Tiszacseke, almost all the long-term unemployed are drawn into the program, which includes about 200 to 240 beneficiaries yearly, although only 80 to 120 people are employed at a time and usually only for a short period. The mayor of Tiszacseke treats the maintenance of the large public works program as one of his major responsibilities. The LG is the only large-scale employer in the village, and the mayor views the public works program as crucial for those who cannot advance by themselves. He employs a very different, rather paternalistic style when talking about his co-villagers: "I look after them a lot. We [the LG] are constantly preoccupied with these people. We don't let them sink into irreversible indebtedness and poverty." Inevitably, most of the work is unskilled and entails maintaining public places and buildings or cleaning the sewage and cutting the grass. Public works projects are deliberately used to fulfill the numerous mandatory tasks of the LG, for which it struggles to find resources. A few work teams are called on for skilled labor; they are usually permanently employed and are viewed locally as accomplishing something valuable, comparable to regular paid work elsewhere. One such example is the women's brigade, the most prestigious of the working units that represents the village at festivals and makes local tablecloths, hence playing a crucial role in the touristic popularization of the village. Work in the women's brigade secures better life opportunities, as we can see in the case of Marika, the mayor's dance partner in the opening vignette. Earlier, Marika was employed in the public works as a street cleaner and was doing cemetery maintenance, but becoming a permanent member of the brigade helped her to educate her children.

Housing Allowance

Like the organization of public works services, housing assistance was also distributed in accordance with particular state images in each locality. Housing allowance is a means-tested benefit to support those who are unable to cover their housing costs. The benefit has two forms. The 'normative housing allowance' is centrally set and regulated by Act III of 1993. However, the central law also allows for local social regulations to specify their own set of criteria within the centrally determined frames and provide a so-called local housing allowance. In practice, local authorities have considerable discretionary power when it comes to housing allowances. The mayor of Sziroda, for example, transformed housing allowances from an infrequent occurrence (when he took over in 2006 there were only four beneficiaries) to a more dominant form of social aid, applying central—and modifying local—regulations that were in force. However, here again, the mayor applied the rules in a way that supported the 'self-advancing' poor more than those suffering deep poverty as the following example, taken from field notes, reveals:

In 2009, Schwarcz first met Juli, a 43-year-old Roma mother of eight, living in one of the small houses on the hill, who had been continuously unemployed since 1997. Her second partner, also unemployed, had not been offered any public work by the LG in the past 10 years because of his alcohol problems. For similar reasons, the local unofficial employment options were also closed off for him. Juli and her partner had moved to Sziroda only a few years ago because—as she put it—it has "better possibilities for children." The opportunity arose just recently to lease their present house on the vineyard hill. Most of these houses were built as wine cellars, so the actual living space is small and damp. Juli, her partner, and her three youngest children share the less than 20 square meters of living space. However, the family uses only the 6 square meter room on the upper level, as the lower floor has mold on the walls. Their arrangement with the owner is to pay 600,000 forint [ca. 2,248 euros at the time] for the house within a two-year period, at monthly installments of 20,000 to 25,000 forints [ca. 77 to 94 euros at the time] each month. When Schwarcz met the family, they talked about getting an electric connection, which was missing from the house along with the water and gas mains. Showing Schwarcz around in their small living quarters, they complained that even though they had applied for a housing allowance, the social worker, after checking their living circumstances, was not optimistic that they would receive assistance. Yet the mother of the large family, struggling to improve their living circumstances, could not understand why her application was refused.

Juli and her family did not qualify for either form of housing allowance. On the one hand, the centrally regulated housing assistance favored small households (of one or two members) with low incomes. On the other hand, local housing assistance applied only to real housing costs because the regulation takes the real housing costs into account rather than pre-set fixed ones set by central law. Thus, local regulations favored large families whose actual housing expenses were high, and therefore families living in houses fitted with modern conveniences like gas, water, and electricity were more likely to be declared eligible. Since Juli and her family had no such amenities in their home, their housing costs were well below the local average. Furthermore, leasing was not considered a valid housing cost under the local regulation, so the family could not claim valid expenses through this allowance. In Sziroda, this form of benefit thus has an exclusionary character similar to the public works program. Despite the considerably large number of newcomer families living in conditions like those of Juli, local regulation favors slightly better-off families, namely, those who formerly belonged to the lower level of the medium strata and now need help to prevent them from slipping into poverty.

In contrast, the mayor of Tiszacseke stipulated that fixed costs qualified as the eligibility criterion, but he set the eligibility threshold so high that it could absorb a wide range of applicants. Thus, while in Sziroda the number of housing allowance recipients in the year of 2009 was 83, in Tiszacseke 250 people received this benefit, which ranged from 9 to 50 euros per month.[15] The next example reveals that in Tiszacseke not just the poor receive housing assistance:

> Márton was in the Véndiófa pub when Szőke arrived for the interview. He and his wife had bought the former peasant house on one of the backstreets of

Tiszacseke three years ago. By now, the freshly renovated building, with its big veranda, indoor dance floor, and well-stocked jukebox, was one of the most popular local pubs. The middle-aged couple also owned a 200 square meter garden behind the pub, which at the time was full of cabbages, ready to be sold to wholesalers. The family had two children; however, both spent the majority of the week in their places of study. The couple nevertheless maintained a large house of three rooms and a side building renovated for their daughter's rare visits. Although the house could be found at the start of "Roma Road," as the locals referred to the part of the village that most of the Roma inhabitants lived in, by local standards it was rather large, with expensive amenities such as a flat screen television, microwave, and washing machine. While we were discussing how they set up their present enterprise, another middle-aged man came in to ask when he should help Márton pick apples, which they would sell to a nearby company that would use them to produce apple juice. Despite their comparatively better living conditions in the context of the village, Márton and his wife received about 20 euros a month in housing allowances.

In Tiszacseke, similar to public works, the local housing allowance is used as a general aid. A large number of beneficiaries from varied backgrounds receive housing assistance, both the destitute and more fortunate families. This is partly related to the local social situation and the mayor's understanding of it: "Here everyone is in need, without exception, because even if someone has a job in the local government office, which is already the best here, the rest of the family is still unemployed."

Crisis Aid

Local governments can also distribute a number of irregular benefits—such as crisis aid, funeral aid, and irregular allowances for families—according to locally set criteria. These benefits also reflect important differences in state ideas, which are translated into different practices of social redistribution in the two localities.

The irregular crisis aid is given as a one-time cash benefit (which can also partly be given as in-kind assistance) for emergency situations, including economic circumstances that "threaten the personal integrity and human existence of a person," as it is phrased in central law. While the phrasing of local regulations is rather vague in both villages, local authorities (the mayor in Sziroda and the LG in Tiszacseke) decide on the actual cases and beneficiaries. Whereas the number of housing allowance and public works recipients is kept low by the highly exclusive local regulations in Sziroda, almost 200 inhabitants receive this crisis aid each year, hence serving as a regular form of social aid for needy individuals who do not benefit from the public works or housing allowances. While these latter forms of social welfare are reserved for the somewhat better-off, self-advancing groups (as determined by the mayor), these one-time benefits are mainly extended to "less self-advancing" individuals, many of whom are Roma and most of whom are among the poorest in the village. In contrast, in Tiszacseke, a comparatively large number of individuals benefit from public works or housing assistance, with only around 10 individuals receiving crisis benefits each year. In Tiszacseke, crisis aid is granted only in exceptional cases because, as the mayor explained, the LG has no budget for such aid.

Local Benefits as a Means of Exclusion and Inclusion

The large differences in the local organization of benefits and their different outcomes for local inclusion/exclusion in the two localities are rooted in various factors. The mayors, having strong legislative and executive power, may form the local regulatory framework according to their own image of the state. However, as state representatives, and also as elected local leaders, they are embedded in different relations, which shape their image of the state. On the one hand, their role within the administrative structures is to 'make' the local state work. In the exercise of their regulatory and executive power, mayors must take into account the relations that link them to higher and/or other state authorities. On the other hand, they have to maintain their relations with their electorate and the different segments of the local society, whom they serve as elected leaders (see Dorondel and Popa, chap. 7). These different forms of embeddedness make up the relational setting of two distinct welfare regimes that we see emerging in the two villages.

Both mayors emphasized that financial considerations and the availability of resources play crucial roles in determining how benefits are locally regulated. Regular benefits such as public works programs and housing allowances are mostly financed from central contributions, but irregular benefits like crisis aid must rely entirely on local resources. This can pose serious problems for LGs with scant resources, particularly in Tiszacseke, where the majority of the local population is without formal employment and thus largely relies on assistance from the local government. In addition, the LG in Tiszacseke lacks income from entrepreneurial taxes, which provide Sziroda with additional revenues.[16] Even the mandatory social provisions that are funded by the central state budget require some degree of local contribution, the amount of which is not insignificant when there are many applicants.[17] This means that local officials are often pushed to prioritize between the various compulsory and assumed tasks, as well as among the different local claims/needs. Consequently, in both villages benefits financed entirely by local contributions are quite limited.

However, such financial considerations in themselves cannot satisfactorily account for the differences in how benefits are locally organized. The state images of local state actors as they translate into different practices are decisive. The mayor of Sziroda explained that he believes the local government's primary aim should be to develop human resources and material infrastructure in the village. During our research period, the local school was being reconstructed and modernized, some sidewalks were being embellished with decorative pavements, and a local market was being set up. In terms of social considerations, the mayor explained how he would like to "educate" local people to become responsible, "self-advancing" citizens. He stated that he rewards such efforts with long-term involvement in the public works program. Furthermore, he applies the same approach to the local government, which, he believes, should not disburse central funds irresponsibly. As a result, the LG in Sziroda has no outstanding debts and no unpaid bills. The mayor declared: "No matter what, here the bills are always paid, and we don't go into debt. We decrease our spending and introduce budget restriction measures if we have to, but we have no unpaid bills or debts." His image of the state (and himself) as educator is mirrored in his local interactions—rather than joyful dancing and joking, he maintains a respectful distance from the public workers.

In contrast, the mayor of Tiszacseke is primarily concerned with maintaining a certain level of well-being for all local citizens and preventing social problems from escalating. Thus, the most significant spending in Tiszacseke, and where the LG personnel also invest most of their efforts, is in social assistance. Given the limited resources, however, this requires considerable restructuring of the local budget, which has already led to housing allowances being withheld for two to three months in order to pay off the public works wages. It also puts great financial burdens on the LG, which has been forced to take bank loans and has outstanding debts to public utility companies. The LG in Tiszacseke obtains as much funding as possible from the central budget and spends it on locally significant issues, even if other obligations or local needs cannot be attended to fully.

Nuijten and Lorenzo (2009: 100) point out that effective elected officials must be willing to understand and be influenced by the point of view of other members of the community they lead. While the two mayors clearly approach benefits provision differently, they are motivated by a common desire to meet the demands of the majority of their respective local constituents. As elected officials, they seek to resonate with dominant local views about state responsibilities. Both mayors enjoy wide support in their respective villages: the mayor of Tiszacseke has managed to stay in office since 1990, while the mayor of Sziroda had no challenger in the 2010 local elections. However, local images of need differ in critical ways in the two villages. While most residents in Sziroda have permanent or temporary jobs and belong more to the middle segments of society, 90 percent of local families in Tiszacseke subsist on social benefits, public works projects, temporary (frequently informal) work, or minimum wage jobs. The more inclusive approach to social benefits in Tiszacseke aims to prevent people from sinking into deep poverty and thereby to decrease criminality, ethnic tensions, and social crises. This seems to be partly successful, as in Tiszacseke, notwithstanding widespread unemployment, most families manage to maintain a minimal standard of living.

In Tiszacseke, most inhabitants support this more 'generous' approach to social support. As one middle-aged teacher, who was one of the few permanent employees in the village, explained: "Even those of us who now have a job could get there [i.e., could become unemployed and have to live on benefits] at any time, or have experienced unemployment at some time in the past." However, sustaining large public works programs poses serious difficulties for the LG, which is not viewed in positive terms by other local officials. This especially includes officials who are not dependent on relations with the electorate and are less integrated into personal local networks. One such local official is the notary, whose role is to ensure the lawful working of the local government. She often complains that the public works program takes immense human and financial effort, from which the LG sees little return in terms of actual work. She also believes that social aid beneficiaries receive too much support. During Szőke's field research, the mayor and notary clashed numerous times over similar issues, which always ended with the mayor reaffirming his personal power. Eventually in the year following the research, the notary resigned from her position in response to these clashes, an option that she had often mentioned to Szőke. Numerous local officials explained that in Tiszacseke various notaries came and went with regularity, owing to frequent confrontations with the mayor. This incident further demonstrated that in Tiszacseke the mayor holds a particularly strong personal position, which leaves little room for effective criticism, especially of his views about the state and deservingness.

In Sziroda, the mayor's image of the state and opinion about deservingness also remain dominant. He has no major opponents among LG members and officials of his office despite the fact that budget restrictions led to cutbacks in extra pay for officials. His law-abiding attitude, reflected above with his remodeling of the local housing allowance, has set an example for other officials. For instance, the social affairs official moaned about how frustrating it had become to refuse benefit claims in cases when eligibility criteria exceeded the threshold by only a few forints. Her complaint shows to what extent personal norms and feelings collide with written regulations, a matter that could theoretically be resolved through discretion. But as a law-abiding official, her viewpoints and feelings were being overridden by the official norm. As the opening vignettes reveal, other local state officials share not only the law-abiding but also the pedagogical and disciplinary approach of Sziroda's mayor, which creates a vulnerable situation for those who are 'rewarded' for their efforts with employment in the public works, since there are many applicants for only a few available positions.

The mayors must maneuver differing and even conflicting ideas about the purpose and proper role of the state in order to implement their own ideas. Even though some residents oppose how welfare provisioning is implemented, most people in Tiszacseke do not question it. In contrast, according to mainstream public opinion in Sziroda, those who live off social benefits are undeserving of state assistance and are criticized for abusing aid and for not contributing to the 'communal good'. These broader ideologies are also reflected in the comparatively limited budget designated for social expenditures in Sziroda.

However, these webs of relations and the local embeddedness of the mayors not only influence local regulations and the distribution of benefits; they also have important effects on the day-to-day life of the locals and groups at the material and normative levels (see also Dorondel and Popa, chap. 7). Not only do people with certain needs have very different prospects for state assistance in the two villages, but how benefits are locally organized affects conceptions and practices of belonging. In Sziroda, as a result of the mayor's approach, which is conditioned by local public opinion, nationally dominant notions of who does or does not deserve state support are not only replicated but also strengthened. By supporting those who are depicted as 'deserving' in dominant national discourse, the mayor reinforces these notions locally through his social policies and recreates the lines of exclusion/inclusion that materialize through them, which most often hits Roma families like Juli's the hardest.

In comparison, the supportive approach and inclusive policies of the mayor of Tiszacseke, which run counter to nationally dominant notions, establish a more inclusive basis for communal belonging that extends also to those who are depicted as undeserving in the dominant national discourse—that is, the long-term unemployed. These individuals are believed to rely on extensive state assistance and are often conflated with the Roma as an ethnic group, thereby further reinforcing the exclusion and segregation of this ethnic group on a nationanl level. Moreover, even if the mayor's policy is not accepted by some local officials and inhabitants (mostly local 'elite' with permanent jobs), Roma and long-term unemployed inhabitants of Tiszacseke enjoy a better position in local society and are better equipped to make claims on the local state because of the mayor's inclusive approach, as we saw in the case of Marika and her children.

Conclusion

In this chapter, we looked at the differing practices of distributing social assistance in two villages situated within the same central regulatory framework of the country. We particularly focused our attention on the villages' mayors and how their regulatory power can lead to dissimilar local practices of distribution, resulting in very different outcomes for local citizens. Our findings resemble the case studies discussed by Dorondel and Popa (chap. 7), insofar as we also show that these local practices relate to social belonging and (re)create lines of exclusion and inclusion. With regard to a broader theory of the state, the focus on the consequences of radical decentralization helped to underline some significant aspects.

Central regulations impact the provision of social assistance on a local level and convey particular images of the state—its role in social care and the need to determine who is deserving of its support. Our analysis captures 'state dynamics' (Migdal and Schlichte 2005) in the field of social assistance, but it also goes further to show not only that state images and practices influence each other. It also demonstrates that in the case of strong local states, local practices may overwrite or reconfigure a centrally transmitted idea of the state, replacing it with a locally constructed idea.

One might say that elected mayors are not very effective bureaucrats, since they prioritize electoral considerations in the fulfillment of their administrative tasks, as our examples show, especially in the case of Tiszacseke. But on the other hand, being an effective elected local leader and reflecting on how the state is perceived among the local population (cf. Nuijten and Lorenzo 2009) is the only way for mayors to fulfill their administrative tasks and establish their own 'social regime'. According to the 'hidden' agenda of the Hungarian central state (Gyulavári and Krémer 2006), the state itself provides the possibility for local bureaucrats to overwrite central ideas locally, although doing so does not affect the central idea of welfare (see also Dubois, chap. 2). Nonetheless, this results in scattered images of the state since each locality might create its own local state (as an idea and as a practice), each of which may differ to a greater or lesser extent from the central idea and from one another.

Therefore, we see these mayors not as mediators who integrate different state actors/institutions through their relational strategies, as Forbess and James (chap. 4) describe the role of legal aid advisers in post-welfare Britain. These village mayors create their own idea of the state—one that is rooted in the local relations where they exercise their regulatory and executive power. In this sense, mayors can create coherence as they implement solutions that 'best' adjust to dominant local norms, although along differing conceptions about the role of the state and its responsibilities. Thus, in our example, it is not the citizens who offer coherence to the notion of the state through their interactions with state actors, as Vetters (chap. 1) shows in the case of the fragmented, post-war Bosnian state. Rather, it is the local state actors, particularly mayors, who imagine and practice the state as a result of the legal autonomy accorded to them.

As such, our examples demonstrate first that the state as an image can be established on multiple levels, embedded not only in differing cultural conceptions (Sharma and Gupta 2006) but also in differing social relations, thereby underlining the state's multi-layered and relational character (cf. Frödin 2012; see also the introduction to this book). Second, our examples also highlight the importance of looking at the specific position of local state actors within the bureaucratic structures as well as the particular socio-spatial aspects of their locality, as these play crucial roles in how images of the state are (re)created locally and translated into practice. Finally, it can be said that the co-existence of multiple locally constructed states enables the decentralized Hungarian state to work, even if it results in social inequality.

Acknowledgments

The authors would like to express their gratitude to Monica Heintz and Ștefan Dorondel for their helpful comments, to the editors of this book, and, last but not least, to all members of the project group Local State and Social Security in Rural Hungary, Romania, and Serbia, which was funded by the Volkswagen Foundation and hosted by the Max Planck Institute for Social Anthropology.

Gyöngyi Schwarcz earned her PhD in European ethnology from Eötvös Loránd University in Budapest in 2012 and currently works for the Research Institute for National Strategy in Budapest. Her research interests include the ethnography of Hungary, ethnicity, ethnic economy, rural poverty, and local economic development.

Alexandra Szőke is a Postdoctoral Researcher at the Centre for Regional and Economic Studies of the Hungarian Academy of Sciences. She obtained her PhD in 2013 at the Central European University in Budapest. Her research interests include anthropology of the state, citizenship, and rural development.

Notes

1. The names of the villages and interviewees throughout this chapter are pseudonyms.
2. Officially, inhabitants in Hungary are designated to be of Roma ethnicity through self-identification, which often does not coincide with identification by the majority population. As a consequence of the prevailing practice of discrimination and exclusion of this ethnic group in contemporary Hungary, the majority of the society recognizes people as Roma by their skin color, family name, way of life, or poverty level (Kovács 2002). Because such 'ethnicization' by the majority non-Roma population has significance and is strongly built into dominant notions of deservingness, we use this ethnic 'category of practice' (Brubaker and Cooper 2000: 4–6) to describe those who are considered Roma by local officials and by a majority of local inhabitants. In most cases, this coincides with the interviewees self-identification, although not in every situation.
3. In the case of central and local regulations, we refer only to the situation during our research. Note 6 summarizes the more recent and the most significant legislative changes that have since taken place.
4. Act III of 1993 on social assistance enumerates the list of benefits that LGs need to distribute, while allowances for children in need are governed under Act XXXI of 1997 on child protection. While there is no intermediary level between the central and local state to implement social provision, the specific laws assign duties of social provision according to settlement types and population size.
5. According to a survey, the central funds distributed to LGs in 2000 constituted only 49 percent of the amount distributed in 1991 (Pálné Kovács 2008: 152).
6. In 2013, a new intermediary level (county or *járás*) was created and accorded considerable regulatory, distributive, and decision-making powers.
7. The authors carried out extensive fieldwork in both villages (6 months in Sziroda and 10 months in Tiszacseke), conducting interviews, participating in local events, and accompanying local state officials during their daily routines. The qualitative material gained from these methods was also complemented with 60 survey questionnaires. In addition to the demographic data of respondents and their household members, the questionnaire focused on four larger issues: the local state, support networks, landed and land-related productive resources, and household assets and income.
8. Data are from the National Development and Town and Country Planning Information System (TeIR) and the National Employment Service National Labour Office,

December 2010. See http://nfsz.munka.hu/engine.aspx?page=full_afsz_havi_reszletes_adatok_2010 (accessed 14 June 2017).
9. However, according to official statistics, the unemployment rate is only 34.4 percent. Data are from the National Employment Service National Labour Office, December 2010. See http://nfsz.munka.hu/engine.aspx?page=full_afsz_havi_reszletes_adatok_2010 (accessed 14 June 2017).
10. At the time of writing, Hungary was in the middle of crucial transformations that were implemented by the Fidesz government, which had been in power since 2010. These involved numerous institutional and regulatory reforms that substantially altered social provisions along with the distribution of tasks and responsibilities among the different levels of the state. These changes reflect a strong tendency toward centralization: several tasks have been taken away from the LGs, and their centrally allocated financial resources have been severely curtailed. Meanwhile, the central state is increasingly rolling back its former tasks of social service provision, devolving its responsibilities to other levels (local and intermediary), and to non-state providers (religious organizations and charities). Consequently, centrally regulated universal social aid no longer exists. Similarly, two of the benefits discussed here (housing allowance and crisis aid) are no longer available. Social beneficiaries must now apply at either the LG or the (newly created) county level (*járás*) for aid; these two aid forms are supposed to cover all types of formerly existing social provisions. With these reforms, the central government delegated the responsibility of offering universal social support entirely to the local and intermediary levels, which now have sole regulatory and decision-making power. In addition, the public works program became even more significant: it is used as the primary tool of job creation by the current government. Overall, the 'punishing/disciplining' face of the state has become dominant, along with exclusionary practices, while the idea of solidarity and inclusion has disappeared even from political rhetoric, let alone practice.
11. Our data and analysis are restricted to the social regulations in force during our period of field research.
12. Since January 2009, the former 'regular social aid' has been distributed only to individuals incapable of working because of age, health, or family situation.
13. LGs have to cover 20 percent of the provisions for recipients of availability benefit while covering only 5 percent of the minimum wage for public workers.
14. 'Self-advancement' is a general category that is widespread in public discourse in present-day Hungary, and it was prevalent in both of our field sites. It denotes people who make no use of state assistance in their dire situation (unemployment, poverty) but try to obtain additional income on their own, or who at least decrease their expenses in acceptable ways according to the local norms (e.g., by raising animals, growing fruits/vegetables in their gardens, or taking occasional jobs). The categories of 'self-advancing' and 'deserving needy' greatly overlap.
15. All data used in reference to aid recipients were obtained from local reports of social aid allocation for the year 2009–2010, when the research was conducted.
16. The budgets of LGs consist of two principal resources: central funds and contributions and local financial resources. The latter is obtained mostly from taxes (e.g., income, car ownership, and business taxes) and from national or EU grants for which LGs can apply.
17. According to the notary in Tiszacseke, in 2009 the local government needed to match the central contribution with over 1 million forint each month to cover housing benefits for 224 recipients.

References

Benda-Beckmann, Franz von, and Keebet von Benda-Beckmann. 1998. "Where Structures Merge: State and Off-State Involvement in Rural Social Security on Ambon, Indonesia." In *Old World Places, New World Problems: Exploring Resource Management Issues in Eastern Indonesia*, ed. Sandra N. Pannell and Franz von Benda-Beckmann, 143–180. Canberra: Australian National University, Centre for Resource and Environmental Studies.

Brubaker, Roger, and Frederick Cooper. 2000. "Beyond 'Identity.'" *Theory and Society* 29 (1): 1–47.

de Koning, Peter. 1988. "Bureaucrat-Client Interaction: Normative Pluralism in the Implementation of Social Security Disability Laws." In *Between Kinship and the State: Social Security and Law in Developing Countries*, ed. Franz von Benda-Beckmann, Keebet von Benda-Beckmann, Eric S. Casino, Frank Hirtz, George R. Woodman, and Hans F. Zacher, 367–397. Dordrecht: Foris Publications.

Ferge, Zsuzsa, and Katalin Tausz. 2002. "Social Security in Hungary: A Balance Sheet after Twelve Years." *Social Policy & Administration* 36 (2): 176–199.

Ferguson, James, and Akhil Gupta. 2002. "Spatializing States: Toward an Ethnography of Neoliberal Governmentality." *American Ethnologist* 29 (4): 981–1002.

Frödin, Olle J. 2012. "Dissecting the State: Towards a Relational Conceptualization of States and State Failure." *Journal of International Development* 24 (3): 271–286.

Gluckman, Max, James C. Mitchell, and John A. Barnes. 1949. "The Village Headman in British Central Africa." *Africa: Journal of the International African Institute* 19 (2): 89–106.

Gyulavári, Tamás, and Balázs Krémer. 2006 "Why Is the System of Cash Benefit Obscured?" [In Hungarian.] *Esély* 2: 29–48.

Heyman, Josiah McC. 2004. "The Anthropology of Power-Wielding Bureaucracies." *Human Organization* 63 (4): 487–500.

Kovács, Éva. 2002. "Identity and Ethnicity in Central and Eastern Europe." [In Hungarian.] In *Social Knowledge and National Identity in Central Europe*, ed. Csilla Fedinec, 7–24. Budapest: Teleki László Alapítvány.

Lipsky, Michael. 1980. *Street-Level Bureaucracy: Dilemmas of the Individual in Public Services*. New York: Russell Sage Foundation.

Migdal, Joel S., and Klaus Schlichte. 2005. "Rethinking the State." In *The Dynamics of States: The Formation and Crises of State Domination*, ed. Klaus Schlichte, 1–40. Aldershot: Ashgate.

Milbourne, Paul. 2010a. "Scaling and Spacing Welfare Reform: Making Sense of Welfare in Rural Places." In Milbourne 2010b, 1–18.

Milbourne, Paul, ed. 2010b. *Welfare Reform in Rural Places: Comparative Perspectives*. Bingley: Emerald Group Publishing.

Nuijten, Monique, and David Lorenzo. 2009. "Ruling by Record: The Meaning of Rights, Rules and Registration in an Andean *Comunidad*." *Development and Change* 40 (1): 81–103.

Pálné Kovács, Ilona. 2008. *Local Governance in Hungary*. [In Hungarian.] Budapest: Dialóg Campus Kiadó.

Pickering, Kathleen A., Mark H. Harvey, Gene F. Summers, and David Mushinski. 2006. *Welfare Reform in Persistent Rural Poverty: Dreams, Disenchantments, and Diversity*. University Park: Pennsylvania State University Press.

Schwarcz, Gyöngyi. 2012. "Ethnicizing Poverty through Social Security Provision in Rural Hungary." *Journal of Rural Studies* 28 (2): 99–107.

Sharma, Aradhana, and Akhil Gupta. 2006. "Introduction: Rethinking Theories of the State in an Age of Globalization." In *The Anthropology of the State: A Reader*, ed. Aradhana Sharma and Akhil Gupta, 1–41. Malden, MA: Blackwell Publishing.

Tickamyer, Ann R., and Debra A. Henderson. 2010. "Devolution, Social Exclusion, and Spatial Inequality in U.S. Welfare Provision." In Milbourne 2010b, 41–59.

Váradi, Monika M. 2010. "The Roads and Dead Ends of Public Employment in a Small Village Area." [In Hungarian.] *Esély* 1: 79–100.

Virág, Tünde. 2010. *Being Excluded: Rural Ghettos at the Edge of the Country*. [In Hungarian.] Budapest: Akadémiai.

INDEX

Abrams, Philip, 9, 74
administration. *See* bureaucracy
aid
   housing, 10, 21–31, 79, 147–149
   humanitarian, 12, 31, 63–64, 100, 110, 124–125, 130
   legal, 11, 73–87, 88n4, 110, 154
   material, 34, 63, 68, 133
   monetary, 15, 103, 110
   social, 41–42, 53, 60–63, 65, 69, 79–80, 125, 129, 131, 133, 135, 146–153
   state, 28, 110, 112, 156n10, 156n11
   See also welfare
anthropology of the state, 1–4, 6, 14–15, 16n1–2, 16n6, 21, 38, 108, 119, 136
assistance. *See* aid; welfare
authority
   central, 14, 41, 57, 59, 67, 143
   international, 22
   local, 9, 20, 24, 28–32, 34, 59–61, 65, 78–81, 88n8, 102, 142–143, 146–147
   regional, 57, 61–62, 65–69, 93, 101, 134
   state, 4–5, 9–12, 30–31, 35, 39, 59, 66–67, 91–92, 94, 97, 109, 136, 144–145, 150, 153–154
   See also power; municipality

belonging, 2, 13, 24–25, 30–31, 34, 37, 99 127, 132, 138n5, 143, 145, 148, 151, 153
Benda-Beckmann, Franz und Keebet von, 8, 59–60, 64–65, 126, 137, 144

Bierschenk, Thomas, 5, 126
Bornemann, John, 4, 109, 117
boundaries
   blurred, 3, 81, 120
   state, 1, 8, 13–15, 53, 84, 90–92
   state-civil society, 11, 86–87, 91, 97, 100–104
   state-kinship, 108, 112, 115, 117, 119–120
boundary work, 2, 8–9, 11, 13, 68, 76, 81, 86–87, 91–92, 97, 104, 108–109, 117, 119–120
Bourdieu, Pierre, 3, 38, 43
bureaucracy
   encounters, 5, 7, 9, 34, 39, 41, 46–47, 62, 69
   institutions, 5, 39, 109, 136
   practice, 24, 34, 39, 40, 41, 43, 54n1, 76–77, 80, 127, 131, 133, 153–154
   rules, 45, 51, 53, 131
bureaucrats, 5, 12–14, 21, 39–43, 59, 71n4, 74, 124–128, 132–137, 153–154

care
   child, 64, 71n2, 85, 113
   elder, 11, 97, 107, 109–112, 117–120, 121n3
   expert, 95, 97, 104, 111
   family, 67, 109, 113–114, 118
   health, 60, 80, 90–104, 121n3, 121n5, 122n7, 122n9
   home, 62, 65, 100–101, 107–120, 121n4
   obligation, 63–64, 69–70, 117

care (cont.)
  recipients, 13, 109-110, 113, 117-119
  state, 11, 24, 76, 92, 94-95, 104, 108-109, 111-112, 114, 116-120, 142
  work, 62, 65, 97, 104, 107, 111, 113
  workers, 62, 65, 77, 82-83, 85, 107, 115
categorizations
  bureaucratic, 21, 24, 27, 29-31, 33, 38-41, 43-46, 53, 125, 128-134, 143, 156
  ethnic, 6, 21, 36n8, 50, 53 132, 155n2
charity, 74, 76, 86-87, 92, 94, 98, 101-102, 125, 156
citizenship, 31-34, 79, 83, 85, 91, 97
civil society, 8, 10-11, 20, 22, 31-34, 86-87, 90-98, 100-104, 112
clientelism, 10, 22, 27, 29, 31, 33-35, 57, 66, 70. *See also* patronage
common good, 29, 34, 66
community
  building, 4, 125, 130, 132, 135-136, 138n5
  local, 2, 8, 12-14, 24, 57, 61, 79, 82, 109, 112, 127, 136, 151
  political, 3, 29, 31-33, 64
control. *See* verification
corruption, 27-28, 69, 92, 133-134
cross-cutting ties. *See* embeddedness

Das, Veena, 4, 127
decentralization, 14, 58, 91, 94 100, 142-145, 153
dependence, 29, 40, 81, 97, 102, 116, 127, 132-133, 135, 144, 152
deservingness, 10-14, 24, 29-30, 40-43, 73, 114, 118, 142, 145-146, 152-153. *See also* need
dichotomy
  rural and urban, 14, 21-30, 32-34, 56, 68, 92, 116, 126-127, 129, 136, 138n4, 154, 155nn3-4
  state and civil society, 91-92, 95-97, 100, 102, 110, 119
  state and family/kinship, 8, 112, 117, 119-120
  state images and practices, 1-3, 5-11, 14, 22, 58, 62, 64, 69-70, 108, 115, 144, 150
discretion, 8, 10, 12, 39-40, 42-44, 57, 70, 73, 78, 84, 86, 125-127, 134-136, 144, 147, 152

distribution, 24, 31-32, 42, 125-126, 130-135, 146-153, 152. *See also* redistribution
distrust. *See* trust
Dubois, Vincent, 5, 39-41, 47, 53, 54n1, 73

economy, 4, 22, 26-27, 36n12, 40-41, 51-52, 56, 60, 91, 93, 102, 129-130, 142-143, 145, 149
elections, 14, 29, 131, 134-135, 151
eligibility, 29-30, 75, 78, 112-113, 115, 127-128, 142-144, 146, 148, 152
embeddedness
  forms of, 2, 6-15, 80, 145, 150-154
  of local actors, 22, 28-29, 33-34, 36n12, 57, 59, 61, 65-69, 74, 79, 83, 85, 98, 102-104, 117-118, 124, 130, 133, 135, 142-146
  of state actors, 10, 14, 44-46, 61, 65-66, 74, 77, 86, 124-127, 130-137, 143-146, 151-154
  See also intermediaries
entitlement, 24, 40, 51-52, 76-77, 79, 82, 133, 136, 143
equality, 27, 48, 75, 110, 154. *See also* inclusion
ethnic divisions, 12, 21-23, 25-26, 33-34, 36n12, 109, 125, 130, 136, 139n19, 143, 151
ethnic groups, 23, 25, 29, 34, 36n8, 128-130, 136, 138n9, 153, 155n2
ethnicity, 109, 125, 130, 155n2
exclusion, 4, 8, 13, 83, 109, 136, 138n5, 144, 148, 150, 153, 155n2, 156n10

family, 4, 44, 67, 85, 108-111, 122n7, 156n12. *See also* kinship
Ferguson, James, 10, 29, 144
Foucault, Michel, 4, 16n3, 39, 131
fragmentation
  state, 5-6, 10, 35, 86
  welfare, 39-40, 42, 56, 74, 154

gift, 14, 77, 92, 116, 133, 135
Gluckman, Max, 6, 8, 12, 16n1, 58, 63-64, 66, 86, 126, 144
governance, 14, 21-22, 31, 34, 40
government
  central, 9, 11, 14, 88n8, 91, 93-94, 97, 104, 125, 128, 156n10

levels of, 32, 36n6, 112, 126, 128, 130, 138n4, 156n10
local, 7, 9-11, 20-21, 60, 77, 81-82, 85, 92, 98, 100-102, 104, 124-126, 129-135, 141-143, 149-152, 156n17
Gupta, Akhil, 3-4, 58-59, 63, 109, 144, 154

Hann, Chris, 8, 31, 86, 91-92, 95, 104
Hansen, Thomas B., 3, 7, 35n3
Herzfeld, Michael, 4, 59, 109, 131
Heyman, Josiah McC., 5, 6, 73, 128, 134, 137, 144
hierarchies, 7-8, 14, 43, 66, 125-126, 130
hospital, 11, 60, 90-104, 105n1, 116-118
household, 23, 27-28, 32, 36n10, 42, 62, 113, 115-116, 118, 134, 148, 155n7
housing, 11, 21-32, 36n3, 42, 44, 67-68, 74-85, 77-79, 85, 88n8, 118, 147-150, 156n10, 156n17

ideology, 3, 5, 11, 26-27, 30, 36n5, 80, 86, 90, 95-97, 117, 152
inclusion, 2, 10, 156n10. *See also* equality
indebtedness, 52, 74-75, 81-82, 85, 87, 147, 151
inequality. *See* equality
infrastructure, 57, 60, 62, 145, 150
interaction
  client, 10, 75, 77, 80-85
  state-citizen, 2, 4-5, 9-10, 13-14, 21-22, 33, 36n4, 47-48, 56, 58-61, 74-75, 77, 80-81, 83, 144, 154
intermediaries, 8, 13, 21, 44, 61, 65, 74, 83, 86, 98, 126-128, 143-144, 155n4, 155n6, 156n10. *See also* embeddedness
international organizations, 24, 31, 33, 100
intimacy, 57, 63-64, 68-70, 107-108, 110-111, 120

Jansen, Stef, 10, 31, 108, 111, 119, 127, 134

kinning, 107-109, 111-120.
kinship, 11, 28, 64, 68, 86, 97, 108-109, 114-118, 120. *See also* family; relatives
Krohn-Hansen, Christian, 9, 58
Kuper, Adam, 8, 63, 65, 86, 126

legalism, 38-39, 41-42, 45, 51, 68-70, 82, 84, 86, 147
legibility, 5, 31, 39, 80, 119, 126-128, 136. *See also* visibility
legislation, 38, 42, 45, 75, 77-78, 132, 144
legitimacy, 7-8, 23, 27, 30-32, 52, 59, 64, 79, 111, 135
Lipsky, Michael, 5, 39, 43, 74, 126-127, 136, 144
local state, 8-10, 12, 31-34, 57-70, 78, 81, 102, 109, 112, 122n8, 125-128, 131-137, 143-145

Marxism, 3-4, 16n3, 90, 96
mayor, 10, 12, 14, 20, 30, 61, 63-64, 66-67, 102, 126, 130-135, 138n4, 138n12, 141-154
Migdal, Joel S., 3, 5-6, 36n4, 58, 144, 153
Mitchell, Timothy, 3, 8, 53, 91, 97, 108
morality, 4, 10-11, 13, 25, 28-29, 40, 52-53, 58, 69-70, 73, 118
municipality, 14, 21, 24-25, 29-32, 34, 36n6, 68, 102, 109-110, 112-113, 116, 121n4. *See also* authority
mutuality, 4, 13, 41, 48, 58, 68, 70, 78, 81-82, 115-116

nation, 4-5, 7, 12, 14, 16n10, 22, 30-31, 33, 77, 109-111, 115, 130
nationalism, 4, 21-23, 25, 33, 36n12, 109
need, 28, 60, 62-63, 65, 67, 69-70, 81, 93, 100-101, 110-112, 122n8, 125, 128, 133-136, 142, 149-153, 156n14. *See also* deservingness
neo-liberalism, 2, 14, 39, 56, 76, 97, 104, 110-111, 119
non-governmental actors, 5, 9, 31-32, 91-94, 104
non-profit organizations, 11, 75, 100-101
norms
  institutional, 43, 45, 53, 68, 131, 144, 152
  legal, 13, 39, 51, 84, 125-126, 132, 152
  local, 7-8, 28, 43, 58, 64, 67, 70, 108, 114, 142-143, 154, 156n14. *See also* values
Nuijten, Monique, 58, 144, 151, 154

Olivier de Sardan, Jean Pierre, 5, 126

patronage, 10, 20, 27, 29, 31, 34, 57, 65–66, 70. *See also* clientelism
personalized relationships. *See* embeddedness; relational modality, personalized
policy
  implementation, 39, 53, 110, 130, 136, 138n7, 144
  makers, 26–27, 34, 74–75, 88n2
  national, 11, 108, 135
  transnational, 12, 136
  welfare, 14, 34, 40, 53, 110–111, 119
political party
  functionaries 28, 29, 34, 65, 80, 131
  leaders 21, 23, 27
politics, 5, 7, 9, 21–22, 25, 29, 31–34, 90, 93, 125, 131, 133
positionalities. *See* embeddedness
post-socialism, 2, 13–14, 22, 56–58, 93, 104, 138n7, 142–143, 145, 153
post-war period, 10, 13, 21–22, 24, 26, 28–34, 92, 154
poverty, 5, 12, 14, 38, 40–41, 46, 66, 75, 115, 130, 133–134, 136, 143, 147–149, 151, 156n14
power, 12–14, 41, 43, 60, 66, 136. *See also* authority
privatization, 22, 59, 69, 91, 111, 129
professional
  authority, 82, 96–97, 104
  ethos, 32–33, 45–47, 64, 67–70, 78–79, 93, 111, 113, 127, 133
  status, 43, 62, 70, 74–76, 113
property, 22, 24, 27, 29–30, 71n2, 92–93, 129, 138n7, 145, 156n16
protest, 20–22, 30–32, 36n10, 36n12, 93, 132–133
public services, 39, 76, 86–87
public work, 10, 68, 141–142, 146–152, 156n10, 156n13

Read, Rosie, 56, 91, 94, 110
reciprocity, 29, 66, 71n3, 112, 115, 117
redistribution, 21–22, 33, 35n3, 93, 133, 149. *See also* distribution
regulation
  framework, 7, 12, 42–43, 77, 93, 127, 135, 142–143, 150, 153, 156nn10–11
  local, 144, 146–150, 152, 155n3

power, 7, 14, 144–145, 150, 153–154, 155n6, 156n10
practice, 9, 51–52, 142, 146–150, 152–153
relational modality
  adversarial, 69, 75, 78–81, 97
  coercive, 4, 9, 13–14, 40–42, 53, 64, 94
  cooperative, 11, 47, 81, 111
  educative, 10, 52, 61, 85, 142, 146–147, 150–151
  emotional, 108, 97, 115
  hybrid, 10, 64, 70
  paternalistic, 10, 14, 22, 40, 69, 85, 147
  personalized, 10–11, 13, 22, 27–29, 33, 53, 57–59, 61, 66–70, 86, 96–97, 102
  rule-centered, 68–69, 84, 96
relatives, 26, 28, 46, 68, 103, 111–112, 117–118, 135. *See also* kinship
religion, 6, 46, 96, 98, 100, 130, 139n20, 156
resistance, 13, 85, 131
ritual, 118–119, 125, 130, 131, 139n20

Sampson, Steven, 91–92, 104, 127
Schlichte, Klaus, 3, 5–6, 36n4, 58, 144, 153
Scott, James C., 4–5, 39, 127
sharing, 49, 65, 120, 134
socialism, 2, 26–27, 29–33, 36n5, 90–96, 104, 110, 127, 129, 138n7, 145
social security, 10, 22, 45, 57–61, 65, 69, 71, 74–78, 80, 91, 118, 125, 143, 56n10. *See also* welfare
social worker, 41, 46, 48, 59, 67, 85, 110–116, 119, 133, 138n4, 148
solidarity, 27–29, 33, 51, 81, 91, 110, 124, 156n10
sovereignty, 4–5, 7, 16n5
stability, 6, 35, 52, 99, 118
standards, 44–45, 51, 54n1, 66, 79, 127–128, 134, 136, 149, 151
state images, 1–14, 35, 56–58, 66, 69, 91, 96, 107, 109–118, 120, 127, 142–144, 147, 153
state practices, 1–14, 21, 24, 35, 38–39, 56–59, 70, 108–109, 111–112, 125
Stepputat, Finn, 3, 7, 35n3

Street, Alice, 10, 31, 108, 117, 119, 127, 134
symbolic capital, 7, 82, 132, 135

technologies
  bureaucratic, 10, 41, 124–125, 128, 137
  government, 4, 33–34, 41, 59–60, 76, 125–126, 128, 137
Thelen, Tatjana, 8, 56, 91, 97, 108, 110, 130, 139n18
transformation
  state, 2, 22, 34–35, 40, 53
  welfare, 2, 12–14, 40–41, 56–57, 91, 143, 154, 156n10
translation, 52, 54n3, 81, 83–84, 110, 121n5, 142, 149, 154
Trouillot, Michel-Rolph, 4, 35n3, 38–39, 91
trust, 1, 67–70, 78, 82, 86, 110, 117, 131

uncertainty, 33, 40–42, 46–47, 51, 79
unemployment, 40, 42, 46, 52, 124–125, 128, 145–149, 151, 153, 156n9, 156n14

values, 13, 26, 28, 46, 49, 51, 68, 76, 86, 99, 103, 108–112, 121, 127, 142. *See also* norms
Verdery, Katherine, 2, 59, 71n2, 138n7, 139n19
verification, 14, 21, 30–31, 38–53, 82–83, 85, 101, 105n1, 114, 118, 120, 128, 131, 139n17

Vetters, Larissa, 57, 61, 70, 154
violence, 7, 13, 21–23, 94
visibility, 31, 92, 99, 101, 103–104, 119, 127, 129, 136, 146. *See also* legibility
volunteering, 11, 21, 29, 76–77, 80–81, 85, 88n2, 91–104, 105n1, 105n4, 112
vulnerability, 40, 46, 56, 69, 79, 82, 100, 152

Weber, Max, 3–8, 16n9–10, 126–127, 136
welfare
  benefits, 12–14, 24, 30, 40–47, 50–52, 56, 67–68, 81–82, 85, 132, 135, 138n, 142–143, 146–153, 155n4, 156n17
  institutions, 5, 39, 41, 47, 60, 94–95, 100–101, 112
  local, 57–58, 62, 65, 80, 107, 110, 146, 150
  policies, 2, 9, 13, 34, 40, 53, 75–76, 108, 111, 119, 132, 142
  recipients, 13–14, 21, 29, 40–43, 46, 49, 51–53, 73, 77, 86, 124–125, 128–136, 142–143, 147, 149, 152, 156n10, 156n15
  state, 2, 13, 40–41, 52–53, 54n3, 73–75, 86, 110, 119, 129
  system, 14, 24, 61, 75, 78, 91, 97, 109–111, 143, 150
  See also aid; social security
workfare. *See* public work